# FEMALE AUTONOMY, FAMILY DECISION MAKING, AND DEMOGRAPHIC BEHAVIOR IN AFRICA

**Cover Illustration**:

A portrait of an African couple sitting under a cocoa tree pondering over family decisions. Art work from the author's private collection.

**Cover design** by Mark S. Huff, Professor of Art, SUNY Potsdam, Potsdam, NY.

# FEMALE AUTONOMY, FAMILY DECISION MAKING, AND DEMOGRAPHIC BEHAVIOR IN AFRICA

Yaw Oheneba-Sakyi

With Contributions From
Kofi Awusabo-Asare

Studies in African Economic and Social Development
Volume 12

The Edwin Mellen Press
Lewiston•Queenston•Lampeter

**Library of Congress Cataloging-in-Publication Data**

Oheneba-Sakyi, Yaw.
  Female autonomy, family decision making, and demographic
behavior in Africa / Yaw Oheneba-Sakyi ; with contributions from
Kofi Awusabo-Asare.
      p.  cm.  --  (Studies in African economic and social development
; v. 12)
  Includes bibliographical references and index.
  ISBN 0-7734-7981-3
      1. Women--Ghana--Social conditions.   2. Family size--Ghana.  3.
Ghana--Social conditions.   I. Awusabo-Asare, Kofi.   II. Title.   III.
Series.
HQ1816 .O38   1999
305.42' 09667--dc21                                                                99-34530
                                                                                              CIP

This is volume 12 in the continuing series
Studies in African Economic & Social Development
Volume 12  ISBN 0-7734-7981-3
SAESD Series  ISBN 0-88946-514-2

A CIP catalog record for this book is available from the British Library.

The Edwin Mellen Press                              The Edwin Mellen Press
            Box 450                                                          Box 67
Lewiston, New York                                Queenston, Ontario
  USA  14092-0450                                  CANADA  L0S 1L0

The Edwin Mellen Press, Ltd.
Lampeter, Ceredigion, Wales
UNITED KINGDOM SA48 8LT

Printed in the United States of America

# CONTENTS

# TABLES

**Chapter 7**

# FIGURES

# PREFACE

The family is central to the social and economic fabric of sub-Saharan African societies. With rising levels of urbanization and migration and widespread stresses induced by economic restructuring and the HIV/AIDS epidemic, many African families have had to make rapid adjustments in both structure and function. Gender relations and women's autonomy lie at the core of recent changes in the family, and are particularly relevant for study for both policy reasons and reasons specific to the African context.

Major world-wide conferences in the last decade—the 1994 United Nations-sponsored International Conference on Population and Development in Cairo, Egypt and the 1995 International Women's Conference in Beijing, China—have brought improvements in women's status to the forefront of population policy priorities. Addressing gender inequity has meant focusing on a number of often-divisive issues that had previously been ignored, issues such as sexual coercion, domestic violence, and girls' schooling. However, it is within the family that many of these issues find their strongest roots in opposition to change. If governments and communities are to formulate effective policies to meet the challenges of Cairo and Beijing, it is clear that more attention must be devoted to empirical research on the family as a sound basis for policy decision making.

Apart from policy concerns, the very meaning of women's autonomy in Africa is bound up in the family. Female autonomy is not only measured by women's control over their own bodies or their freedom to express their sexuality, as the issues of Western feminism embrace. Nor is women's autonomy captured completely by formal education or economic independence, though it is inextricably linked to these broad developments in human capital. Women's autonomy in Africa is inherently part of the structure and meaning of larger family systems since women bear the major brunt of support and daily sustenance for dependent children. In short, women's status in Africa cannot be divorced from many of the activities necessary for children's welfare. The study of reproductive behavior and ways to bring about related change in gender equity in rights, representation and economic power thus means that the family is a necessary focal point of research.

This book presents an important, in-depth study that addresses these multiple links between reproduction, women's status, and the family. The original research, conducted as the Ghana Female Autonomy Micro Study (GFAMS), was designed to collect information about the nature of spousal relations and the extent to which changes in the position of women affect demographic change in Ghana. This valuable study of women's autonomy and reproductive behavior frames research questions, measures, and analyses in terms of women's many roles in the African family as well as women's roles in political, legal and economic spheres of life. This multi-dimensional and multi-level picture of women's status is necessary since change on one level, such as a woman's level of formal schooling, does not automatically mean change on a broader level, such as legal protections for child custody or support in the case of death or divorce. Furthermore, the views and behaviors of women *and* their husbands are included in the analyses in this book. This approach carries research on women's status and demographic behavior forward by bringing in *men* as an important but often absent aspect of reproductive decision making.

The book is organized into 9 chapters that highlight many aspects of women's status. Chapter 1 is an introduction to the relationship between women's autonomy and reproductive behavior. It also outlines the goals and objectives of the study, the study rationale, and a conceptual framework for analysis. Chapter 2 discusses the methodology of the study. Chapter 3 presents evidence about marriage systems and fertility behavior. The next chapter focuses on the link between contraception and reproductive intentions followed by a chapter on spousal communication and household decision making, including the influence of other family members on couples' reproductive decision making. Chapter 6 describes the degree to which women and men retain control over their own economic resources and contribute to household expenditures. The next two chapters present evidence about how women and men view gender roles and responsibilities, female education, women's roles in politics, and perceptions of marital, sexual and property rights. The concluding chapter reviews main findings of the GFAMS and the critical policy and programmatic consequences.

This valuable study serves as a basis for understanding how family systems change and the consequences of family change for women's position in society. The concepts, methodology, and main findings constitute useful tools for teachers and researchers in the social sciences (e.g., sociology, anthropology, African/ethnic studies and women's studies). Likewise, organizations involved with practical implications of population research (e.g., non-governmental organizations or donor agencies) will find discussions in this volume of relevance and interest.

*Ann E. Biddlecom, Ph.D.*
*Institute for Research*
*University of Michigan*
*Ann Arbor, MI 48106*
*U.S.A.*

*March 1999*

# ACKNOWLEDGEMENTS

This book represents the findings of the Ghana Female Autonomy Micro Study (GFAMS) conducted between 1992 and 1993 by the State University of New York (SUNY) Potsdam, Potsdam, NY, in collaboration with the Regional Institute for Population Studies (RIPS), University of Ghana, Legon, Accra. The GFAMS began in June 1992 with a generous grant from the Rockefeller Foundation, New York, NY. The Project Director and Principal Investigator of the GFAMS was Dr. Yaw Oheneba-Sakyi, SUNY Potsdam. The other collaborators were Dr. Kofi Awusabo-Asare, University of Cape Coast, Ghana; Ms. Edna Gbortsu, Ghana Statistical Service, and Dr. Andrew F. Aryee, University of Ghana, Legon. We would also like to thank Dr. John K. Anarfi, University of Ghana, Legon, for his assistance in organizing the GFAMS seminar in Accra, Ghana, August, 1995.

We wish to acknowledge additional financial contributions from the Dr. Nuala McGann Dresher Fellowship Program; the Population Investigation Committee of the London School of Economics and Political Science; the Population Studies and Training Center of Brown University, Providence, RI; the Faculty-Undergraduate Research Program, SUNY Potsdam, NY; the Research and Creative Endeavors Program, SUNY Potsdam, NY; and the SUNY/UUP Joint Management Professional Development and Quality of Working Life Program.

We are enormously grateful to our colleagues, Dr. Ann Biddlecom, University of Michigan, Ann Arbor, MI for contributing the Preface, and Professor Mark Huff, SUNY Potsdam for the cover illustration. We also wish to express our appreciation to Dr. David Hanson, Dr. Philip Neisser, Dr. Caroline Danielson, and Ms. Kathleen Chapman all of SUNY Potsdam, NY; Dr. George K. Arthur, Marshall University, WV; and other anonymous reviewers who read final drafts of the manuscript and provided valuable comments. We also wish to express our sincere thanks to Ms.

Jackie Rush for her technical support in the preparation of tables, illustrations, and indexes for the book. Our research assistant, Ms. Shelitha Dickerson, provided a variety of services including library research, cataloguing and cross-checking references, compiling the indexes as well as reading drafts and offering comments, for which we are very grateful. The director of The Edwin Mellen Press, Professor Herbert Richardson, and the production editor, Ms. Patricia Schultz, have been very cooperative and supportive of this work.

Finally, we extend our deep and earnest thanks to our families for their patience, understanding and support. We hope the value of this volume justifies the enormous sacrifices they have made on our behalf during the period of our pre-occupation with researching and writing this book.

1

# INTRODUCTION: THE CONTEXT OF WOMEN'S
# AUTONOMY AND FERTILITY BEHAVIOR

The recent reported evidence of fertility decline in Botswana, Kenya, Zimbabwe, and South Africa have created interest among researchers and policy makers on the factors that have been responsible for the decline (Caldwell, et al., 1992; Caldwell & Caldwell, 1993; Muhuri et al., 1994; Thomas & Muvandi, 1995). In Ghana, the 1993 Demographic and Health Survey (GDHS) reported an overall total fertility rate of 5.5 children, an apparent decline of more than a child from the results of the 1988 GDHS (Ghana Statistical Service [GSS] and Macro International Inc. [MI], 1994).

One of the factors that has been linked to fertility decline is the level of autonomy of women within the society. The general thesis is that when women are able to make independent decisions on a wide range of issues including those on reproductive health, fertility begins to decline (Mason, 1993). This general theme does not seem to play out in parts of Ghana (such as among the Akan and Gas) where, in spite of the relative economic autonomy of females, fertility rates are high (Gaisie, 1981; Oppong, 1987; Clark, 1994). Caldwell & Caldwell (1987) have argued that women in West Africa, although economically autonomous, are constrained by a lineage system which takes precedence over conjugal bonds. To them, economic and emotional nucleation are low within the system leading to differential interests which translate into high fertility outcomes. However, as Mason (1987) points out, the concept of "female autonomy" has not been well defined to distinguish between individual autonomy and institutional factors. This anomalous situation of a gap between individual level factors and institutional forces in fertility behavior seems to exist in Ghana.

The present study seeks to explore the relationship, if any, between the autonomy of females and fertility behavior among couples in Ghana. Cognizant of the fact that there is no single and simple measure of the status of women that will accurately reflect the diversity of women's experiences relative to men, we employ a multi-dimensional approach (Oppong, 1983a; Mason, 1984; Dormor, 1994). At the individual level, variables such as level of formal education, employment status, independent source of income and control over earnings, nature of communication, and patterns of decision making will be used as measures of autonomy within marriage. At the institutional level, societal perceptions of gender roles, rights and obligations in the context of existing socio-economic institutions will be examined in the selected communities.

## SPECIFIC GOALS AND OBJECTIVES

The goals of this project were to pursue further studies to examine the impact of female decision making autonomy on contraception and ultimate fertility, and the intervening factors influencing this relationship in Ghana. This project was designed to test some existing ideas from Mason's (1987) work about female autonomy and fertility decision making among third world populations. Our aim was to assess the decision-making process among selected rural and urban couples in Ghana on matters affecting them as couples, their children and other relations.

The specific objectives were:

- to examine the nature of interaction and communication between couples and how they influence contraceptive knowledge, method choice, discontinuation, and other fertility-related matters;

- to examine how communication influences couple equality in decision making on contraception and fertility-related issues;

- to assess couples' control over their own resources and their individual contributions to household expenditure;

- to assess perception of gender roles, family responsibilities, sexual rights, and views on women in national leadership positions; and

- to assess the significant social contextual factors that impact the effects women's autonomy has on their contraceptive use and ultimate fertility behavior.

## RATIONALE FOR STUDY

In spite of the elaborate efforts of the Demographic Health Surveys (DHSs) to create the much needed data bank on human fertility for developing countries, the data are inadequate in addressing couple communication, household decision making, couples' earnings and disposal of earned income, and gender roles. For the purpose of seeking additional information to supplement the data from the GDHS, the Ghana Female Autonomy Micro Study (GFAMS) was designed. We collected information on women as well as men as the main actors so we could assess gender differentials in our analysis on resources and fertility goals of couples (Mason, 1984; Gage, 1995). The focus of our micro study, then, was to collect data on the following six areas:

- *Couple Communication* in various areas like children's educational matters, current affairs, politics, acquisition of household items, and acquisition of physical property (e.g., land, house, etc.).

- *Couple Conjugality,* to measure the extent that couples do things together like sitting at the table to eat, visit relations, visit hometown, attend church, attend funerals, and attend other social functions, etc.

- *Discussion of Fertility-Related Topics,* such as the number of children desired, birth spacing, resumption of sex after child birth, breast-feeding, pregnancy prevention, and contraceptive method choice.

- *Decision-Making Process,* to address the dynamics of how decisions are arrived at in the household on general matters, fertility-related matters, and contraceptive matters.

- *Disposal of Income,* to measure how independent money earned is spent, who influences the decision, and the extent of their individual contributions to household expenditure.

- *Gender Roles,* to ask couples about their perceptions of appropriate gender roles, rights, and obligations, and about women in positions of authority.

The GFAMS field work was successfully carried out between December, 1992 and March, 1993, giving us access to current and comparable data for analyses on the family dynamics of Ghanaian couples.

**CONCEPTUAL FRAMEWORK**

**Women's Autonomy and Fertility Change**

The general notion that women's position in society is related to fertility levels is not new. Female autonomy and its relationship with socio-economic and demographic factors have been extensively explored in the last two decades. Several of these studies have focused on the differential access by females to economic, cultural, and political resources for empowerment and the effects of that on reproductive choices (Cain et al., 1979; Mason & Palan, 1981; Dyson & Moore, 1983; Oppong, 1983a; Cain, 1984; Mason, 1984; Knodel et al., 1987; Costello & Palabrica-Costello, 1988; Lim, 1988; Kritz & Gurak, 1989). However, as noted by Mason (1987), more specific ideas about the impact of female autonomy on fertility thus far remain scattered in the literature. She argues that there is often confusion on the use of the concept "female autonomy" in relation to the statuses of individual women vis-a-vis the impact of patriarchal social institutions on fertility behavior. This makes it difficult to assess the impact of the hypothesized factor on women's fertility behavior.[1]

Using a Euro-American world view, female autonomy has come to be equated with education, occupation and control of independent income as well as sexuality. But as pointed out by Caldwell (1986:202), female education is not co-terminal with female autonomy, "... although the former may contribute to the latter." Social conditioning brings about autonomy more so than female education per se. Indeed, in some cases higher female education may result in a loss of autonomy since such women may marry wealthier husbands who could restrict their activities (Kaufmann & Cleland, 1994, quoted in Mason, 1995). Such individual characteristics as education or employment do not address the social context in which people operate.

The position of individuals in a group is a social construct, as the range of reactions is influenced by perceptions molded by the larger society. Goldscheider (1995:472) stresses that the causes of demographic behavior can best be understood by moving beyond the individual and focusing on what people derive from "... belonging to various kinds of families, and hence why they should form them, remain in them, and contribute to them." She is convinced that it is within this larger community/societal context that we are able to comprehend the content of long-term intergenerational and gender relations that make up the core of the lives of many people. Thus, any measure of autonomy should include the social conditions that shape the individual's decision making and practices. Toward this end, Schuler & Hashemi (1994, quoted in Mason, 1995:8) have identified six specific components of female empowerment in Bangladesh. These are: (1) sense of self and vision of a future; (2) mobility and visibility; (3) economic security; (4) status and decision-making power within the household; (5) ability to interact effectively in the public sphere; and (6) participation in non-family groups.

---

[1]The nature of these confusions and alternative concepts employed by various authors are discussed in detail by Mason (1987).

Although there is no consensus as to what constitutes female autonomy, one of the attempts to measure "autonomy" has been to use "a basket of issues." Among them are those issues involving the individual (e.g., educational attainment, occupation, and age), and those derived from the social milieu within which people operate (e.g., family of orientation, involvement of females in public life, involvement in household and community decision making, expression of rights on issues such as occupation and disposal of income, right to own property and dispose of property acquired, etc.).

The focus of the present study, then, is to utilize multiple indicators to examine the concept and the implications of women's autonomy on a wide range of factors including contraception and fertility behavior in Ghana. In this study, women's autonomy at the individual level is conceptualized as a composite of: (1) formal educational level, (2) employment status, (3) control and disposal of independently-earned income, and (4) communication and decision making on a wide range of issues including contraception and ultimate fertility. At the institutional level, the concept of female autonomy is used to capture: (1) levels of involvement in the family decision-making process, (2) gender role expectations and obligations, (3) societal norms on issues such as "gender-appropriate" behavior for females and males, (4) leadership positions for females and males, and (5) rights within marriage including sexual rights as well as inheritance of property.

● **Formal Education**

In developed and developing countries, numerous studies have shown that formal education is a prerequisite for greater social autonomy for women, and in several ways, helps shape their biological destiny as well (Gaisie, 1969; Cochrane, 1979; Oppong, 1982; Caldwell, 1982; Bulatao, 1984; Farooq & Simmons, 1985; Kasarda et al., 1986). For instance, formal education socializes the individual into new behavior patterns which may undermine the traditional norms of procreation and facilitates the application of scientific knowledge. Through formal education, a woman gets access to printed materials and information--a major link to the modern world--which enhances her knowledge and practice of modern contraception (Kasarda et al., 1986; Oheneba-Sakyi, 1992; Oheneba-Sakyi & Takyi, 1997).

Furthermore, the formal education system frees girls from their parents' control for many hours of the week. Once in school, they form new social networks, and are encouraged to ask questions and express ideas which the traditional system may discourage them from doing (Kritz & Gurak, 1989). All these skills can eventually facilitate women's autonomy in decision making. Formal education also exposes women to better nutritional practices and health care facilities. For instance, Caldwell (1986) argues that better educated women have the tendency to diagnose illness and seek professional help promptly. With access to quality care, infant/child mortality is reduced, thereby minimizing the motivation to have additional children in the expectation that some will die. For the reasons discussed above, therefore, women's autonomy in decision making is expected to increase with formal education.

The absolute necessity of education in the lives of individuals and nations the world over was reaffirmed at "The World Conference on Education for All," organized by the United Nations in 1990 at Jomtien, Thailand. For citizens of the world's economically poorest countries, (most of which are in Africa), an essential element of this conference was its affirmation that female education is an important priority in order to empower them so they can be protected from sexual and economic exploitation and live to their fullest potential (UNICEF, 1998). Overall, the educated woman is more likely to translate the autonomy she has into egalitarianism, improved communication with her spouse, and a desire to be involved in decision making in areas that directly affect her lifestyle such as choice of a marriage partner, and control of natural fertility via the adoption of modern contraception.

- **Employment Status**

Another indicator of women's decision making autonomy which affects fertility behavior is their participation in paid work. Various studies in industrial economies have found linkages between fertility decline and economic change resulting from a decline in the agricultural labor force and a shift to industrial labor (see e.g., Birdsall, 1977; Lesthaeghe & Wilson, 1986). In general, it is believed that women's involvement in non-familial work has the tendency to enhance their status outside the home. For instance, Knodel et al.'s (1987) study in Thailand concluded that high rates of labor force participation were among the significant factors that contributed to rapid fertility decline in that country.

As documented in the literature, a high proportion of West African women have always engaged in productive work outside the home (Oppong, 1970; Ware, 1977; Robertson, 1983, 1989; Kritz & Gurak, 1989; Lloyd & Gage-Brandon, 1993; Clark, 1994). The high rates of non-familial productive work among Ghanaian women was confirmed by a United Nations report in 1985 on women's work rates in 38 developing countries. With work rates of over 90 percent, the U.N. study ranked Ghana the highest in terms of productive activity other than housework.

However, in spite of the high involvement of women in several aspects of the productive life of Ghana, and the significant progress in terms of female education over the years, women generally occupy subordinate positions even in occupations where they dominate (Date-Bah, 1982; Ghana Government, 1984; ROG Statistical Service, 1989; Akuffo, 1990; Republic of Ghana [ROG] & UNICEF, 1990). This disparity means that even though female participation in the labor force is higher (51.4 percent) than that of males (48.6 percent), a greater proportion of males compared to females are found in the organized or formal sector of the economy.

On the whole, though, it is believed that the socio-economic incentive that non-familial work offers to women increases their domestic power, stimulates better communication in their relationships, and could create a desire to reduce the number of children born.

- **Control of Earnings**

It is not only the woman's employment status that affects her autonomy in decision making, but also her control of money independently earned. Studies have demonstrated that money is an important strategic resource that increases women's power in relationships (see e.g., Blau, 1964; Edwards, 1969; Oppong, 1970).

Traditionally, Ghanaian women, and indeed, West African women in general, have always been involved in non-familial work, specifically, participating in agricultural production, fishing, weaving, pottery, and other crafts either on their own or jointly with husbands or kin (Oppong, 1970; Fiawoo, 1978a; Kritz & Gurak, 1989; Blanc & Lloyd, 1990; ROG & UNICEF, 1990). Furthermore, they have been allowed to sell the surplus of their farm produce, and also engage in other kinds of trading activities to earn additional income for saving, personal use and/or family expenditure (Lesthaeghe, 1989; Blanc & Lloyd, 1990). The need for women to secure an independent source of income and control of earnings in marital relations is linked to the "unreliability of financial contributions from husbands" which may come about as a result of death, divorce, illness, or even an unanticipated polygyny (Clark, 1994:338). It is suggested that a woman's financial independence will to a large extent enhance her decision making ability.

● **Communication and Decision Making**

In spite of the history of high levels of economic activities and some financial autonomy among Ghanaian women, birth rates are high. The extent of the translation of the socio-economic autonomy into fertility decision making is not clear. Caldwell & Caldwell (1988) argue that African women have less autonomy in matters of reproduction due to a lineage system and networking that fosters kin interests over the interests of the smaller nuclear family unit.

In most African cultures, the husband is normatively regarded as the provider, the household head and patriarch, who commands respect from his dependent children and wives (O'Laughlin, 1974). While for women marriage is supposed to mark the transfer of dependence from father to husband, for men marriage is to help them accumulate social status and dependents (Henn, 1989). These relations of patriarchal dominance remain a prominent feature in most Ghanaian households. It is suggested that these practices may reduce effective communication between couples and restrain a wife's freedom to make reproductive decisions. To a large extent then, the decisions pertaining to fertility-related behavior could be understood in terms of the dynamic aspects of the household power structures.

A major feature of Ghanaian marriages is that they occur at an early age, particularly for females, most of whom marry soon after puberty. Marriage at an early age not only increases their risk of childbearing, but also results in most women marrying men who are often older than themselves (Central Bureau of Statistics [CBS], 1983; GSS & IRD, 1989; Takyi, 1993a). In Ghana, the mean age between spouses is 9 years (Casterline, et. al, 1986). Age-discrepant marriages create power in favor of the men and may be held responsible for inadequate communication and weak conjugal bonds for couples.

In the present study, we expound further on the power relations within marriage, and how such relations affect contraceptive use in Ghana. Since some of the methods of contraception--especially condom use, withdrawal, periodic abstinence or rhythm--require the support and cooperation of the husband, it is imperative to look at his perceptions and characteristics as well.

• **Gender Role Expectations**

The common variables in the transition to adulthood for men and women in Ghana are separation and segregation of roles, frequent duo-locality, and a large measure of independence from each other (Oppong, 1987). Traditional notions about gender/sex roles whereby husbands are regarded as the providers, heads of household and patriarchs can be found among Ghanaians. As such, men are supposed to be respected, served the best food, and be freed from performing certain household tasks labeled as demeaning (Akuffo, 1987; ROG & UNICEF, 1990; Lloyd & Gage-Brandon, 1993). Men are responsible for the maintenance and debts of their wives and children, willful neglect of which are grounds for divorce (Kuenyehia, 1978; Nukunya, 1978).

In several essays and reviews, Oppong and others have documented the multi-faceted nature of the role of the Ghanaian woman in marriage and family life. Their studies provide insights into the woman's roles as mother, mate/wife, worker outside the home, housekeeper/worker inside the home, kinswoman, community member, and individual (see e.g., Oppong, 1974, 1982, 1983a, 1983b, 1987, 1993; Oppong & Abu, 1984). These involvements vary by ethnic group and family system. However, it is primarily the responsibility of the Ghanaian mother to provide the basic household needs such as cooking, cleaning, washing clothes and dishes, fetching water, taking care of the frail (children, the sick, the elderly), and ensuring the good health and well-being of all family members (Caldwell, 1982; Oppong, 1987).

African women and men generally accept the traditional distinctions of female and male roles based on their beliefs that nature and culture are inseparable. Hence, gender relations are negotiated and manipulated, and responsibilities are performed to meet complementary interests and needs of the household, economic, and socio-political domains (Mikell, 1997).

Even though Ghanaian fathers' contribution to household responsibilities have traditionally been limited to the provision of educational and housing costs and the support of kin, their familial roles have been changing due to the levels of formal education, migration, and formal employment,. Socially mobile fathers tend to have a greater sense of the importance of individual parenting responsibility, and high aspirations for their children's educational attainment (Oppong, 1987). Also, there is evidence in Ghana to support the thesis that the more marital resources wives have (such as education, employment and income for the maintenance of the conjugal family), the more likely husbands will share domestic and parental activities and responsibilities (Oppong, 1970; Oppong, 1982; Oppong, 1987). Undoubtedly, cultural capital would stimulate better communication between spouses and lead to culturally enriched lives.

- **Societal Norms on Gender-Appropriate Education and Leadership**

Societal attitudes toward female education have over the years created educational inequalities throughout most countries in Africa. For example, among the Masai people of eastern Africa, there is the perception that when girls are sent to school they may learn that they are more valuable than cattle, thus, threatening the Masai traditional cultural values (Slakey, 1997; Kaufmann & Meekers, 1998; Fisher,

1999). Schooling in Ghana has been primarily for the benefit of males, although there are recent reports showing general improvement in educational attainment for females as well (GSS & MI, 1994; United Nations Children's Fund [UNICEF], 1994). In both absolute and relative terms, female enrollment always lags behind that of males at all levels of the educational ladder.

The educational disparity between females and males in Ghana increases as the level of education increases. In the 1989/90 academic year, for instance, of the total number of children enrolled in primary school, 45.1 percent were females and the rest males. While at the secondary school level females accounted for 38 percent of the enrollment, they only constituted 18.3 percent of the university enrollment (Republic of Ghana [ROG] Statistical Service, 1989:59; Ghana Statistical Service [GSS], 1991:81-95). Thus, the proportion of Ghanaian females in educational institutions declines as the level of education increases.

The obstacles to female education in Ghana have included early marriage, adolescent pregnancy, and financial constraints. Traditionally, most illiterate parents have taken on the attitude that higher education is not "appropriate" for females because of the risk of pregnancy which often leads to school drop-out, ultimately followed by marriage (Bukh, 1979; Bleek, 1981; Akuffo, 1987). This situation leads to low educational aspiration of girls who then perceive their future roles largely as mothers and homemakers. In West Africa, generally, women are valued for their reproductive as well as productive abilities, thus they may readily be encouraged to choose marriage as a means to gain power in the society (Lesthaeghe, 1989; Kaufmann & Meekers, 1998).

Although societal attitudes of educating girls are gradually changing in Ghana and elsewhere in Africa, it is still the practice that whenever cash-strapped families are faced with cost-cutting measures in their fiscal choices, they frequently choose to invest more in their sons' education than their daughters in the hope that the men will give the family a better return on their investment. This perception is in contrast to Harrison's (1997) study which estimates that when all things are considered, providing education for girls gives a 20 percent financial return because of the high probability that an educated mother will raise healthy educated daughters and sons, and thus so will the succeeding generations in the family for years to come.

Because formal education throughout Africa, and in most parts of the world, has traditionally been a male preserve, so has the bureaucracy. Therefore, it is no coincidence that at economic, social, and political levels of society, the number of women at senior level decision-making positions remains abysmally low. Globally, it has been documented that women constitute only 3 percent of political ministerial positions, 4 percent of executive positions, 10 percent of law and justice positions, and 14 percent of ministerial positions in the category of social services (World Wide Government Directory, 1996).

Similarly, Ghanaian men dominate in the professional, technical, administrative, managerial, production and related occupations, while women tend to be more involved in trading, service, and agricultural-related work although among the Akans menopausal women and those of royal birth are given some opportunities to occupy leadership positions in their communities. When Ghanaian women do go to school it is typically at a vocational, commercial or technical institution which prepares them for low paying jobs such as hairdressers, dressmakers, beauticians, cooks, secretaries, typists, nurses and such (Ghana Government, 1984). Because their low level of education qualifies them only for low paying jobs, even females with formal education, still become subordinates at the work place. This makes them socially and economically dependent and vulnerable to their well placed, highly educated and better paid male counterparts. With a change in traditional societal standards and attitudes about gender-appropriate education and leadership, increased opportunities for women in the public as well as the private domain could enhance the cause of social progress and sustainable development for the society as a whole.

- **Sexual Rights and Inheritance**

The issue of rights within marriage in the African context is complicated by the "legal pluralism" that permits various codified customary laws and practices to operate side-by-side with those imposed through the introduction of Islam and Christianity, the colonial and post-colonial states (Allot, 1960; Woodman, 1988; Owen, 1996). Hence, marital rights vary depending on factors such as the ethnic group, lineage group, type of marriage contracted, and which European country was the colonizer. In spite of the variations of marriage laws and customs, several studies have documented that gender inequity is a significant feature inherent in most of the existing laws (see e.g., Vellenga, 1971; Owen, 1996; Manuh, 1997, Toungara, 1997). The two issues that impact women and children the most and that we are especially concerned with in this study, are sexual rights and the right to inherit a deceased spouse's self-acquired property.

The persistence of polygyny in many African societies where husbands are legally allowed to marry more than one wife indicates the appearance of double standards with regards to sexual rights within marriage. These double standards are quite obvious under the Customary and Islamic law, both of which legally permit husbands to acquire additional wives but denies wives similar legal rights to be married to additional husbands. While the impact of the Ghanaian marriage systems on reproductive behavior are discussed in Chapter 3, the focus of Chapter 8 is on the effects of marriage systems on sexual rights.

Throughout Africa, as the use of communally-owned land became important for the farming of cash crops such as cocoa, coffee, rubber, and tea, the issue of how proceeds from the land should be shared became contentious. Equally touchy has been how to adequately compensate surviving wives and children who often work the land. Since it is within one's lineage group that one can inherit property, land, and other material possessions, traditional culture recognizes the transfer of lineage property while being fussy about individual property (Ollennu, 1966; Mikell, 1997).

Although transformations in inheritance laws in African societies are slow to produce because of traditions, pressure from women's groups and new economic realities have encouraged countries to make attempts at reforms. The Intestate Succession Law in Ghana is examined as one such attempt to reform inheritance.

From the theoretical discussion above, the following inter-related hypotheses, modified from Mason's (1987) ideas concerning the link between women's autonomy and fertility in third world populations, will be tested in Ghana.

**Hypothesized Effects:**

Women's autonomy is influenced by individual characteristics and also by institutional factors such as family of orientation, societal norms, perception and gender roles. The impact of these background factors on autonomy will be positive or negative depending on the amount of socio-economic capital (e.g., age, education, employment, income, etc.) that the individual brings into the relationship, as well as the extent of sexual double standards embedded in societal practices that create power differentials between women and men.

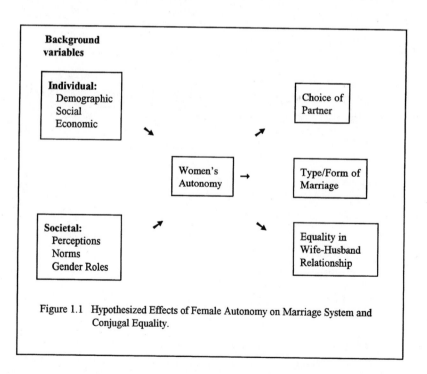

Figure 1.1   Hypothesized Effects of Female Autonomy on Marriage System and Conjugal Equality.

- The extent of women's autonomy influences choice of partner, the type of marriage (e.g., Customary, Ordinance, Islamic, Consensual) and form of marriage (monogamy versus polygyny), and equality in wife-husband relationship as illustrated in Figure 1.1 above.

- The nature of equality in wife-husband relationship, level of participation in partner choice, and marriage type and form influence couple communication which is assumed to include discussions about fertility control. Figure 1.2 shows the hypothesized effects of female autonomy on couple communication.

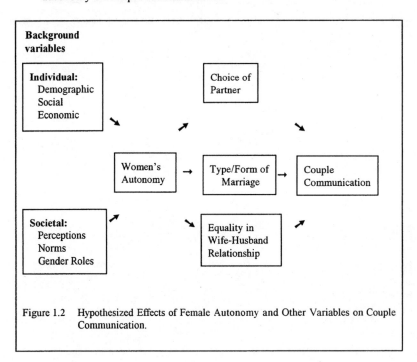

Figure 1.2    Hypothesized Effects of Female Autonomy and Other Variables on Couple Communication.

- Couple communication is likely to influence decision making in several familial domains including family planning. The hypothesized paths are shown in Figure 1.3.

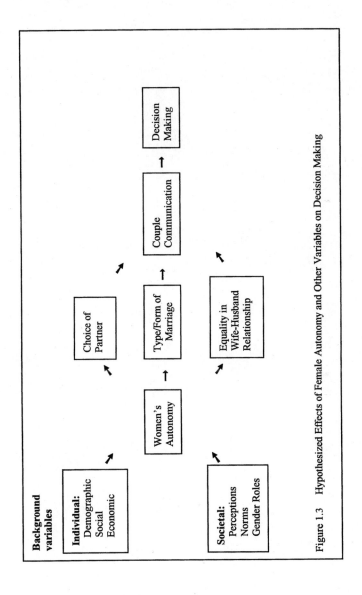

Figure 1.3    Hypothesized Effects of Female Autonomy and Other Variables on Decision Making

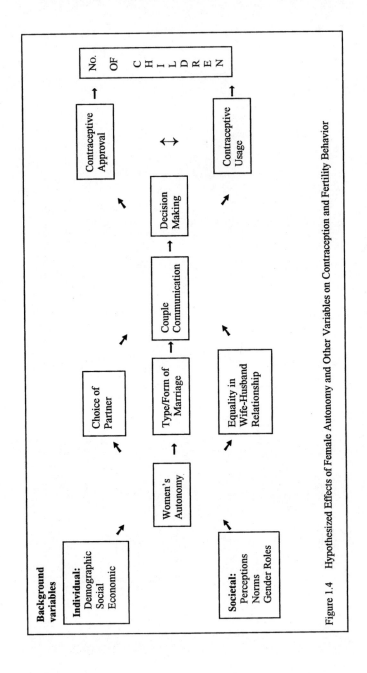

Figure 1.4    Hypothesized Effects of Female Autonomy and Other Variables on Contraception and Fertility Behavior

- The final model is presented in Figure 1.4, showing all the hypothesized paths through which women's autonomy may influence decision making which then affects contraceptive approval and usage, and ultimately fertility.

The complete model, then, indicates that women's autonomy (which is itself influenced by individual and societal factors) is predicted to influence contraception and fertility outcomes through conjugal equality, couple communication and decision making among other things.

In summary, it seems clear from the literature that women's autonomy in decision making at the individual level may be attained through the acquisition of formal education which increases one's willingness to engage in innovative behavior, through the ability to work and earn money independently of the husband and the power to control the earnings, and through egalitarianism and the ability to discuss and communicate family-related issues such as reproduction with one's spouse.

At the societal level, a woman's autonomy may be a function of the society's perception of gender roles, gender-appropriate education, customary practices, and the rights and obligations of married couples. The context that may condition the relationship between female autonomy and fertility behavior is the level of "modernization" (see e.g., Bukh, 1979; Lloyd, 1986; Mason, 1987; Henn, 1989). Although the concept of "modernization" has been widely discussed in the literature to include the attainment of formal education, wage-labor, "modern" political systems, foreign religions, and urbanization, to better appreciate modernization's impact in the African context, Eyetsemitan (1997) distinguishes between two types of modernization: (1) modernization from within--defined as the gradual evolving of new ways of life and behavior patterns by the people and for the people based on collective experience, with or without outside contact, and (2) modernization from outside--defined as others outside the culture imposing new ways of life and patterns of behavior on the people as was the case of the colonial experience of most African peoples, which resulted in "Western" ideas being viewed with cynicism and suspicion.

The social context of analysis is essential because of the varying normative and socio-political circumstances within which individuals make decisions on the patterning and sequencing of the key events in their lives (Teachman, 1985; Namboodiri & Suchindran, 1987). In different cultural settings, variations in socio-economic resources and value systems produce different arrangements of life-course events like marriage and childbearing because of the differential impact these processes have on social change from within and from without on the individual and society as a whole. For example, for the highly educated, external pressures that may influence their behavior could be coming from professional colleagues, while with illiterates the pressure might from in-laws, friends, or religious leaders.

How would greater women's autonomy in decision making, as discussed above, affect contraception and fertility behavior among couples in contemporary Ghana, where as in many African countries, "modernization from within" and "modernization from the outside" have been operating side by side as a continuous process of adjustments and reactions with the indigenous social institutions? And what are the intervening factors that may impact the process of social change? The present study was designed to shed some light on these issues.

**2**

---

# METHODOLOGY

## PREPARATION

Before the Ghana Female Autonomy Micro Study survey was conducted, a one-week training session was organized by the three project associates for 12 field assistants, made up of two supervisors and 10 interviewers at the University of Ghana, Legon. This was in September, 1992. Initially, the survey was to be held in October-November, 1992. But it was suspended due to the campaigns for the country's Fourth Republic Presidential and Parliamentary elections in November-December, 1992. The period following the Presidential election was politically charged when the opposition parties challenged the results of the Presidential election alleging that it was rigged (New Patriotic Party, 1993). As a result, the opposition parties boycotted the Parliamentary election that was scheduled to be held two weeks after the Presidential election. Although the date for the Parliamentary election was postponed with the hope that the opposition parties would change their stand, they still refused to take part. The survey was eventually held between December, 1992, and March, 1993, after the elections. In spite of the above observations, people were cooperative especially in the rural areas. Therefore, the quality of the data collected was not likely to have been influenced by the political situation in the country at the time the survey was administered.

In each of the selected settlements, both the traditional (chiefs and elders) and the modern (district assembly members and members of the Committee for the Defence of the Revolution--[CDR]) political structures were informed about the survey. Because there has been a lot of discussion on the effects of prior information or lack of it on survey responses in Ghana (see e.g., Agyeman et al., 1990), our intention was to solicit the support and cooperation of the members of the various communities before the field work began. Experience from the GFAMS and other studies indicate that gaining support from existing traditional and modern community leaders gives credence and enhances cooperation in such surveys.

### DATA COLLECTION

For the GFAMS project, the Accra metropolitan area and four rural districts in the Central Region were purposively selected to provide contrast regarding the variables of interest. The Accra metropolitan area, as the most urbanized place in Ghana, was chosen to provide information on "modern" trends in demographic behavior. On the other hand, the rural communities in the Central Region were expected to represent traditional views and practices. The settlements in the latter were also selected to reflect the occupational differences in the region. These are the fishing communities along the coast and the interior farming communities.

The target was 1,000 couples with 600 selected from the Accra sub-sample and 400 in the Central Region. The sample frame was electoral areas and the selection of areas for the study was based on the results of the November 1992 Presidential Elections.[2] The selected electoral areas for the GFAMS are shown in Appendix A. The selection of areas for the survey then varied according to the region. In the Greater Accra region, considerations of the cost of data collection and supervision of the field-work made it imperative to use Self-Weighted Multi-Stage Sampling. The decision was made to use three-stage sampling of the following kind:

---

[2]Initially, the sampling frame for the Ghana Living Standards Survey was going to be used but this was not readily available; and so after the Presidential elections, it was felt that the electoral areas presented another sampling frame which could be used for the selection of specific study areas.

(1) As first-stage sampling units, constituencies for the 1992 presidential elections were used. (2) As second-stage sampling units constituency areas were used. (3) As third-stage sampling units, dwelling units were used and all households in the selected dwelling units were included in the sample.  In the Central region, a number of settlements were selected from each electoral area by simple random sampling.  These settlements were then sampled according to size.  The settlements were then clustered and couples were chosen from every other house (one couple per household) till the number of expected couples from that settlement was obtained.  The choice of couple in a household was the availability of that couple for interview.

Data collection was through the use of questionnaires.  However, most of the questions were open ended so that respondents could express themselves.  And since the interaction of the interviewers and the respondents was one-on-one, it provided an avenue for in-depth discussion of some of the issues covered. (Helitzer-Allen, et al., (1994) provides an excellent critique of in-depth interview in sub-Saharan Africa.) The original questionnaire for the interview was written in English.  Ideally, it should have been written in a Ghanaian language or translated into the various languages in the areas where the questionnaire was administered as was the case with GFS and the GDHSs questionnaires.  The debate on the translation and re-translation of questionnaires in demographic surveys is still alive (see for instance, Lucas & Ware, 1981).  However, given the numbers involved and the range of Ghanaian Languages spoken in the areas of the survey, it was decided that the original questionnaire be kept in English and translated on the spot when necessary.  Consequently, efforts were made to translate some of the concepts into Ghanaian languages during the training session.

The questionnaire for each couple had three parts.  The first part involved a listing of all household members and the socio-economic background of the selected couple.  Eligibility was defined as married with both husband and wife present either in the same or separate household/dwelling places. From the household schedule, the eligible couples were identified.  The second part of the questionnaire was for the eligible female while the third was for the selected female's spouse. Both the female and male questionnaires were identical (except for the question on polygyny where polygynous wives were asked about their rank). Each couple questionnaire had questions soliciting information on the following areas: (1) Background Characteristics, (2) Marriage Systems, (3) Childbearing, (4) Contraceptive Use, (5) Couple Communication, (6) Couple Decision Making, (7) In-law Influence, (8) Disposal of Income Intestate Succession, (9) Gender Roles, and (10) Marital Rights.

The GFS of 1979/80 and DHSs of 1988 and 1993 were not designed to measure issues dealing with female autonomy. Education, employment and age between couple, which have been widely used as measures of autonomy, are at best only "proxies" (Mason, 1995). The GFAMS was designed specifically to capture a number of issues in female autonomy. Thus, the questionnaire has face validity for the measurement of female autonomy.

In order to avoid spousal interference, the interviews were held separately for the wife and the husband. Where the two were physically available in the same house, one was interviewed first based on availability away from the hearing of the other person, and after that the other was interviewed. At times it became important to distract the men in particular by offering to buy them drinks away from the house. In the fishing communities, the potential source of interference for the men was from colleagues during group activities such as the mending of nets. In such cases, the respondent was taken outside the hearing distance of the others.

The quality of responses using the direct interview or canvasser method has been found to partly depend on some of the terminologies used, the gender and age of the interviewers vis-a-vis the respondents, the interviewing environment and the recall lapse time (Awusabo-Asare & Agyeman, 1993; Caldwell et al., 1994; Dare & Cleland, 1994). There was every attempt to keep some of these potential interferences to a minimum, such as the use of both male and female interviewers. In some cases respondents were interviewed by people of the opposite sex. But overall, the survey appeared to have been well received and the communities cooperated.

## DATA PROCESSING AND ANALYSES

Following the interviewing, the questionnaires were edited by the supervisors for completeness. All the completed questionnaires were then sent to SUNY Potsdam, for data entry and processing in July, 1993. Under the supervision of the Project Director and Principal Investigator, the data coding was done by a team of trained research assistants between September, 1993, and May, 1994. In the summer of 1994, the data were cleaned by locating out-liers, out-of-range response categories, missing cases, and matching identification numbers with "questionable" response codes and original questionnaire. For the data analyses of the GFAMS project, the Statistical Package for the Social Scientist (SPSS-X) software was used. From September 1994 to July 1995, data analyses and write-ups of preliminary reports were undertaken.

A descriptive research design was used in the present study to describe the distribution of both discrete and continuous variables and examine the joint distributions of two or more variables (Knoke & Bohrnstedt, 1994). Summaries of distribution of variables in the form of simple frequencies, percentages, arithmetic means, bar charts, histograms, and pie charts have been used wherever appropriate to help in the interpretation of the data. In addition to describing the data, bivariate crosstabulations or joint contingency tables were used for the most part to assess the relationship between relevant background variables, taking a number of female autonomy indicators--including choice of partner, type of marriage, equality in conjugal communication and decision making, contraception, and fertility behavior-- as dependent variables.

## DISSEMINATION OF PRELIMINARY RESULTS

The preliminary results of the GFAMS project and policy implications for development were presented at a conference in Accra, Ghana, in August, 1995 to a national audience. The organizations/groups represented included the University of Ghana, Legon; the University of Cape Coast; Ghana Statistical Service; National

Population Council (NPC); Population Impact Project (PIP); Ministry of Health, Planned Parenthood Association of Ghana (PPAG); National Council on Women and Development (NCWD); United Nation Children's Fund (UNICEF); AIDS Control Program; Department of Social Welfare; Ministry of Education; Institute of Adult Education; Christian Council of Ghana; Muslim Council of Ghana; and the National Press Corps. Several of these groups are generally involved in policy making, administration and implementation of family and population programs in the country. At this forum, participants examined, discussed, and critiqued the conceptual framework, methodology, and research findings of this study, and made suggestions for future research on the family and the improvement of women's lives.

## BACKGROUND CHARACTERISTICS OF RESPONDENTS

Of the 1,000 households selected, 940 were successfully interviewed, giving us a household response rate of 94 percent. Out of the 940 eligible wives in the household schedule, 933 were successfully interviewed, a response rate of 99 percent. Of the 940 eligible husbands, 916 were successfully interviewed, representing a response rate of 97 percent. Thus, when wives were matched to their husbands, the resulting sample was made up of 909 couples. While 61 percent of the couples resided in the urban area (identified in this study as the Greater Accra region), the remaining 39 percent lived in the rural area (identified with the selected settlements in the Central region). The rural-urban distribution reflects our purposive sampling.

In Ghana, as in a number of non-literate societies, vital events are not normally recorded. Often, dates of events are estimated with reference to major historical occurrences in the country (such as political elections, death of presidents or chiefs, major natural disasters), estimates which might not be accurate. Exact dates of occurrence of events are likely to be misreported, particularly among illiterate people. For events such as marriages, which have the tendency to involve long processes of customary ceremonies, exact dates may not be reported. One manifestation of the poor dating is "age heaping," whereby preference for numbers ending with "zero" and "five," and for even numbers, are reported. As a result, age data have to be viewed with some caution.

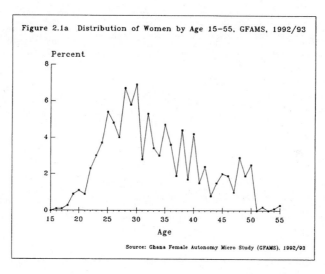

Figure 2.1a   Distribution of Women by Age 15-55, GFAMS, 1992/93

Source: Ghana Female Autonomy Micro Study (GFAMS), 1992/93

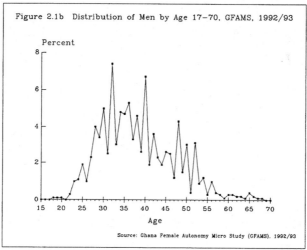

Figure 2.1b   Distribution of Men by Age 17-70, GFAMS, 1992/93

Source: Ghana Female Autonomy Micro Study (GFAMS), 1992/93

**Table 2.1**    Percentage Distribution of Couples by Age, GFS (1979/80), GDHS (1988), GFAMS (1992/93)

| | COUPLES | | | | | |
| | GFS[1] | | GDHS[2] | | GFAMS | |
| AGE | Wife | Husband | Wife | Husband | Wife | Husband |
|---|---|---|---|---|---|---|
| 15-19 | 8.3 | 0.3 | 4.3 | 0.6 | 1.3 | 0.2 |
| 20-24 | 20.9 | 4.0 | 15.0 | 3.7 | 10.9 | 2.2 |
| 25-29 | 20.6 | 12.1 | 24.9 | 12.3 | 26.3 | 12.5 |
| 30-34 | 16.5 | 15.2 | 18.7 | 17.5 | 21.5 | 22.8 |
| 35-39 | 14.2 | 12.8 | 16.6 | 15.0 | 16.6 | 20.5 |
| 40-44 | 11.2 | 12.9 | 10.0 | 14.6 | 10.1 | 16.4 |
| 45-49 | 8.2 | 11.2 | 10.5 | 13.3 | 9.9 | 12.1 |
| 50+ | ** | 31.5 | ** | 23.2 | 3.1 | 12.8 |
| Not reporting | 0.0 | 0.0 | 0.0 | 0.0 | 0.3 | 0.6 |
| TOTAL | 100.0 | 100.0 | 100.0 | 100.0 | 100.0 | 100.0 |
| NUMBER | [4436] | [4436] | [1010] | [1010] | [909] | [909] |

**Note:**
[1]Data are computed from Ghana Fertility Survey (GFS) data files, 1979/80
[2]Data are computed from Ghana Demographic and Health Survey (GDHS) data files, 1988
** Data were not collected on women aged 50+

As was the case in the GFS, 1979/80, and the GDHS, 1988, Figures 2.1a & 2.1b show that there were disproportionately large numbers of both women and men in the sample reporting ages with terminal digits of 0 and 5, an evidence of "age heaping." In most of the analysis, the conventional five-year age groups had been used to reduce the impact of age heaping on certain digits. As shown in Table 2.1, the distribution of the couples looked quite similar to those found in the GFS, 1979/80 and the GDHS, 1988.

Although recent indications point to an increasing trend of female-headed households and the marginalization of husbands and fathers in Ghana (Bleek, 1987; Lloyd & Gage-Brandon, 1993), the households in the selected sample areas were overwhelmingly male-headed as indicated in Table 2.2.

Table 2.2    Percentage Distribution of Households by Head of Household, Type of Residence,
Number of Rooms, Co-residential Status, and Living Arrangement of Children,
According to Residence, GFAMS, 1992/93

| | COUPLES | | | |
| | URBAN | | RURAL | |
| Characteristic | Percent | Number | Percent | Number |
|---|---|---|---|---|
| **HOUSEHOLD HEAD** | | | | |
| Male | 97.6 | 1071 | 93.5 | 664 |
| Female | 2.4 | 26 | 6.5 | 46 |
| Total | 100.0 | 1097 | 100.0 | 710 |
| **TYPE OF RESIDENCE** | | | | |
| Owner occupier (bungalow) | 3.5 | 38 | 7.6 | 54 |
| Owner occupier (shared) | 4.7 | 51 | 6.9 | 49 |
| Family house | 20.1 | 219 | 34.8 | 248 |
| Hired premises (alone) | 7.1 | 77 | 8.4 | 60 |
| Hired premises (shared) | 58.6 | 638 | 33.0 | 235 |
| Other | 6.1 | 66 | 9.4 | 67 |
| Total | 100.0 | 1089 | 100.0 | 713 |
| **NUMBER OF ROOMS OCCUPIED** | | | | |
| One room | 23.2 | 256 | 56.3 | 403 |
| Two rooms | 44.7 | 493 | 27.5 | 197 |
| Three rooms | 18.1 | 199 | 8.4 | 60 |
| 4 or more rooms | 14.0 | 154 | 7.8 | 56 |
| Total | 100.0 | 1102 | 100.0 | 716 |
| **LIVE IN SAME HOUSE** | | | | |
| Yes | 93.7 | 1027 | 82.4 | 589 |
| No | 6.3 | 69 | 17.6 | 126 |
| Total | 100.0 | 1096 | 100.0 | 715 |
| **LIVING ARRANGEMENT OF CHILDREN** | | | | |
| Live with both parents | 87.8 | 893 | 71.6 | 479 |
| Live with wife only | 5.3 | 54 | 14.1 | 94 |
| Live with husband only | 1.2 | 12 | 6.0 | 40 |
| Live with wife's relatives | 2.4 | 24 | 2.1 | 14 |
| Live with husband's relatives | 0.4 | 4 | 2.2 | 15 |
| Other | 2.9 | 30 | 4.0 | 27 |
| Total | 100.0 | 1017 | 100.0 | 669 |

The fact that the majority of the households in the GFAMS were headed by males may be because, unlike other studies that included single parents (most of whom are women), the present study utilized a sample of married couples only. The data also showed that while the type of residence predominant in the urban area was hired premises shared by other occupiers, over one third of rural couples lived in family houses. In the rural area, well over half of the couples occupied only a single dwelling room, whereas over two-thirds of urban couples occupied two or more rooms. While almost 20 percent of the rural couples in the sample did not live in the same house, only 6 percent of urban couples lived apart from each other.

In terms of the living arrangement of children, Table 2.2 indicates that while the majority of children lived with both parents, about three times as many children in rural areas lived with their mothers only as compared to children living in urban areas. Consistent with high fertility desires and attitudes towards childrearing, Ghanaians, as do others in West Africa, participate in widespread child fostering (Goody, 1973; Fiawoo, 1978a; Isiugo-Abanihe, 1983, 1985; Page, 1989). Child fostering is defined by Isiugo-Abanihe (1994:163) as "the assumption by surrogate or non-biological parents of the responsibility of raising a child." The data indicate some incidence of fostering--8 percent for children in the rural area and 6 percent for children in the urban area.

The percentage distribution of couples by age and selected background characteristics is presented in Table 2.3. The results indicate that the 15-19 year age group comprised less than 2 percent of the sample of both wives and husbands. The 25-29 age group accounted for 26 percent of the wives but only 13 percent of the husbands. For the wives, the proportion of the sample in the older age group declined steadily from 17 percent in the 35-39 age group to 3 percent in the 50+ age group. For the husbands, the decline was from 21 percent in the 35-39 age group to 13 percent in the 50+ age group.

Forty-five percent of wives in the sample did not work in the four weeks preceding the survey compared to only 23 percent of husbands.

**Table 2.3**   Percentage Distribution of Couples by Age and Selected Background Characteristics, GFAMS, 1992/93

| Background Characteristic | COUPLES | | | |
| | WIFE | | HUSBAND | |
| | Percent | Number | Percent | Number |
| --- | --- | --- | --- | --- |
| **AGE** | | | | |
| 15-19 | 1.3 | 12 | 0.2 | 2 |
| 20-24 | 10.9 | 99 | 2.2 | 20 |
| 25-29 | 26.4 | 239 | 12.6 | 114 |
| 30-34 | 21.5 | 195 | 22.9 | 207 |
| 35-39 | 16.7 | 151 | 20.6 | 186 |
| 40-44 | 10.2 | 92 | 16.5 | 149 |
| 45-49 | 9.9 | 90 | 12.2 | 110 |
| 50 + | 3.1 | 28 | 12.8 | 116 |
| | | | | |
| **RESIDENCE** | | | | |
| Urban | 60.6 | 551 | 60.6 | 551 |
| Rural | 39.4 | 358 | 39.4 | 358 |
| | | | | |
| **OCCUPATION** | | | | |
| Professional | 7.3 | 66 | 20.1 | 182 |
| Sub-professional/tech | 1.8 | 16 | 3.8 | 34 |
| Clerical | 6.1 | 55 | 10.6 | 96 |
| Sales | 20.5 | 185 | 3.9 | 35 |
| Service/transport | 5.2 | 47 | 13.5 | 122 |
| Farmer/fisherman | 1.4 | 13 | 3.9 | 35 |
| Craftsman | 12.6 | 114 | 21.5 | 194 |
| | | | | |
| **RELIGION** | | | | |
| Catholic | 17.5 | 159 | 18.9 | 171 |
| Protestant | 67.8 | 614 | 62.7 | 566 |
| Muslim | 4.4 | 40 | 4.7 | 42 |
| Traditionalist | 1.0 | 9 | 2.5 | 23 |
| Other religion | 6.7 | 61 | 6.6 | 60 |
| No religion | 2.5 | 23 | 4.5 | 41 |
| | | | | |
| **LEVEL OF EDUCATION** | | | | |
| No education | 17.0 | 151 | 4.5 | 40 |
| Elementary | 56.8 | 504 | 43.7 | 388 |
| Sec/tec/trg.college | 22.3 | 198 | 33.6 | 298 |
| Higher | 3.9 | 35 | 18.2 | 162 |
| | | | | |
| **TOTAL** | 100.0 | 909 | 100.0 | 909 |

The high proportion of women reporting themselves as not working is consistent with similar reports from Ghana censuses. Women tend to report themselves as homemakers, even when engaged in "economic activities." For all working wives, the common employment was in the sales sector (21 percent), followed by craftsmen (13 percent), with less than 10 percent as professionals or sub-professionals. Twenty-two percent of husbands worked as craftsmen, about a quarter as professionals, 11 percent as clerical workers, about 4 percent as farmers/fishermen, and the rest were almost evenly divided between, clerical/sales and service/transport.

A majority of wives (68 percent) and husbands (63 percent) were affiliated with the Protestant religion, followed by approximately 20 percent who were Catholics, with the remainder divided between Muslims, Traditionalists, and those with other religion and no religion. Except in the categories of Traditionalist religion and those without religion where there were about twice as many husbands as there are wives, it appeared that there were no significant differences between wives and husbands in religious affiliation.

While a mere 5 percent of husbands had never been to school, over three times as many wives (17 percent) reported having no formal education. Of those educated, 57 percent of wives had only elementary school education compared to 44 percent of husbands. As expected, almost a fifth of the husbands in the sample had attained some form of higher education beyond the secondary/technical/training college level while only 4 percent of wives had done so.

Educational differences between the age groups among wives and husbands are presented in Tables 2.4. Overall, the results indicate a general improvement in educational attainment with time, with the majority of both wives and husbands in the younger cohorts attaining basic education or higher. For instance, while 26 percent of women aged 40-44 never attended school, only 13-15 percent of women aged 20-29 had no formal education. These results echo a recent UNESCO report which listed Ghana as one of the 10 nations with the largest rises in literacy rates over the last two decades (UNICEF, 1994:23).

Table 2.4    Percentage Distribution of Couples by Level of Education, According to Age
             and Residence, GFAMS, 1992/93

| | | | LEVEL OF EDUCATION OF WIVES | | | |
|---|---|---|---|---|---|---|
| Background Characteristic | No Education | Elementary | Sec/tec/ Trg. Coll | Higher | Total | Number |
| AGE | | | | | | |
| 15-19 | 0.0 | 100.0 | 0.0 | 0.0 | 100.0 | 12 |
| 20-24 | 13.3 | 78.6 | 7.1 | 1.0 | 100.0 | 98 |
| 25-29 | 14.5 | 59.0 | 21.1 | 5.3 | 100.0 | 227 |
| 30-34 | 16.1 | 55.2 | 25.5 | 3.1 | 100.0 | 192 |
| 35-39 | 18.7 | 55.3 | 22.0 | 4.0 | 100.0 | 150 |
| 40-44 | 26.1 | 48.9 | 22.8 | 2.2 | 100.0 | 92 |
| 45-49 | 19.8 | 40.7 | 32.6 | 7.0 | 100.0 | 86 |
| 50+ | 10.7 | 39.3 | 42.9 | 7.1 | 100.0 | 28 |
| RESIDENCE | | | | | | |
| Urban | 11.2 | 53.3 | 30.5 | 5.0 | 100.0 | 538 |
| Rural | 26.0 | 62.0 | 9.7 | 2.3 | 100.0 | 350 |
| TOTAL | 16.8 | 56.8 | 22.4 | 4.0 | 100.0 | 888 |

| | | | LEVEL OF EDUCATION OF HUSBANDS | | | |
|---|---|---|---|---|---|---|
| AGE | | | | | | |
| 15-19 | 0.0 | 50.0 | 50.0 | 0.0 | 100.0 | 2 |
| 20-24 | 0.0 | 73.7 | 26.3 | 0.0 | 100.0 | 19 |
| 25-29 | 4.4 | 57.5 | 30.1 | 8.0 | 100.0 | 113 |
| 30-34 | 4.5 | 46.5 | 31.2 | 17.8 | 100.0 | 202 |
| 35-39 | 2.7 | 41.8 | 37.9 | 17.6 | 100.0 | 182 |
| 40-44 | 2.8 | 44.1 | 35.2 | 17.9 | 100.0 | 145 |
| 45-49 | 8.3 | 35.2 | 36.1 | 20.4 | 100.0 | 108 |
| 50+ | 7.1 | 30.4 | 29.5 | 33.0 | 100.0 | 112 |
| RESIDENCE | | | | | | |
| Urban | 0.9 | 35.4 | 39.7 | 24.0 | 100.0 | 537 |
| Rural | 10.0 | 56.4 | 24.2 | 9.4 | 100.0 | 351 |
| TOTAL | 4.5 | 43.7 | 33.6 | 18.2 | 100.0 | 888 |

According to the report, literacy rates in Ghana rose from 30 percent in 1970 to 60 percent in 1990, signifying a 30 percentage-point rise for the period. Urban-rural differences in educational attainment come as no surprise. People living in the urban areas, all things being equal, have more access to formal education than their rural counterparts. Moreover, formal education is an important factor in rural-urban migration. Urban areas tend to be the point of destination for a number of people with formal education. The results indicate that there were three times as many wives with post-elementary school education living in the urban area (36 percent) as wives living in the rural areas (12 percent), and that 64 percent of husbands residing in the urban area had at least a post-elementary education compared to 34 percent of husbands residing in rural areas.

In summary, this chapter has examined the methodology of our study including the data collection procedures and background characteristics of respondents. Among the highlights are that the households in the selected sample areas were predominantly male-headed. And that while the type of residence predominant in the urban area was hired premises shared by other occupiers, over one third of rural couples lived in family houses. This phenomena leads to the tendency for most rural couples to live apart from each other. The data also indicated that while the majority of children lived with both parents, about three times as many children in the rural area lived with their mothers alone compared to children in the urban area. There were significant rural-urban differences in educational attainment with people living in the urban area having more access to formal education than their rural counterparts.

The effects of these background characteristics are often ambiguous if examined in isolation. In the following chapters, an attempt will be made to use many of these variables to explore the interrelationships among them, and evaluate their influence on marriages, fertility behavior, contraception, communication, decision making, and gender roles.

## 3

---

# MARRIAGE SYSTEMS AND FERTILITY BEHAVIOR

## MARRIAGE SYSTEMS

Theoretically, the institution of marriage marks the beginning of family formation and the approved means for procreation for two individuals in most societies. However, in the African context, marriage goes beyond the individual since it was and is still one of the structures for building alliances between corporate clans. As a result, the choice of marriage partner has always been of concern to kin group. Among all the ethnic groups in Ghana, it is expected that any "normal" person will marry, at least once, in his/her lifetime. The condition of a never-married adult is unacceptable since the person is considered to be living an unfulfilled life. Due to this expectation, marriage is near universal.

An examination of the concept "marriage," as has been used in the contemporary Western societies, implies a single definitive act; a clearly defined legal state with socially sanctioned rights and obligations attendant upon that status. To the contrary, marriage in Ghana, and many societies in Africa, is defined as a developmental process which could take anywhere between a month to several years to complete because of the involvement of whole families of the bride and the groom (Radcliffe-Brown, 1950; Nukunya, 1978; Aryee, 1985).

Every cultural system has preferred forms of marriage. Among the matrilineal Akan and the patrilineal Ewe, the most preferred form of marriage is the one between cross cousins: marriage to one's father's sister's child or mother's brother's child. This is allowed because in each case the individuals involved belonged to different clans.  Among the Akan, cross-cousin marriage ensured that the self-acquired property of a man, which became extended family property after death in intestate, would also be available to his children through marriage (Rattray, 1929).  The Anlo Ewe also believe that couples who are relatives are more likely to think about kinship obligations and, therefore, such marriages tend to be stable (Nukunya, 1969).

Among the various Ghanaian ethnic groups in Ghana, it was the traditional responsibility of a father to perform the rites for the first marriage for a son.  Often, the prospective spouse was acquired either through betrothal or selection, in some cases, in consultation with the young people involved.  As an honor to the family name and also due to the wish to gain respect of the would-be husband, young women were expected to be virgins at first marriage while that was not expected of males. Before marriage, a father was expected to set his son up in life, an act that involved apprenticing him to a master craftsman, and/or giving him land for farming and a gun for hunting.  For a girl, setting her up in life involved giving her land for farming and or trinkets, in some cases including gold ornaments (Rattray, 1929).

In contemporary Ghana, however, the various norms governing marriage have changed and the expectations are not as they used to be.  For example, setting up a son or a daughter in life now often involves sending him or her to school or an urban area to acquire the necessary skills to cope with life in the modern world. Schooling and urban living, among other things, facilitate new social networking which loosens parental control over the economic and sexual activities of young women and men, hence opening up more options for family life than existed in the traditional system.

**Form of Marriage**

In this study, marriage implies all forms of sexual unions between males and females, irrespective of whether or not any marriage ceremonies have been performed. Three types of marriages are recognized by law in present day Ghana: (1) Customary law marriages [expected to be registered under PNDCL 112], (2) Marriage under the Ordinance [Cap 127], and (3) Marriage under the Islamic law [Cap 129]. Marriage under the Ordinance may be civil or religious (some people do marry both in church and at the registry/court). Every marriage under the Ordinance first goes through the Customary process. Both Customary and Islamic marriages have the potential of developing into polygyny. A fourth type of marriage called consensual union or common law marriage, also occurs in Ghana. This type of union is without statutory backing, is more likely to breakdown and also is more likely to involve some amount of extra-marital sex.

Since the GFAMS sample was made up of only married couples, the analysis did not include other marital statuses. In Figure 3.1, the percentage distribution of the form of marriage among couples in our sample is presented.

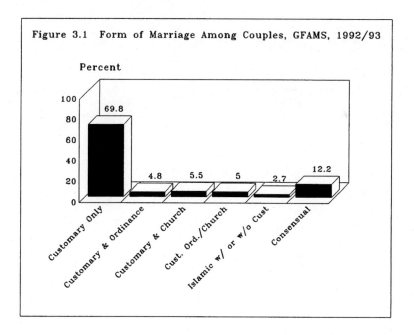

Figure 3.1   Form of Marriage Among Couples, GFAMS, 1992/93

**Marriage Systems and Fertility Behavior**

In spite of the fact that the first Marriage Ordinance in Ghana was passed in 1884, 70 percent of the marriages contracted in our sample were under Customary law only. Another 12 percent were in consensual union and 15 percent being various combinations of Customary, Ordinance and Church. The patterns observed in this study are similar to those reported from analysis of national data (Gaisie & DeGraft Johnson, 1976; Awusabo-Asare, 1990). Table 3.1 shows the percentage distribution of couples by type of marriage according to selected background characteristics.

**Table 3.1**  Percentage Distribution of Couples by Type of Marriage, According to Selected Background Characteristics, GFAMS, 1992/93

| Background Characteristic | Customary Only | Customary & Church/ Ordinance | Mutual Consent/ Consensual | Islamic w/ or w/o Customary | Total | No. |
|---|---|---|---|---|---|---|
| CHOICE OF PARTNER | | | | | | |
| Entirely by me | 69.2 | 13.2 | 16.0 | 1.6 | 100.0 | 1291 |
| Help/consent of family | 74.8 | 19.9 | 0.2 | 5.1 | 100.0 | 433 |
| Arranged by family | 72.7 | 13.6 | 2.3 | 11.4 | 100.0 | 44 |
| Other | 21.7 | 30.4 | 47.8 | 0.0 | 100.0 | 23 |
| | | | | | | |
| AGE | | | | | | |
| 15-19 | 71.4 | 0.0 | 28.6 | 0.0 | 100.0 | 14 |
| 20-24 | 63.6 | 3.4 | 33.1 | 0.0 | 100.0 | 118 |
| 25-29 | 68.9 | 10.0 | 17.7 | 3.4 | 100.0 | 351 |
| 30-34 | 73.5 | 11.0 | 12.5 | 3.0 | 100.0 | 400 |
| 35-39 | 71.0 | 15.2 | 11.9 | 1.8 | 100.0 | 335 |
| 40-44 | 68.8 | 22.5 | 5.4 | 3.3 | 100.0 | 240 |
| 45-49 | 69.3 | 23.6 | 3.0 | 4.0 | 100.0 | 199 |
| 50+ | 66.0 | 29.2 | 3.5 | 1.4 | 100.0 | 144 |
| | | | | | | |
| RESIDENCE | | | | | | |
| Urban | 61.7 | 17.6 | 18.1 | 2.5 | 100.0 | 1100 |
| Rural | 82.4 | 11.7 | 3.1 | 2.8 | 100.0 | 709 |
| | | | | | | |
| LEVEL OF EDUCATION | | | | | | |
| No education | 71.4 | 5.8 | 10.1 | 12.7 | 100.0 | 189 |
| Elementary | 76.1 | 7.9 | 14.1 | 1.9 | 100.0 | 887 |
| Sec/tec/trg.college | 64.2 | 22.6 | 12.1 | 1.0 | 100.0 | 495 |
| Higher | 56.1 | 37.8 | 5.6 | 0.5 | 100.0 | 196 |
| | | | | | | |
| TOTAL | 69.8 | 15.3 | 12.2 | 2.7 | 100.0 | 1809 |

The data indicate that couples were more likely to contract consensual marriages if they had chosen their partners entirely by themselves than if there had been family involvement. There also seemed to be an inverse relationship between age and consensual relationship. While 33 percent of couples aged 20-24 had consensual unions, only 18 percent of the 25-29 age cohort had consensual unions, and the proportion steadily declined to 5.4 percent for the 40-44 age cohort. This phenomena may be explained by the weakening of the role of kinsmen over the younger generation in mate selection. Moreover, since many of the consensual unions are prelude to marriage, older women might have had time to regularize their relationships into formal marriages. Such transformations may be the result of childbirth and the need to be accepted by members of the extended family to ensure full rights and obligations as married couples.

In considering rural-urban differences in the type of marriage, the data indicate that while 82 percent of couples living in rural areas were in customary marriages, 62 percent of the couples living in urban areas were in a similar marriage; 18 percent of those in urban areas reported being in consensual unions while only 3 percent of their rural counterparts were in consensual relationships. Furthermore, compared to couples who had not had any formal education, or only elementary school education, those with post-elementary education were less likely to marry under Customary law alone. The rural-urban and educational differences may be explained by the modernizing influences of schooling, urban residence, religion and the weakening role of members of the corporate clan in the marriage process.

**Choice of Partner**

Respondents were asked to indicate how they chose their current partners. We were interested in finding out if the traditional practice of one's parents and other family members influencing the choice of one's partner was operating. In some cases family members play facilitating roles rather than being "match makers."

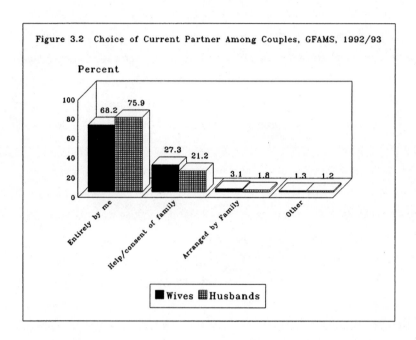

Figure 3.2  Choice of Current Partner Among Couples, GFAMS, 1992/93

Figure 3.2 indicates that over two-thirds of the couples chose their partners entirely by themselves, while the rest had some form of family involvement in the choice of a partner. We need to stress that in the sample only a tiny proportion of couples had their marriages entirely arranged by the family (3 percent of wives and 2 percent of husbands). However, it is worth noting that slightly more husbands (76 percent) reported that they chose their partners entirely by themselves, compared to 68 percent of wives. These results indicate that while Ghanaian couples now have the freedom to choose their own partners, the family still has some influence in their choice of a partner for some people. This influence is higher for females than males.

An overview of the relationship between age, residence, and the level of education in the amount of influence that the family has over choice of partner is presented in Table 3.2. All things being equal one would expect the practice of family involvement in marriages to be low or non-existent among the younger couples (under 25 years of age) and those with post-elementary school education. Indeed, the results of this study confirm our expectations. The data show that in general, younger couples were more likely to choose their partners entirely by themselves compared to older couples although more older wives than husbands had some kind of family involvement in their choice of partners.

There also appeared to be an inverse relationship between level of education and arranged marriages. For instance, while about five percent of couples with no education had their marriages entirely arranged by family, only about one percent of couples with secondary education had entirely arranged marriages and no arranged marriage at all were reported by couples with higher education.

Similarly, consistent with our expectations, urban couples were more likely to choose their partners entirely by themselves, thus having less family involvement than their rural counterparts. For instance, while only under 20 percent of urban couples chose their partners with the help or consent of the family, twice as many rural couples (43 percent for wives and 37 percent for husbands) did so.

The data also indicate that while only 51 percent of women with no education had chosen their partner entirely by themselves, the proportion systematically increased to 80 percent for women with a post-secondary education. On the contrary, the proportion of women who had chosen their partners with the help/consent of family decreased from 43 percent for those with no education to 20 percent for their counterparts with higher education. And as for women whose marriages had entirely been arranged by family, there was a steady decline of the proportions as educational level increased. Similarly, there appeared to be an inverse relationship between level of education and family control over choice of partner with regard to the experiences of the men in the sample. Thus, as the level of education increased, both women and men were more likely to choose their partners entirely by themselves.

**Table 3.2**   Percentage Distribution of Couples by Choice of Partner, According to Age, Residence, and Level of Education, GFAMS, 1992/93

| | CHOICE OF PARTNER | | | | | | | | | | | |
|---|---|---|---|---|---|---|---|---|---|---|---|---|
| | Entirely By Me | | Help Or Consent Of Family | | Entirely Arranged By Family | | Other Avenue | | Total | | Number | |
| | Wife | Hus. | Wife | Hus. | Wife | Hus. | Wife | Hus. | Wife | Hus. | Wife | Hus. |
| **AGE** | | | | | | | | | | | | |
| Under 25 | 82.7 | 95.5 | 15.5 | 4.5 | 0.9 | 0.0 | 0.9 | 0.0 | 100.0 | 100.0 | 110 | 22 |
| 25-29 | 71.1 | 84.2 | 24.7 | 14.9 | 2.6 | 0.9 | 1.7 | 0.0 | 100.0 | 100.0 | 235 | 114 |
| 30-34 | 71.7 | 77.7 | 23.0 | 19.9 | 4.2 | 1.5 | 1.0 | 1.0 | 100.0 | 100.0 | 191 | 206 |
| 35-44 | 63.7 | 71.2 | 30.4 | 24.0 | 3.8 | 2.7 | 2.1 | 2.1 | 100.0 | 100.0 | 237 | 333 |
| 45+ | 51.8 | 74.4 | 45.6 | 23.3 | 2.6 | 1.3 | 0.0 | 0.9 | 100.0 | 100.0 | 114 | 223 |
| **RESIDENCE** | | | | | | | | | | | | |
| Urban | 79.4 | 86.7 | 16.9 | 10.9 | 2.0 | 0.9 | 1.7 | 1.5 | 100.0 | 100.0 | 540 | 549 |
| Rural | 50.9 | 59.0 | 43.4 | 37.0 | 4.9 | 3.1 | 0.9 | 0.8 | 100.0 | 100.0 | 350 | 354 |
| **LEVEL OF EDUCATION** | | | | | | | | | | | | |
| No education | 51.4 | 71.1 | 43.2 | 23.7 | 4.8 | 5.3 | 0.7 | 0.0 | 100.0 | 100.0 | 146 | 38 |
| Elementary | 70.4 | 69.0 | 24.6 | 27.4 | 4.0 | 2.6 | 1.0 | 1.0 | 100.0 | 100.0 | 496 | 387 |
| Sec/tec/trg.college | 72.0 | 80.5 | 24.9 | 17.2 | 0.5 | 1.3 | 2.6 | 1.0 | 100.0 | 100.0 | 193 | 297 |
| Higher | 80.0 | 81.9 | 20.0 | 15.6 | 0.0 | 0.0 | 0.0 | 2.5 | 100.0 | 100.0 | 35 | 160 |
| **TOTAL** | 68.2 | 75.9 | 27.3 | 21.2 | 3.1 | 1.8 | 1.3 | 1.2 | 100.0 | 100.0 | 890 | 903 |

**Residence of Couples**

Although marriage in Ghana is defined as two people of the opposite sex living together as husband and wife, it does not necessarily imply that married couples would live together in the same household. Figure 3.3 shows that 11 percent of all couples lived apart from each other. Of all the couples who did not live in the same house, almost half lived in another part of town, 29 percent lived in their extended family house in town, and 15 percent lived in another town. Thus, not all Ghanaian marriages lead to co-residence especially so among the matrilineal Akans, who achieve greater autonomy for the wife by encouraging continued residence with the couples' respective lineages (Nukunya, 1978, Bleek, 1987).

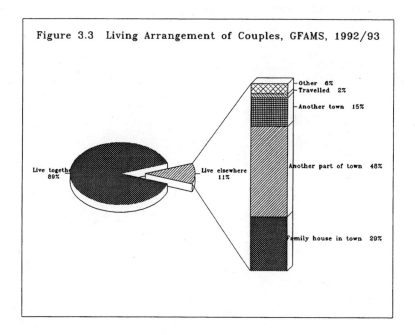

Figure 3.3   Living Arrangement of Couples, GFAMS, 1992/93

**Age at First Marriage**

Table 3.3 compares the mean age at first marriage for wives and husbands across selected socio-demographic background variables. Mean age at first marriage in the sample was 22.0 years for wives and 26.2 years for husbands. The reported mean age at first marriage among the wives was about 4 years higher than had been reported from the GFS and the GDHSs. This is because the present study sampled only married people whereas the other studies included single people.

As expected, urban respondents, and respondents with higher education marry later than their counterparts in rural areas and those with little or no education. The mean age at marriage rose from 20.5 years for wives with no formal education to 25.1 years for those with education beyond the secondary level. Similarly, the mean age at marriage for husbands also increased from 24.8 years for those without any schooling to 27.9 years for those with higher education. As observed in other surveys, age at first marriage among females increases with increasing education. But it appears the effect of education on age at first marriage begins to be felt after basic education (Awusabo-Asare, 1988).

The variability by education was also reflected in the relatively high age at first marriage reported by females in professional, sub-professional, technical and clerical occupations. Husbands and wives with no work and farmers and fishermen were more likely to enter into a union relatively earlier than their counterparts in the other occupational groups. The results also reveal that among the female respondents those whose choice of partner was influenced by family members married slightly earlier than the rest. For men, there was no difference in age at marriage according to how their partners were chosen. And wives and husbands waited about three years longer to contract Ordinance or Church marriages than those who performed Islamic marriages. Nevertheless, there was only a slight difference in the mean age at first marriage for respondents who married customarily or consensually.

**Table 3.3** Mean Age at First Marriage Among Couples by Selected Background Characteristics, GFAMS, 1992/93

| Background Characteristic | COUPLES | | | | |
| | Wife | | | Husband | |
| | Mean | Number | | Mean | Number |
| --- | --- | --- | --- | --- | --- |
| **RESIDENCE** | | | | | |
| Urban | 22.7 | 544 | | 26.6 | 539 |
| Rural | 20.8 | 349 | | 25.4 | 345 |
| **LEVEL OF EDUCATION** | | | | | |
| No education | 20.5 | 142 | | 24.8 | 40 |
| Elementary | 21.3 | 499 | | 25.1 | 380 |
| Sec/tecltrg.coll | 24.2 | 197 | | 26.6 | 287 |
| Higher | 25.1 | 35 | | 27.9 | 156 |
| **OCCUPATION** | | | | | |
| Professional | 24.4 | 66 | | 27.2 | 176 |
| Sub-professional/tech | 24.0 | 15 | | 25.9 | 33 |
| Clerical | 24.1 | 55 | | 27.6 | 94 |
| Sales | 21.9 | 179 | | 26.4 | 33 |
| Service/transport | 23.0 | 47 | | 25.9 | 119 |
| Farmer/fisherman | 20.4 | 13 | | 26.0 | 34 |
| Craftsman | 22.9 | 113 | | 26.0 | 192 |
| **RELIGION** | | | | | |
| Catholic | 21.9 | 157 | | 26.4 | 165 |
| Protestant | 22.1 | 604 | | 26.3 | 555 |
| Muslim | 21.0 | 39 | | 25.6 | 41 |
| Traditionalist | 22.0 | 8 | | 25.1 | 21 |
| Other religion | 22.2 | 59 | | 26.1 | 57 |
| No religion | 19.5 | 23 | | 24.0 | 39 |
| **CHOICE OF PARTNER** | | | | | |
| Entirely by me | 22.0 | 598 | | 26.2 | 666 |
| Help/consent of family | 22.0 | 240 | | 26.0 | 187 |
| Arranged by family | 20.2 | 27 | | 26.1 | 15 |
| Other | 21.8 | 12 | | 28.1 | 11 |
| **TYPE OF MARRIAGE** | | | | | |
| Customary | 21.6 | 611 | | 26.0 | 626 |
| Ordinance/Church | 24.4 | 137 | | 28.0 | 132 |
| Consensual | 21.4 | 118 | | 24.9 | 101 |
| Islamic | 20.2 | 25 | | 25.0 | 22 |
| **TOTAL** | 22.0 | 893 | | 26.2 | 884 |

## Polygyny

Another marriage form that needs to be discussed here is polygyny. Polygyny as a marriage institution had been predicted to disappear in Ghana almost a quarter of a century ago because of increasing urbanization, industrialization, formal education, and other "modernization" and "westernization" influences (Goode, 1963). However, the direction and stages of the predicted declines in polygyny have not been very clear because there is the tendency for many monogamous marriages contracted under Customary or Islamic law to develop into polygyny (Clignet & Sween; 1969; Pool, 1972; Aryee, 1978; Brabin, 1984).

As the data in Table 3.4 show, about 11 percent of husbands in the sample reported that they were in polygynous unions while slightly more wives (12 percent) said they have co-wives. Older couples were more likely to be in polygynous unions than younger couples, suggesting that the practice of polygyny may be declining with time. For instance, while only 9 percent of women aged 15-29 years were in polygynous unions, about twice as many (16 percent) of women aged 40+ years were engaged in polygyny. Similarly, higher proportions of older men reported having more than one wife compared to younger men. Then again, it takes time to marry more than one wife.

The data also indicate that couples residing in rural areas were more likely to practice polygyny than those living in the urban area. Generally, the incidence of polygyny seemed to decrease with increasing education. The practice of polygyny ranged from an average of 22 percent for couples with no schooling to 9 percent for couples with higher education. Marriages that had been arranged by family were more likely to be polygynous than those in which the partners had chosen their spouses by themselves. This is because a high proportion of arranged marriages are contracted under Customary law alone. As expected, none of the couples who married under the Ordinance (civil or religious) reported being in polygynous relationships compared to an average of 41 percent for Islamic marriages.

**Table 3.4** Percentage in Polygyny by Age and Selected Background Characteristics, GFAMS, 1992/93

| | AGE GROUPS | | | | | | | |
|---|---|---|---|---|---|---|---|---|
| | 15-29 | | 30-39 | | 40+ | | Average | |
| Background Characteristic | Wife | Hus. | Wife | Hus. | Wife | Hus. | Wife | Hus. |
| **RESIDENCE** | | | | | | | | |
| Urban | 8.5 | 1.5 | 9.1 | 6.2 | 13.4 | 13.5 | 10.0 | 8.8 |
| Rural | 9.5 | 4.5 | 19.0 | 14.1 | 21.4 | 17.2 | 15.4 | 13.4 |
| **LEVEL OF EDUCATION** | | | | | | | | |
| No education | 19.6 | 0.0 | 15.3 | 30.8 | 28.6 | 23.8 | 20.4 | 23.1 |
| Elementary | 8.6 | 5.1 | 16.9 | 12.9 | 15.9 | 23.1 | 13.0 | 14.9 |
| Sec/tec/trg.college | 3.7 | 0.0 | 3.7 | 4.6 | 6.6 | 5.7 | 4.6 | 4.4 |
| Higher | 0.0 | 0.0 | 0.0 | 4.5 | 20.0 | 13.1 | 5.9 | 8.8 |
| **CHOICE OF PARTNER** | | | | | | | | |
| Entirely by me | 9.7 | 3.4 | 14.0 | 9.4 | 10.5 | 13.3 | 11.5 | 9.9 |
| Help/consent of family | 6.7 | 0.0 | 10.3 | 9.0 | 21.3 | 16.1 | 12.8 | 11.7 |
| Arranged by family | 14.3 | 0.0 | 26.7 | 0.0 | 40.0 | 37.5 | 25.9 | 18.8 |
| Other | 0.0 | 0.0 | 14.3 | 14.3 | 0.0 | 25.0 | 8.3 | 18.2 |
| **TYPE OF MARRIAGE** | | | | | | | | |
| Customary | 9.3 | 2.2 | 13.4 | 10.6 | 20.7 | 16.9 | 13.5 | 12.0 |
| Ordinance/Church | 0.0 | 0.0 | 0.0 | 0.0 | 0.0 | 0.0 | 0.0 | 0.0 |
| Consensual | 5.8 | 2.8 | 23.8 | 8.3 | 12.5 | 31.3 | 12.6 | 10.0 |
| Islamic | 45.5 | 100.0 | 42.9 | 18.2 | 42.9 | 54.5 | 44.0 | 39.1 |
| **RELIGION** | | | | | | | | |
| Catholic | 7.4 | 0.0 | 12.7 | 6.8 | 11.8 | 4.3 | 10.2 | 4.8 |
| Protestant | 6.8 | 2.5 | 13.9 | 9.1 | 13.8 | 14.1 | 11.3 | 10.3 |
| Muslim | 23.5 | 0.0 | 7.7 | 19.0 | 37.5 | 37.5 | 21.1 | 23.8 |
| Traditionalist | 50.0 | 0.0 | 0.0 | 10.0 | 0.0 | 20.0 | 25.0 | 13.6 |
| Other religion | 15.4 | 6.7 | 15.8 | 15.0 | 28.6 | 30.4 | 18.6 | 19.0 |
| No religion | 9.1 | 10.0 | 9.1 | 5.0 | 0.0 | 20.0 | 8.7 | 10.0 |
| **OCCUPATION** | | | | | | | | |
| Professional | 0.0 | 0.0 | 5.9 | 5.9 | 15.8 | 10.3 | 6.2 | 7.5 |
| Clerical | 5.9 | 0.0 | 4.5 | 0.0 | 12.5 | 4.4 | 7.3 | 2.1 |
| Sales | 12.1 | 0.0 | 8.5 | 0.0 | 16.4 | 0.0 | 12.0 | 0.0 |
| Farmer/fisherman | 0.0 | 14.3 | 25.0 | 13.3 | 100.0 | 15.4 | 30.8 | 14.3 |
| Service/transport | 4.8 | 10.5 | 4.8 | 13.0 | 0.0 | 22.9 | 4.3 | 16.5 |
| Craftsman | 10.3 | 0.0 | 8.8 | 7.9 | 13.2 | 20.3 | 10.8 | 10.5 |
| **TOTAL** | 8.9 | 3.0 | 13.3 | 9.2 | 15.6 | 14.8 | 12.1 | 10.6 |

## CHILDBEARING

In Ghana, as in many African countries, parents want more children for a number of reasons. Parents throughout sub-Saharan Africa are known to have large families as a source of income, labor, and security for old age (Caldwell, 1982; Boserup, 1985; Akuffo, 1987; Lesthaeghe, 1989; Dasgupta, 1994). The labor resource argument is particularly true for parents employed in the service and agricultural sectors of the economy. To the extent that children are considered part of the family wealth, high fertility is used as a buffer against high infant and child mortality which is still a problem in the country. Caldwell & Caldwell (1987) have argued that in many African societies, barrenness is a matter of fundamental social and theological significance. In Ghana, infertility, whether caused by ill health or not, is often abhorred. A woman incapable of reproducing is regarded differently from one who is likely to do so. So great is the premium attached to children that barren women have been regarded as witches or evildoers. Such is the fear of infertility that women go to all lengths of spending their wealth in order to procure both traditional and modern treatment which can make them fertile (Gaisie, 1968; Ebin, 1982; United Nations Economic Commission for Africa [UNECA], 1984; Bleek, 1987).

Since the 1970s, the GFS and the GDHSs have provided comprehensive national data on fertility levels and trends, and general reproductive behavior in Ghana. The focus of this chapter is on the number of male and female children ever born (CEB), number still alive, current fertility, age at birth, determinants of fertility, and reasons for a gap, if any, between desired and actual fertility.

### Children Ever Born (CEB)

The distribution of CEB to wives and husbands according to age is presented in Table 3.5. The mean number of CEB to wives was 3.2, slightly lower than 4.0 reported for currently married women in the GDHS.

**Table 3.5** Percentage Distribution of Children Ever Born (CEB) to Couples, According to Age, GFAMS, 1992/93

| AGE | 0 | 1 | 2 | 3 | 4 | 5 | 6 | 7 | 8 | 9 | 10+ | Total | N | CEB |
|---|---|---|---|---|---|---|---|---|---|---|---|---|---|---|
| | | | | | CHILDREN EVER BORN TO WIVES | | | | | | | | | |
| 15-19 | 25.0 | 58.3 | 8.3 | 8.3 | 0.0 | 0.0 | 0.0 | 0.0 | 0.0 | 0.0 | 0.0 | 100.0 | 12 | 1.0 |
| 20-24 | 18.6 | 38.1 | 32.0 | 9.3 | 0.0 | 2.1 | 0.0 | 0.0 | 0.0 | 0.0 | 0.0 | 100.0 | 97 | 1.4 |
| 25-29 | 11.4 | 24.9 | 30.8 | 19.4 | 6.8 | 5.5 | 0.8 | 0.0 | 0.4 | 0.0 | 0.0 | 100.0 | 237 | 2.1 |
| 30-34 | 3.6 | 6.2 | 26.9 | 26.9 | 15.5 | 13.5 | 4.1 | 2.6 | 0.5 | 0.0 | 0.0 | 100.0 | 193 | 3.2 |
| 35-39 | 2.0 | 2.7 | 12.7 | 22.0 | 25.3 | 16.7 | 8.7 | 4.0 | 4.0 | 0.7 | 1.3 | 100.0 | 150 | 4.1 |
| 40-44 | 0.0 | 2.2 | 6.6 | 22.0 | 17.6 | 19.8 | 15.4 | 6.6 | 4.4 | 4.4 | 1.1 | 100.0 | 91 | 4.7 |
| 45-49 | 1.1 | 0.0 | 4.5 | 16.9 | 30.3 | 16.9 | 5.6 | 9.0 | 6.7 | 2.2 | 6.7 | 100.0 | 89 | 5.1 |
| 50+ | 0.0 | 3.6 | 7.1 | 14.3 | 50.0 | 14.3 | 0.0 | 3.6 | 0.0 | 0.0 | 7.1 | 100.0 | 28 | 4.3 |
| ALL AGES | 6.6 | 13.6 | 21.0 | 20.1 | 15.7 | 11.5 | 4.7 | 2.9 | 2.0 | 0.8 | 1.2 | 100.0 | 897 | 3.2 |
| | | | | | CHILDREN EVER BORN TO HUSBANDS | | | | | | | | | |
| 15-19 | 0.0 | 100.0 | 0.0 | 0.0 | 0.0 | 0.0 | 0.0 | 0.0 | 0.0 | 0.0 | 0.0 | 100.0 | 2 | 1.0 |
| 20-24 | 26.3 | 36.8 | 26.3 | 0.0 | 0.0 | 10.5 | 0.0 | 0.0 | 0.0 | 0.0 | 0.0 | 100.0 | 19 | 1.4 |
| 25-29 | 15.8 | 16.8 | 26.3 | 13.2 | 4.4 | 0.9 | 2.6 | 0.0 | 0.0 | 0.0 | 0.0 | 100.0 | 114 | 1.7 |
| 30-34 | 12.1 | 20.3 | 23.7 | 22.7 | 10.1 | 7.2 | 2.9 | 0.5 | 0.5 | 0.0 | 0.0 | 100.0 | 207 | 2.4 |
| 35-39 | 0.5 | 7.1 | 26.8 | 23.5 | 19.7 | 10.9 | 4.9 | 2.7 | 1.6 | 1.1 | 1.1 | 100.0 | 187 | 3.5 |
| 40-44 | 0.7 | 2.0 | 10.8 | 25.7 | 18.2 | 14.9 | 13.5 | 4.7 | 3.4 | 0.0 | 6.1 | 100.0 | 148 | 4.6 |
| 45-49 | 0.9 | 0.9 | 7.4 | 21.3 | 25.0 | 17.6 | 8.3 | 5.6 | 4.6 | 2.8 | 5.6 | 100.0 | 108 | 4.8 |
| 50+ | 0.0 | 1.7 | 5.2 | 8.7 | 27.8 | 8.7 | 7.8 | 11.3 | 11.3 | 7.0 | 10.4 | 100.0 | 115 | 5.8 |
| ALL AGES | 5.7 | 12.5 | 18.2 | 19.6 | 16.5 | 9.9 | 6.3 | 3.6 | 3.0 | 1.5 | 3.2 | 100.0 | 896 | 3.6 |

In both the GFAMS and the GDHS, the same proportion of wives (7 percent) have never had a child. Childlessness, a rare phenomena in Ghana, declines sharply with age. While a quarter of wives in age group 15-19 had never had a child, this percentage was 4 for wives aged 30-34, and one percent for wives aged 45-49. Among wives aged 45 or older, 7 percent had 10 or more children compared to only one percent for wives aged 35-44.

The mean number of CEB to husbands (3.6) was slightly higher than that for wives (3.2). As expected, the mean CEB increases steadily with age. While 6 percent of husbands aged 40-44 had 10 or more children, only one percent of wives did. Among husbands aged 50 or more, 10 percent had 10 or more children compared to 7 percent of wives of similar age group possibly from multiple wives.

An interesting comparison between the mean number of CEB reported by wives and husbands is that in almost all age groups, wives reported higher mean number of CEB compared to husbands except in the 50 or more age group. Among husbands aged 50 or more, the mean CEB was 5.8 while for wives of the same age group the mean was 4.3. A similar pattern of differences was observed in the GDHS report. This picture is an indication that while men continue to have children well beyond age 50, childbearing for women cease around that age.

**Children Ever Born by Background Characteristics**

The data presented in Tables 3.6a & 3.6b give the distribution of CEB to wives and husbands respectively, according to selected background characteristics. Variations in the CEB by place of residence, level of education, choice of partner, and type of marriage are evident for both wives and husbands as also shown in Figure 3.4. There was an almost one child difference between women residing in rural areas and their counterparts living in urban centers.

As expected, there was an inverse relationship between educational attainment and CEB for both wives and husbands. For example, while only 9 percent of husbands with higher education were childless, close to 21 percent of wives with the same level of education reported no children. The results indicate that while higher education may delay or reduce the childbearing activities for Ghanaian women, that does not seem to be the case for the men. In fact, at every educational level, men had significantly more children than women.

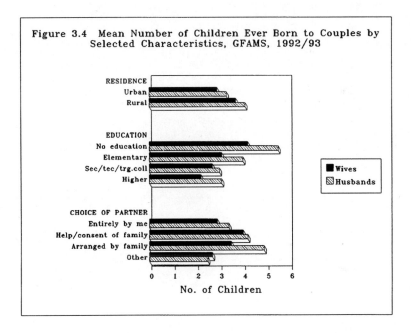

Figure 3.4   Mean Number of Children Ever Born to Couples by Selected Characteristics, GFAMS, 1992/93

Also, if the respondents themselves had chosen their partners, they were more likely to have fewer children compared to those whose families have had a hand in the choice of marriage partners. In terms of occupational groups, the differences were not very pronounced for wives even though professional wives had slightly fewer children than wives in the other categories. However, husbands employed as farmers/fishermen averaged 1.5 more children than husbands employed in other areas, perhaps due to child labor needs.

Table 3.6a    Percentage Distribution of Children Ever Born (CEB) to Wives by Selected Background Characteristics, GFAMS, 1992/93

| Background Characteristics | CHILDREN EVER BORN | | | | | | | N | Mean CEB |
|---|---|---|---|---|---|---|---|---|---|
| | 0 | 1 | 2 | 3 | 4 | 5+ | Total | | |
| RESIDENCE | | | | | | | | | |
| Urban | 7.1 | 16.0 | 21.9 | 22.6 | 16.8 | 15.7 | 100.0 | 549 | 2.9 |
| Rural | 6.0 | 9.7 | 19.9 | 16.0 | 14.0 | 34.5 | 100.0 | 351 | 3.7 |
| LEVEL OF EDUCATION | | | | | | | | | |
| No education | 4.1 | 4.1 | 16.2 | 17.6 | 15.5 | 42.6 | 100.0 | 148 | 4.2 |
| Elementary | 5.5 | 18.2 | 21.0 | 17.8 | 14.0 | 23.6 | 100.0 | 500 | 3.1 |
| Sec/tec/trg.college | 9.6 | 9.6 | 23.4 | 27.9 | 18.8 | 10.7 | 100.0 | 197 | 2.7 |
| Higher | 20.6 | 11.8 | 23.5 | 20.6 | 17.6 | 5.9 | 100.0 | 34 | 2.2 |
| CHOICE OF PARTNER | | | | | | | | | |
| Entirely by me | 7.5 | 16.7 | 23.7 | 20.4 | 14.6 | 17.2 | 100.0 | 604 | 2.9 |
| Help/consent of family | 4.5 | 7.0 | 16.1 | 18.2 | 17.8 | 36.4 | 100.0 | 242 | 4.0 |
| Arranged by family | 7.7 | 7.7 | 11.5 | 23.1 | 15.4 | 34.6 | 100.0 | 26 | 3.5 |
| Other | 16.7 | 8.3 | 25.0 | 8.3 | 25.0 | 16.7 | 100.0 | 12 | 2.7 |
| TYPE OF MARRIAGE | | | | | | | | | |
| Customary | 4.7 | 12.8 | 20.9 | 19.4 | 17.0 | 25.1 | 100.0 | 617 | 3.4 |
| Ordinance/Church | 8.0 | 6.6 | 20.4 | 22.6 | 18.2 | 24.1 | 100.0 | 137 | 3.4 |
| Consensual | 16.8 | 26.9 | 23.5 | 19.3 | 5.9 | 7.6 | 100.0 | 119 | 2.0 |
| Islamic | 0.0 | 8.0 | 20.0 | 20.0 | 16.0 | 36.0 | 100.0 | 25 | 3.9 |
| OCCUPATION | | | | | | | | | |
| Professional | 11.1 | 18.5 | 23.5 | 22.2 | 12.3 | 12.3 | 100.0 | 81 | 2.5 |
| Clerical | 10.9 | 12.7 | 16.4 | 32.7 | 16.4 | 10.9 | 100.0 | 55 | 2.6 |
| Sales | 1.6 | 16.5 | 15.9 | 19.2 | 19.2 | 27.5 | 100.0 | 182 | 3.5 |
| Service/Transport | 12.8 | 10.6 | 31.9 | 23.4 | 14.9 | 6.4 | 100.0 | 47 | 2.4 |
| Farmer/Fisherman | 0.0 | 0.0 | 30.8 | 30.8 | 15.4 | 23.1 | 100.0 | 13 | 3.4 |
| Craftsman | 7.9 | 9.6 | 19.3 | 24.6 | 21.1 | 17.5 | 100.0 | 114 | 3.2 |
| TOTAL | 6.7 | 13.6 | 21.1 | 20.0 | 15.7 | 23.0 | 100.0 | 900 | 3.2 |

**Table 3.6b** Percentage Distribution of Children Ever Born (CEB) to Husbands by Selected Background Characteristics, GFAMS, 1992/93

| Background Characteristic | CHILDREN EVER BORN | | | | | | Total | N | Mean CEB |
|---|---|---|---|---|---|---|---|---|---|
| | 0 | 1 | 2 | 3 | 4 | 5+ | | | |
| RESIDENCE | | | | | | | | | |
| Urban | 6.0 | 13.6 | 20.5 | 21.2 | 16.7 | 22.0 | 100.0 | 551 | 3.3 |
| Rural | 5.1 | 10.6 | 14.6 | 17.4 | 16.3 | 36.0 | 100.0 | 350 | 4.1 |
| LEVEL OF EDUCATION | | | | | | | | | |
| No education | 2.7 | 8.1 | 5.4 | 13.5 | 10.8 | 59.5 | 100.0 | 37 | 5.5 |
| Elementary | 3.4 | 11.4 | 16.9 | 16.6 | 15.1 | 36.6 | 100.0 | 385 | 4.0 |
| Sec/tec/trg.college | 7.1 | 15.5 | 19.9 | 23.6 | 16.2 | 17.8 | 100.0 | 297 | 3.0 |
| Higher | 8.7 | 10.6 | 21.1 | 23.6 | 19.3 | 16.8 | 100.0 | 161 | 3.1 |
| CHOICE OF PARTNER | | | | | | | | | |
| Entirely by me | 5.7 | 13.8 | 19.4 | 20.9 | 16.9 | 23.2 | 100.0 | 680 | 3.4 |
| Help/consent of family | 5.3 | 7.9 | 13.8 | 18.0 | 13.8 | 41.3 | 100.0 | 189 | 4.2 |
| Arranged by family | 6.3 | 6.3 | 12.5 | 0.0 | 25.0 | 50.0 | 100.0 | 16 | 4.9 |
| Other | 9.1 | 18.2 | 27.3 | 18.2 | 18.2 | 9.1 | 100.0 | 11 | 2.5 |
| TYPE OF MARRIAGE | | | | | | | | | |
| Customary | 3.9 | 11.3 | 18.2 | 19.3 | 17.1 | 30.0 | 100.0 | 636 | 3.8 |
| Ordinance/Church | 5.8 | 7.2 | 18.7 | 25.9 | 18.7 | 23.7 | 100.0 | 139 | 3.6 |
| Consensual | 15.7 | 28.4 | 16.7 | 15.7 | 11.8 | 11.8 | 100.0 | 102 | 2.2 |
| Islamic | 4.8 | 4.8 | 23.8 | 14.3 | 4.8 | 47.6 | 100.0 | 21 | 4.4 |
| OCCUPATION | | | | | | | | | |
| Professional | 7.4 | 11.1 | 19.9 | 21.3 | 20.4 | 19.9 | 100.0 | 216 | 3.3 |
| Clerical | 8.3 | 11.5 | 16.7 | 24.0 | 22.9 | 16.7 | 100.0 | 96 | 3.2 |
| Sales | 2.9 | 20.0 | 14.3 | 25.7 | 11.4 | 25.7 | 100.0 | 35 | 3.2 |
| Service/Transport | 4.1 | 11.6 | 22.3 | 15.7 | 14.0 | 32.2 | 100.0 | 121 | 3.6 |
| Farmer/Fisherman | 5.7 | 8.6 | 11.4 | 17.1 | 14.3 | 42.9 | 100.0 | 35 | 4.5 |
| Craftsman | 6.7 | 16.0 | 19.1 | 20.6 | 16.0 | 21.6 | 100.0 | 194 | 3.2 |
| TOTAL | 5.7 | 12.4 | 18.2 | 19.8 | 16.5 | 27.4 | 100.0 | 901 | 3.4 |

### Children Ever Born and Age at First Marriage

The mean number of CEB to wives, by the age at first marriage and duration of marriage is shown in Table 3.7. The evidence indicates that early marriages were generally associated with slightly higher fertility than women who married late. For example, the mean number of CEB decreased from 3.5 for wives who married before their 20th birthday to 2.7 for those who married at age 26 or older. This result is in the expected direction because the earlier a woman marries, the longer her exposure to the risk of childbearing. And in the absence of widespread use of contraception, the more children those women exposed to the highest risk of pregnancy are expected to have by the end of their reproductive years.

**Table 3.7**     Mean Number of Children Ever Born to Wives by Age at First Marriage and Duration of Marriage, GFAMS, 1992/93

| Duration of Marriage (in years) | AGE AT FIRST MARRIAGE | | | | |
|---|---|---|---|---|---|
| | <20 | 20-22 | 23-25 | 26+ | Total |
| 0-4 | 1.9 | 1.8 | 1.5 | 1.1 | 1.6 |
| 5-9 | 3.0 | 2.8 | 2.7 | 2.4 | 2.8 |
| 10-14 | 3.7 | 3.8 | 3.6 | 3.2 | 3.6 |
| 15-19 | 4.7 | 4.2 | 3.8 | 4.1 | 4.3 |
| 20-24 | 6.2 | 4.9 | 4.4 | 3.8 | 4.8 |
| 25+ | 7.1 | 5.4 | 4.9 | 5.6 | 5.7 |
| TOTAL | 3.5 | 3.3 | 2.9 | 2.7 | 3.2 |

### Age at First Birth by Background Characteristics

The importance of age at first birth in fertility decline has extensively been documented. In Table 3.8, we show the mean age at first birth among wives aged 20-49 according to selected background characteristics. For every age group, wives who resided in the urban areas, those with high education, and those who had chosen their partners entirely by themselves were significantly more likely to begin childbearing later than their counterparts living in rural areas, those with no/low education, and those whose families had been involved in their choice of marriage partners. For instance, the average age at first birth for wives with no education was 20.9 followed by 21.7 for those with elementary school education, 24.2 for those with secondary school education or its equivalent, and 26.0 for wives with higher education. Variations in the age at first birth by place of residence is as expected. On the average, urban women waited about 2.1 years longer to begin childbearing compared to their counterparts living in the rural areas.

## DESIRED FERTILITY

Information on desired family size have become important in fertility studies for at least three reasons. First, desired family size among the younger generation (under 25 years of age) can serve as a proxy for future fertility trends. Second, reported ideal family size when compared with actual fertility performance among females aged 40 years and above, give the gap between expectation and reality in fertility (Westoff & Ochoa, 1991). Common among populations yet to achieve fertility decline is the discrepancy between average desired and completed family sizes (Lesthaeghe, et al., 1981). There are those who are not able to achieve their expectation for a variety of reasons, including infertility. On the other hand, there are those who exceed their desired family size--the group described in the literature as having an unmet need for family planning (Bongaarts, 1990; Cochrane & Sai, 1993; Westoff & Ochoa, 1991). Third, between the sexes, questions on desired family size give an idea about the variation in expectations between males and females in family size norms. In general, males tend to want more children than females for economic benefits and status enhancement (Mason & Taj, 1987).

**Marriage Systems and Fertility Behavior**

**Table 3.8** Mean Age at First Birth Among Wives Ages 20-49 Years by Current Age and Selected Background Characteristics

| Background Characteristic | CURRENT AGE | | | | | | Total (20-49) |
|---|---|---|---|---|---|---|---|
| | 20-24 | 25-29 | 30-34 | 35-39 | 40-44 | 45-49 | |
| **RESIDENCE** | | | | | | | |
| Urban | 20.2 | 22.3 | 23.3 | 23.7 | 24.0 | 24.4 | 23.1 |
| Rural | 18.9 | 20.8 | 20.8 | 21.5 | 21.6 | 23.0 | 21.0 |
| **LEVEL OF EDUCATION** | | | | | | | |
| No education | 17.8 | 20.6 | 20.1 | 22.7 | 21.7 | 21.2 | 20.9 |
| Elementary | 19.8 | 21.4 | 21.9 | 22.0 | 23.2 | 23.2 | 21.7 |
| Sec/tec/trg.college | 21.0 | 23.3 | 24.4 | 24.1 | 24.6 | 25.4 | 24.2 |
| Higher | – | 24.0 | 23.0 | 29.3 | 25.0 | 27.7 | 26.0 |
| **CHOICE OF PARTNER** | | | | | | | |
| Entirely by me | 19.9 | 21.9 | 22.2 | 23.1 | 23.5 | 24.2 | 22.3 |
| Help/consent of family | 18.8 | 21.2 | 21.9 | 22.3 | 22.3 | 23.8 | 22.0 |
| Arranged by family | 17.0 | 19.0 | 22.0 | 22.5 | 23.5 | 24.0 | 21.7 |
| Other | 21.0 | 19.3 | 24.0 | 22.0 | – | – | 21.5 |
| **TYPE OF MARRIAGE** | | | | | | | |
| Customary | 19.4 | 21.4 | 21.9 | 22.1 | 23.0 | 23.7 | 21.9 |
| Ordinance/Church | 19.5 | 23.0 | 24.2 | 25.4 | 24.8 | 25.5 | 24.5 |
| Consensual | 20.3 | 22.7 | 23.1 | 23.6 | 20.6 | 23.0 | 22.3 |
| Islamic | – | 20.9 | 20.2 | 21.0 | 19.3 | 19.7 | 20.3 |
| **OCCUPATION** | | | | | | | |
| Professional | – | 23.9 | 24.5 | 24.5 | 24.6 | 26.4 | 24.6 |
| Clerical | – | 22.6 | 24.3 | 25.8 | 23.7 | 26.4 | 24.4 |
| Sales | 19.7 | 21.2 | 21.9 | 22.9 | 22.6 | 24.0 | 22.2 |
| Service/transport | 23.0 | 22.3 | 24.4 | 24.0 | 23.3 | 23.0 | 23.4 |
| Farmer/fisherman | – | 21.4 | 18.7 | 17.0 | 20.3 | – | 20.1 |
| Craftsman | 19.5 | 21.9 | 22.2 | 22.4 | 26.2 | 24.2 | 23.0 |
| **TOTAL** | 19.6 | 21.6 | 22.2 | 22.9 | 23.2 | 24.0 | 22.2 |

**Note:** – fewer than 10 cases

The full features of desired family size issues in Ghana are, to a large extent, obscured by non-numerical answers (up to God; as many as possible; don't know) as well as "ex-post rationalization" of fertility behavior--the tendency to report an ideal family size equal to or close to the actual family size (Pritchett, 1994). Lesthaeghe et al., (1981:190) have observed that questions on desired (ideal) family size "may be rather naive," given the faultiness assumption that people make lifetime calculations on childbearing behavior (see also Awusabo-Asare, 1988). Nonetheless, the concept serves useful purposes in fertility studies as discussed above.

This section of the present chapter discusses the data on the number of sons and daughters desired under ideal conditions and the reasons for the desired number. Table 3.9 gives the distribution of desired number of children by couples and sex of child.

**Table 3.9** Percentage Distribution of Couples by Number of Children Desired According to Sex of the Child, GFAMS, 1992/93

| | SONS DESIRED | | | | DAUGHTERS DESIRED | | | |
|---|---|---|---|---|---|---|---|---|
| | Wife | | Husband | | Wife | | Husband | |
| Number of Children | % | N | % | N | % | N | % | N |
| 0 | 2.2 | 20 | 1.9 | 17 | 1.9 | 17 | 2.3 | 21 |
| 1 | 24.0 | 216 | 15.8 | 142 | 23.6 | 212 | 26.1 | 235 |
| 2 | 51.5 | 463 | 50.1 | 451 | 50.9 | 458 | 45.6 | 411 |
| 3 | 14.9 | 134 | 18.8 | 169 | 16.0 | 144 | 16.1 | 145 |
| 4 | 4.6 | 41 | 7.2 | 65 | 4.3 | 39 | 4.4 | 40 |
| 5 | 2.0 | 18 | 3.6 | 32 | 1.4 | 13 | 2.6 | 23 |
| 6+ | 0.6 | 5 | 2.4 | 22 | 1.6 | 14 | 2.4 | 22 |
| Non-numeric | 0.2 | 2 | 0.2 | 2 | 0.2 | 2 | 0.4 | 4 |
| TOTAL | 100.0 | 899 | 100.0 | 900 | 100.0 | 899 | 100.0 | 901 |
| Mean no. of Chn[1]. | 2.0 | | 2.3 | | 2.1 | | 2.1 | |

**Note:** [1]Excludes respondents who gave non-numeric answers

On the average, couples desired four children: two each of sons and daughters. This is far less than the average completed family size of 5.5 children (GSS & MI, 1994). Between the couples, the men reported, on the average, about 0.3 child (son) more than females. The difference is, however, too small to suggest any preference for sons in the study area. These reported figures are similar to those observed in the 1988 and 1993 GDHSs (GSS & IRD, 1989; GSS & MI, 1994). In fact, the available evidence suggest that there is no obvious sex preference in Ghana, particularly among the matrilineal Akan (who constitute 62 percent of the study population) (Awusabo-Asare, 1988; GSS & IRD, 1989; GSS & MI, 1994).

### Desired Fertility by Background Characteristics

For most age groups and all the background characteristics examined, husbands desired more children than wives. For example, Figure 3.5 shows that rural residents, those with the least education, and those whose marriages were arranged reported slightly higher ideal family size than the other groups, perhaps indicating their adherence to more traditional attitudes on reproduction.

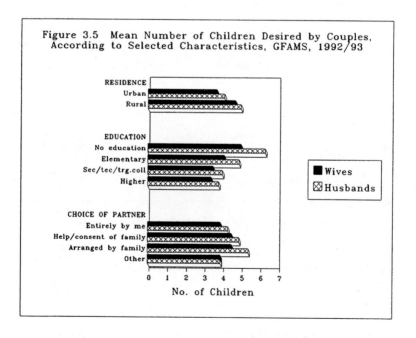

Figure 3.5   Mean Number of Children Desired by Couples, According to Selected Characteristics, GFAMS, 1992/93

Reasons for desiring 4 or fewer children are presented in Figure 3.6. Regardless of residence, a significant majority of couples cited the high cost of raising a child as the reason for their fertility desires.

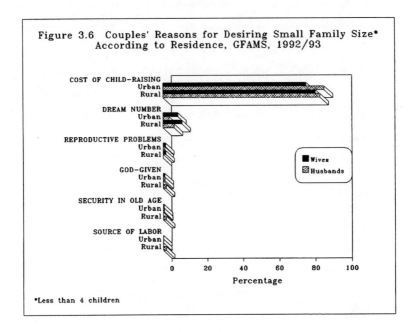

Figure 3.6  Couples' Reasons for Desiring Small Family Size* According to Residence, GFAMS, 1992/93

In summary, it can be said that a number of factors help to explain marriage systems and fertility behavior in Ghana. This chapter shows that a significant majority of all couples contracted their marriages through Customary law, and that over two-thirds of them chose their partners entirely by themselves as opposed to some form of family involvement. Nevertheless, it is worth noting that in comparison with wives, more husbands reported choosing their partners entirely by themselves.

These results indicate that while contemporary Ghanaian couples may have the freedom to choose their own partners, the family still has some influence in their choice of a partner. Such family influence, evidently higher for females than males, may decrease for both women and men as their level of education increase, indicating an element of autonomy. Furthermore, the incidence of polygyny seemed to be declining with time as women and men acquire more education.

The fact that marriage as an institution plays an important role in demographic behavior of Ghanaian women and men alike need not be over-emphasized. However, consistent with other studies, the data from the GFAMS indicate that traditional marriage practices such as family involvement of partner choice and polygyny continue to exist side by side with new forms such as civil and consensual marriages.

Although variations in the number of children born and the ideal number of children desired for both wives and husbands by place of residence, level of education, choice of partner, and type of marriage were evident, for every age group and characteristics, husbands had more children and desired more than wives. And irrespective of residence, the high cost of raising a child in contemporary Ghana prompted the majority of couples to desire fewer children than they normally would have liked to have.

The structural changes that seem to be occurring in the Ghanaian marriage systems and fertility behavior appear to be associated with age, urban residence and formal education, among other things. Perhaps, for women whose achieved family size is higher than desired family size, it is positive changes in their educational status as well as their involvement in their choice of partner which will enhance their capacity to articulate and strive toward the achievement of their desired family size. It is hoped that the use of modern contraception, the focus of the next chapter, will aid in the spacing and reduction of childbearing.

# 4

## CONTRACEPTION AND FAMILY PLANNING

Since the 1960s there has been an increase in contraceptive knowledge in Ghana but a rather low level of their use (Pool, 1972; Appiah, 1985; GSS & IRD, 1989; Oheneba-Sakyi, 1992; GSS & MI, 1994). Various studies in contraceptive knowledge in Ghana have reported near universal knowledge of at least one contraceptive method. For instance, results from the GFS of 1979/80 and the GDHSs of 1988 and 1993 indicate that about 90 percent of Ghanaians know of at least one contraceptive method. Similar proportions have been reported by other small scale studies (e.g., Fosu, 1986). The focus of this chapter is on the prevention of pregnancy and birth spacing with special emphasis on modern contraceptive methods.

Attitudes and beliefs about parenthood as a source of social and economic status, prestige, and psychological fulfillment which are deeply embedded in many African societies also impede the use of contraceptives. Moreover, for fear of a wife's infidelity, some African husbands may disapprove of a wife's use of effective contraception (McGinn, et al., 1989). African men are cautioned against being with women incapable of reproducing to the extent that in some cases, the family may require proof of pregnancy before the sexual relationships are formally recognized. (Bledsoe, 1990). Among Ghanaians, there is the traditional perception that discussion of sexually-related matters such as contraception and family planning is tantamount to sexual promiscuity (ROG & UNICEF, 1990:186). And since sexual promiscuity is believed to be the gateway to reduced fertility, contraception ought to be avoided.

Nonetheless, Ghana developed a population policy in 1969 called "Population Planning for National Progress and Prosperity," in order to parallel birth rates with already falling death rates (Benneh, et al., 1989:1). And in 1986, a non-governmental program called the Ghana Social Marketing Program (GSMP) was established to advertise and deliver contraceptives through chemical sellers, pharmacists, private midwives, and market women. Additional agents of transmission being utilized are the chiefs, folklore and drama, traditional birth attendants, schools and adult education classes, and a variety of media such as radio, television, the press, bumper stickers, and billboards (ROG & UNICEF, 1990). Other non-governmental programs involved in family planning and reproductive health services are the Planned Parenthood Association of Ghana, Ghana Registered Midwives Association, Christian Council, Catholic Secretariat, National Council on Women and Development, and Thirty-First December Women's Movement (Benneh et al., 1989:6).

While family planning programs have yet to produce the expected reductions in fertility, the government and others have made and continue to make concerted efforts to reduce Ghana's rate of population growth. In November 1992, the National Population Council (NPC) was inaugurated as the highest body to advise the government on population issues and to coordinate all population activities in the country (West Africa, 1992). And in 1993, the Ghana Population Policy was revised. The revised draft contains language dealing with children/youth, the aged, the environment, institutional arrangement, and implementation strategies.

In the GFAMS, modern contraceptive methods included the following: the pill, IUD, injection, vaginal methods (foaming tablets, jelly, and diaphragm), condom, female sterilization, male sterilization, and Norplant. This chapter examines the respondents' knowledge, ever use, current use, reasons for non-use, source(s) of knowledge and supply, discontinuation of a method, and reasons for discontinuation.

## Knowledge of Modern Contraceptive Methods

With low contraceptive usage in spite of the reported high knowledge, some observers have begun to question what constitutes "knowledge" of a method. In both the GFS and the GDHSs, a question asked was on "knowledge of methods." This question was stringently defined first in English and subsequently translated into various Ghanaian languages. In the GFAMS, the questions on "knowledge" about modern contraceptive methods were broken into "heard" and "seen." The rationale was that people may have just heard about contraception but may not have heard of a method or seen a contraceptive device/item. It was felt that such an approach will help to put into perspective the responses on contraceptive "knowledge" that have been obtained from various surveys in Ghana about the subject.

**Table 4.1**    Percentage Distribution of Couples Who Know a Modern Contraceptive Method, and Who Know a Source for a Method, According to Residence, GFAMS, 1992/93

| Contraceptive Method | KNOW A METHOD | | | | KNOW A SOURCE | | | |
|---|---|---|---|---|---|---|---|---|
| | Urban | | Rural | | Urban | | Rural | |
| | Wife | Hus. | Wife | Hus. | Wife | Hus. | Wife | Hus |
| Pill | 86.9 | 83.3 | 65.4 | 52.2 | 86.9 | 85.3 | 65.6 | 51.0 |
| IUD | 29.1 | 18.1 | 17.9 | 11.8 | 30.0 | 20.2 | 18.9 | 12.6 |
| Injection | 23.8 | 14.3 | 20.7 | 10.7 | 24.4 | 15.1 | 21.8 | 11.7 |
| Vaginal meth.* | 37.3 | 54.3 | 27.6 | 36.0 | 37.6 | 55.4 | 27.1 | 34.7 |
| Condom | 86.4 | 92.7 | 56.3 | 69.7 | 86.0 | 93.4 | 55.6 | 68.5 |
| Female sterilization | 12.0 | 12.5 | 1.1 | 3.1 | 12.5 | 14.7 | 2.8 | 4.7 |
| Male sterilization | 4.7 | 7.6 | 1.1 | 2.8 | 5.5 | 8.3 | 1.1 | 3.4 |
| Norplant | 1.5 | 1.6 | 0.0 | 0.8 | 2.0 | 2.7 | 1.1 | 2.8 |
| Any modern method | 95.8 | 97.1 | 74.0 | 79.9 | 95.8 | 97.3 | 75.1 | 80.2 |

**Note:** *Vaginal methods include foaming tablets, jelly, and diaphragm

Table 4.1 gives the distribution of respondents who had heard of at least one method and a source where it can be obtained. Nearly all the respondents in urban areas had heard about one method. The proportions were slightly lower among the

**Table 4.2**    Percentage Distribution of Couples Knowing at least One Modern Method, According to Selected Background Characteristics, GFAMS, 1992/93

| Background Characteristic | Wife Know Method | Number | Husband Know Method | Number |
|---|---|---|---|---|
| **AGE** | | | | |
| Under 25 | 78.4 | 87 | 90.9 | 20 |
| 25-29 | 89.1 | 213 | 87.7 | 100 |
| 30-34 | 87.2 | 170 | 92.3 | 191 |
| 35-44 | 90.5 | 220 | 90.4 | 303 |
| 45+ | 84.7 | 100 | 89.8 | 203 |
| **RESIDENCE** | | | | |
| Urban | 95.8 | 528 | 97.1 | 535 |
| Rural | 74.0 | 265 | 79.9 | 286 |
| **LEVEL OF EDUCATION** | | | | |
| No education | 71.5 | 108 | 65.0 | 26 |
| Elementary | 87.5 | 441 | 84.5 | 328 |
| Sec/tec/trg.college | 96.0 | 190 | 96.6 | 288 |
| Higher | 97.1 | 34 | 97.5 | 158 |
| **OCCUPATION** | | | | |
| Professional | 97.6 | 80 | 96.8 | 209 |
| Clerical | 100.0 | 55 | 97.9 | 94 |
| Sales | 88.1 | 163 | 100.0 | 35 |
| Service/transport | 97.9 | 46 | 88.5 | 108 |
| Farmer/fisherman | 69.2 | 9 | 74.3 | 26 |
| Craftsman | 93.0 | 106 | 94.8 | 184 |
| **RELIGION** | | | | |
| Catholic | 80.5 | 128 | 87.7 | 150 |
| Protestant | 90.9 | 558 | 92.8 | 525 |
| Muslim | 77.5 | 31 | 85.7 | 36 |
| Traditionalist | 77.8 | 7 | 78.3 | 18 |
| Other religion | 83.6 | 51 | 91.7 | 55 |
| No religion | 65.2 | 15 | 80.5 | 33 |
| **AGE AT 1ST MARRIAGE** | | | | |
| Under 20 years | 79.9 | 187 | 91.3 | 21 |
| 20-25 years | 89.2 | 456 | 87.6 | 318 |
| 26+ years | 93.9 | 139 | 92.6 | 461 |
| **CHN DESIRED: CHN LIVING** | | | | |
| Desire > Living | 86.0 | 486 | 89.4 | 499 |
| Desire = Living | 90.5 | 257 | 94.2 | 259 |
| Desire < Living | 95.3 | 41 | 90.5 | 57 |
| **TOTAL** | 87.2 | 793 | 90.3 | 821 |

respondents in rural areas--74 percent among the females and 80 percent among males. Among those who had heard of a method, about the same proportion knew of a source. In both the rural and urban areas more wives knew about the feminine methods such as the pill, IUD, and injection whereas more husbands knew of condoms and male sterilization. In the case of vaginal methods more husbands in both rural and urban areas had heard about the methods than wives. The methods most people had heard about were the pill and the condom. These were followed by vaginal methods, IUD and injection, in that order. In most cases, more couples in urban areas knew about methods than those in rural areas. The pattern observed for knowledge of a source for methods is similar to that of knowledge of the methods.

Among the socio-demographic characteristics, residence, education, age at first marriage, and the number of children desired, appeared to be linked to the knowledge of methods as shown in Table 4.2. For instance, for both husbands and wives the proportions of urban residents who knew of at least one method were higher than their rural counterparts. Furthermore, as the level of education increased the proportions of both wives and husbands reported knowing at least one method increased. Among the occupational groups, farmers and fishermen reported the least knowledge of methods, while among religious groups, higher proportions of Protestants knew of modern contraception compared to others. And for wives, the proportions who knew a method increased with increasing age at first marriage.

Reported sources of information about methods are presented in Tables 4.3a & 4.3b. The sources differed markedly between rural-urban residence, husbands and wives, and by method. For wives and husbands in urban areas the main source of knowledge on the pill and vaginal methods was the radio/television. And for the husbands in urban areas the mass media was the main source of knowledge for most methods. On the other hand, for wives in urban areas the hospital/clinic and community and family planning (FP) nurses were the main sources of knowledge for feminine methods. In the case of wives in rural areas the major sources were hospital/clinic and community/FP nurses while for husbands in rural areas the sources

**Table 4.3a** Percentage Distribution of Wives Knowing a Modern Contraceptive Method by Residence and Source of Knowledge, According to Specific Method, GFAMS, 1992/93

**CONTRACEPTIVE METHOD KNOWN TO URBAN WIVES**

| SOURCE OF KNOWLEDGE | Pill | IUD | Injection | Vaginal method | Condom | Female sterilization | Male sterilization | Norplant |
|---|---|---|---|---|---|---|---|---|
| Radio/television | 52.1 | 19.4 | 20.9 | 35.7 | 55.8 | 20.3 | 26.7 | 18.2 |
| Newspaper/magazine | 7.1 | 6.7 | 6.0 | 11.1 | 7.6 | 8.7 | 10.0 | 18.2 |
| Hospital/clinic | 15.3 | 35.8 | 36.6 | 10.6 | 11.8 | 7.2 | 3.3 | 9.1 |
| Community family planning | 8.8 | 18.8 | 14.9 | 10.6 | 6.6 | 8.7 | 6.7 | 18.2 |
| Drug store/pharmacy | 1.0 | 0.0 | 1.5 | 1.4 | 1.7 | 0.0 | 0.0 | 0.0 |
| Friend | 12.3 | 13.3 | 14.9 | 21.7 | 11.8 | 43.5 | 33.3 | 27.3 |
| Spouse/relative | 0.8 | 1.8 | 1.5 | 3.9 | 1.9 | 2.9 | 10.0 | 0.0 |
| TOTAL | 100.0 | 100.0 | 100.0 | 100.0 | 100.0 | 100.0 | 100.0 | 100.0 |
| NUMBER | [478] | [165] | [134] | [207] | [473] | [69] | [30] | [11] |

**CONTRACEPTIVE METHOD KNOWN TO RURAL WIVES**

| SOURCE OF KNOWLEDGE | Pill | IUD | Injection | Vaginal method | Condom | Female sterilization | Male sterilization | Norplant |
|---|---|---|---|---|---|---|---|---|
| Radio/television | 22.7 | 13.4 | 14.3 | 14.6 | 20.3 | 30.0 | 0.0 | 25.0 |
| Newspaper/magazine | 1.3 | 1.5 | 1.3 | 2.1 | 0.5 | 30.0 | 25.0 | 50.0 |
| Hospital/clinic | 36.5 | 46.3 | 53.2 | 38.5 | 38.6 | 10.0 | 0.0 | 0.0 |
| Community family planning | 24.5 | 29.9 | 24.7 | 30.2 | 24.4 | 0.0 | 0.0 | 0.0 |
| Drug store/pharmacy | 0.4 | 0.0 | 0.0 | 1.0 | 0.5 | 0.0 | 0.0 | 0.0 |
| Friend | 9.9 | 4.5 | 5.2 | 7.3 | 8.6 | 10.0 | 0.0 | 0.0 |
| Spouse/relative | 2.1 | 0.0 | 1.3 | 2.1 | 4.1 | 0.0 | 0.0 | 0.0 |
| TOTAL | 100.0 | 100.0 | 100.0 | 100.0 | 100.0 | 100.0 | 100.0 | 100.0 |
| NUMBER | [233] | [67] | [77] | [96] | [197] | [10] | [4] | [4] |

**Table 4.3b** Percentage Distribution of Husbands Knowing a Modern Contraceptive Method by Residence and Source of Knowledge, According to Specific Method, GFAMS, 1992/93

CONTRACEPTIVE METHOD KNOWN TO URBAN HUSBANDS

| SOURCE OF KNOWLEDGE | Pill | IUD | Injection | Vaginal method | Condom | Female sterilization | Male sterilization | Norplant |
|---|---|---|---|---|---|---|---|---|
| Radio/television | 60.6 | 27.9 | 34.9 | 39.5 | 58.7 | 14.8 | 10.9 | 0.0 |
| Newspaper/magazine | 10.4 | 22.5 | 15.7 | 12.8 | 9.9 | 22.2 | 28.3 | 46.7 |
| Hospital/clinic | 2.6 | 9.0 | 3.6 | 3.0 | 1.9 | 2.5 | 2.2 | 6.7 |
| Community family planning | 4.5 | 7.2 | 4.8 | 7.2 | 3.9 | 8.6 | 0.0 | 0.0 |
| Drug store/pharmacy | 2.6 | 2.7 | 2.4 | 4.6 | 3.1 | 1.2 | 0.0 | 0.0 |
| Friend | 13.6 | 16.2 | 14.5 | 25.3 | 17.9 | 33.3 | 37.0 | 33.3 |
| Spouse/relative | 2.6 | 8.1 | 19.3 | 1.6 | 0.8 | 2.5 | 2.2 | 0.0 |
| TOTAL | 100.0 | 100.0 | 100.0 | 100.0 | 100.0 | 100.0 | 100.0 | 100.0 |
| NUMBER | [469] | [111] | [83] | [304] | [513] | [81] | [46] | [15] |

CONTRACEPTIVE METHOD KNOWN TO RURAL HUSBANDS

| SOURCE OF KNOWLEDGE | Pill | IUD | Injection | Vaginal method | Condom | Female sterilization | Male sterilization | Norplant |
|---|---|---|---|---|---|---|---|---|
| Radio/television | 41.4 | 48.9 | 19.0 | 36.3 | 39.8 | 52.9 | 25.0 | 30.0 |
| Newspaper/magazine | 3.9 | 4.4 | 0.0 | 3.2 | 1.2 | 11.8 | 41.7 | 60.0 |
| Hospital/clinic | 11.6 | 15.6 | 19.0 | 9.7 | 11.5 | 0.0 | 0.0 | 0.0 |
| Community family planning | 24.3 | 28.9 | 38.1 | 26.6 | 23.8 | 11.8 | 8.7 | 0.0 |
| Drug store/pharmacy | 2.8 | 0.0 | 2.4 | 5.6 | 2.9 | 0.0 | 0.0 | 0.0 |
| Friend | 9.9 | 0.0 | 9.5 | 12.9 | 16.0 | 17.6 | 16.7 | 0.0 |
| Spouse/relative | 2.8 | 0.0 | 9.5 | 3.2 | 2.0 | 0.0 | 0.0 | 10.0 |
| TOTAL | 100.0 | 100.0 | 100.0 | 100.0 | 100.0 | 100.0 | 100.0 | 100.0 |
| NUMBER | [181] | [45] | [42] | [124] | [244] | [17] | [12] | [10] |

were more diverse. Spouse and friend were among the least mentioned by both males and females. These variations in sources of knowledge are important for the development of strategies for promoting the use of contraceptive methods. Family planning programmers need to take into consideration these group and spatial variations in sources of knowledge.

## Ever-use of Modern Contraceptive Methods

Among those who had ever used a modern contraceptive method, the majority in both rural and urban areas reported using a condom, as illustrated in Figure 4.1. Condom use was followed by the pill and vaginal methods.

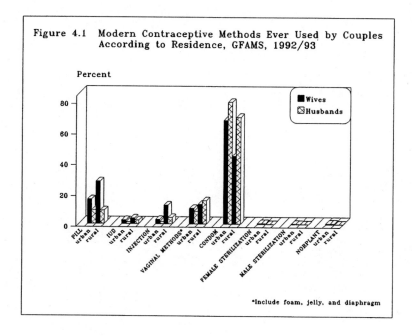

Figure 4.1   Modern Contraceptive Methods Ever Used by Couples According to Residence, GFAMS, 1992/93

The ever use of contraceptive methods by socio-demographic characteristics is shown in Table 4.4. Among the highlights from the table is the observation that younger couples, rural couples, and those with less education were less likely to have

**Table 4.4** Percentage Distribution of Couples Who Have Ever Used a Modern Method, According to Selected Background Characteristics, GFAMS, 1992/93

| Background Characteristic | Wife Ever Used | Number | | Husband Ever Used | Number |
|---|---|---|---|---|---|
| **AGE** | | | | | |
| Under 25 | 48.2 | 41 | | 50.0 | 10 |
| 25-29 | 69.8 | 143 | | 69.4 | 68 |
| 30-34 | 64.4 | 105 | | 75.8 | 135 |
| 35-44 | 75.2 | 155 | | 77.6 | 229 |
| 45+ | 82.0 | 82 | | 80.0 | 156 |
| | | | | | |
| **RESIDENCE** | | | | | |
| Urban | 74.5 | 382 | | 81.9 | 435 |
| Rural | 58.2 | 145 | | 64.5 | 167 |
| | | | | | |
| **LEVEL OF EDUCATION** | | | | | |
| No education | 53.4 | 47 | | 47.4 | 9 |
| Elementary | 63.9 | 274 | | 65.5 | 199 |
| Sec/tec/trg.college | 83.8 | 160 | | 81.9 | 235 |
| Higher | 91.2 | 31 | | 90.6 | 144 |
| | | | | | |
| **RELIGION** | | | | | |
| Catholic | 70.2 | 87 | | 75.7 | 109 |
| Protestant | 71.4 | 387 | | 78.9 | 403 |
| Muslim | 57.7 | 15 | | 60.6 | 20 |
| Traditionalist | 71.4 | 5 | | 66.7 | 12 |
| Other religion | 56.5 | 26 | | 68.6 | 35 |
| No religion | 40.0 | 6 | | 65.5 | 19 |
| | | | | | |
| **TYPE OF MARRIAGE** | | | | | |
| Customary | 67.8 | 341 | | 76.1 | 413 |
| Ordinance/Church | 84.5 | 109 | | 84.0 | 110 |
| Consensual | 57.8 | 63 | | 70.8 | 68 |
| Islamic | 66.7 | 12 | | 50.0 | 9 |
| | | | | | |
| **AGE AT 1ST MARRIAGE** | | | | | |
| Under 20 years | 57.5 | 96 | | 61.1 | 11 |
| 20-25 years | 70.3 | 317 | | 72.1 | 220 |
| 26+ years | 80.7 | 109 | | 80.1 | 358 |
| | | | | | |
| **CHN DESIRED: CHN LIVING** | | | | | |
| Desire > Living | 63.0 | 294 | | 71.9 | 343 |
| Desire = Living | 81.0 | 201 | | 83.9 | 214 |
| Desire < Living | 73.0 | 27 | | 77.4 | 41 |
| | | | | | |
| **TOTAL** | 69.2 | 762 | | 76.2 | 602 |

used any modern contraceptive method. And wives in consensual union were less likely to use modern contraceptive methods compared to those legitimately married. Similarly the proportions of both wives and husbands who reported ever using a method increased with increasing age at first marriage, and if couples had the number of children desired, they were more likely to have used a method than if they desired more children than presently living.

The results point to the general observation that people who have just married are less likely to postpone childbearing. As mentioned above, in a consensual relationship the couple (particularly the female) will be under pressure to prove her fertility as a prelude to marriage and, therefore, is less likely to use a modern contraceptive method. Not surprisingly, then, for couples who have never used a method, Table 4.5 shows that the reasons for non-use range from "wanting to give birth," "no interest in methods," "dangerous side effects," "no knowledge" to "no apparent reason." The fear of side effects is a major concern of non-users and will need to be examined in detail in future studies.

**Table 4.5**  Percentage Distribution of Couples Who Have Never Used a Method by Main Reason for Nonuse, According to Residence, GFAMS, 1992/93

| REASON FOR NONUSE | URBAN | | RURAL | |
|---|---|---|---|---|
| | Wife | Husband | Wife | Husband |
| Dangerous side effects | 14.1 | 14.5 | 13.8 | 9.5 |
| Inadequate knowledge | 10.4 | 9.4 | 14.9 | 13.6 |
| Wants to give birth | 16.0 | 12.8 | 28.2 | 31.3 |
| No interest in methods | 34.4 | 28.2 | 10.5 | 15.0 |
| No apparent reason | 6.1 | 11.1 | 19.3 | 8.8 |
| Other reasons | 19.0 | 23.9 | 13.3 | 21.8 |
| TOTAL | 100.0 | 100.0 | 100.0 | 100.0 |
| NUMBER | [163] | [117] | [181] | [147] |

**Current Usage**

Table 4.6 shows the percentage of couples currently using modern contraceptive methods from the GFAMS and the GDHS I and II. Between 1988 and 1993, data from the DHSs reveal that the proportion of currently married women using modern contraceptive methods increased from 6.0 percent to 10.0 percent and from 9.2 percent to 19.9 percent for males. Thirty-five percent of wives and 39 percent of husbands in the GFAMS reported currently using any method. In terms of methods being used, the majority reported using condoms, perhaps the effect of the government's aggressive media campaign to use the method to prevent the spread of STDs. Similarly, the use of condoms was reported to be on the increase in the GDHS II conducted in 1993.

**Table 4.6** Percentage Distribution of Couples Currently Using a Modern Contraceptive Method by Specific Method, GDHS-I (1988), GFAMS (1992/93), GDHS-II (1993)

| METHOD | GDHS-I[1] Wife | Hus. | GFAMS Wife | Hus. | GDHS-II[2] Wife | Hus. |
|---|---|---|---|---|---|---|
| Pill | 2.4 | 4.1 | 5.7 | 5.7 | 3.2 | 4.7 |
| IUD | 0.5 | 0.6 | 1.4 | 1.5 | 0.9 | 1.1 |
| Injection | 0.3 | 0.2 | 2.2 | 1.0 | 1.6 | 0.9 |
| Vaginal meth* | 0.9 | 1.4 | 2.9 | 3.2 | 1.2 | 2.1 |
| Condom | 0.5 | 1.7 | 19.9 | 24.8 | 2.2 | 10.4 |
| Female sterilization | 1.4 | 1.2 | 2.7 | 2.6 | 0.9 | 0.7 |
| Male sterilization | 0.0 | 0.0 | 0.1 | 0.1 | 0.0 | 0.0 |
| Norplant | 0.0 | 0.0 | 0.2 | 0.1 | 0.0 | 0.0 |
| TOTAL | 6.0 | 9.2 | 35.1 | 39.0 | 10.0 | 19.9 |

**Note:**
*Vaginal methods include foaming tablets, jelly, and diaphragm
[1]Data are computed from GDHS data files, 1988
[2]Data extracted from Ghana Statistical Service (GSS) and Macro International Inc. (MI), 1994, Table 4.6, page 39.

Factors that are associated with knowledge of modern contraceptives are also associated with the use of those methods. For instance, older couples, educated couples, those in formal occupations, those not in arranged marriages, those who married late, those living in the same household, and those desiring less than 4 children, were all generally more likely to currently use modern methods. Also, couples in monogamous marriages were more likely to use modern contraceptive methods. This might be due to the fact that such couples might not practice long durations of post-partum abstinence but use modern contraceptive methods to achieve the same objective.

The major source of procurement of contraceptives for the respondents was drug store/pharmacy shop as shown in Figure 4.2. Pharmacy shops have become major sources of supply for non-prescriptive contraceptive methods through the Ghana Social Marketing Program (GSMP).

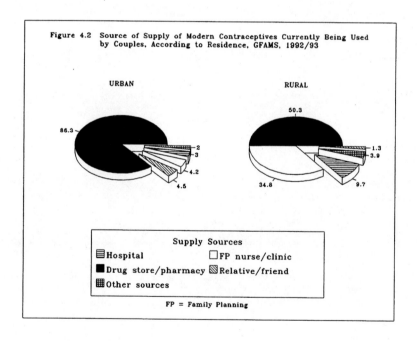

Figure 4.2   Source of Supply of Modern Contraceptives Currently Being Used by Couples, According to Residence, GFAMS, 1992/93

Couples who had discontinued the use of a modern method and the reason(s) for discontinuing are given in Tables 4.7. Three methods stand out among the few respondents who reported discontinuing a method. These were the pill, condom, and vaginal methods. The main reasons for the discontinuation were inconvenience, side effects, and partner disagreement. Cost did not appear as an important deterrent to use. Thus, the reasons for stopping the use of a method are medical and psycho-social which will have to be addressed in contraceptive evaluation programs.

**Table 4.7**  Percentage Distribution of Couples Who Have Ever Used a Modern Method by Reasons for Discontinuing the Method, GFAMS, 1992/93

| | CONTRACEPTIVE METHOD | | | | | | | |
| | WIFE | | | | HUSBAND | | | |
| REASON TO DISCONTINUE | Pill | Vaginal Meth[1] | Condom | Other Meth[2] | Pill | Vaginal Meth[1] | Condom | Other Meth[2] |
| --- | --- | --- | --- | --- | --- | --- | --- | --- |
| Distance to source | 0.0 | 0.0 | 0.0 | 5.3 | 0.0 | 9.1 | 0.0 | 0.0 |
| Costs too much | 0.0 | 0.0 | 0.0 | 0.0 | 0.0 | 0.0 | 1.6 | 0.0 |
| Inconvenient to use | 8.7 | 18.2 | 8.5 | 0.0 | 11.1 | 45.5 | 7.3 | 0.0 |
| Side effects | 39.1 | 54.5 | 31.9 | 63.2 | 50.0 | 27.3 | 38.7 | 63.6 |
| Partner disapproves | 34.8 | 9.1 | 45.7 | 21.1 | 16.7 | 0.0 | 28.2 | 27.3 |
| Other reasons | 17.4 | 18.2 | 13.8 | 10.5 | 22.2 | 18.2 | 24.2 | 9.1 |
| TOTAL | 100.0 | 100.0 | 100.0 | 100.0 | 100.0 | 100.0 | 100.0 | 100.0 |
| NUMBER | [23] | [11] | [94] | [19] | [18] | [11] | [124] | [11] |

**Note:**
[1]Vaginal methods include foaming tablets, jelly, and diaphragm
[2]Other methods include IUD, injection, female and male sterilization, and Norplant

It is evident from Table 4.7 that more wives than husbands reported discontinuing the use of modern contraceptive because of spousal disapproval. For instance, while only 17 percent of husbands said their wives had stopped using the pill due to the wives' own decision, twice as many wives (35 percent), reported discontinuation due to husbands' disapproval. Similarly, a higher percentage of wives than husbands reported that they had discontinued the use of condoms because of partner disapproval.

The fact that partner disapproval plays a major role in the discontinuation of contraception is a reflection of power relations between couples in patriarchal societies. With having children still an important priority among African couples, the wife may have little choice but to avoid contraception to restrict childbirth in order to keep her husband and in-laws happy, and prevent the husband from marrying additional wives to achieve his fertility desires (Ezeh, 1993; Bledsoe, et al., 1994; Lockwood, 1995, Oheneba-Sakyi & Takyi, 1997).

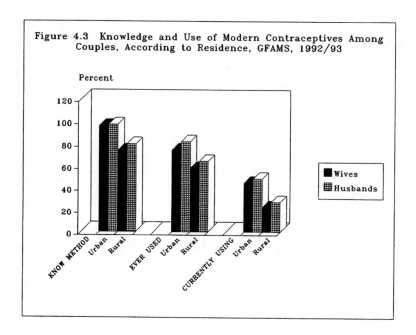

Figure 4.3   Knowledge and Use of Modern Contraceptives Among Couples, According to Residence, GFAMS, 1992/93

The overall picture of knowledge and use of modern contraceptives among couples according to rural-urban residence is shown in Figure 4.3. It seems clear from the GFAMS data that the known gap between knowledge and the use of modern contraceptive methods in Ghana reported in other studies was also observed in this study regardless of residence. However, compared to previous studies there appears to be a trend toward increasing the use of modern methods. The use of condoms seems to be on the increase from both the GDHS II and the GFAMS. One is, however, not sure whether condoms are used for contraception purposes or for protection against STDs. It will be important to distinguish between both uses since they have different implications for family planning programming.

The reasons for not using or discontinuing usage of modern methods are more psycho-social and medical than economic. This implies that women and men can be persuaded to become contraceptive adopters. It is believed that when their genuine concerns are taken care of their motivation levels may be raised for effective contraception. The dynamics of gender relations and communication within the household, and the role of family members in decision-making processes are essential not only for the understanding of family planning programs, but also of other family-related activities. Chapter 5 focuses on communication and decision making among couples in some family activities.

# 5

# COMMUNICATION AND DECISION MAKING

## COMMUNICATION

The frequency of a couple's discussions of family planning is positively related to contraceptive approval and its adoption in general. Indeed, it has been reported that successful practice of contraception is highly influenced by effective communication between couples (Olusanya, 1971; Shah, 1974; Simmons & Culagovski, 1975; Brody et al., 1976; Kar & Talbot, 1980; Kasarda et al., 1986). In much of Africa, however, a lineage system that takes prominence over the conjugal interests invokes an emotional commitment to kin and other social networks, thus weakening conjugal bonds (Caldwell & Caldwell, 1988; Clark, 1994). This loyalty to kinsmen and others beyond the "nuclear" unit, particularly among the matrilineal Akans, may often times translate to inadequate communication and discussions among married couples.

Thus, the social networks theory would offer better explanation for the pattern of interaction observed among Ghanaian couples. As is the practice in most parts of the country, a number of social events and interactions are organized along gender lines. One's spouse is often not the person with whom one would attend social functions such as funerals. Furthermore, family planning, when introduced into the country, followed the line of least resistance by utilizing the existing gendered pattern for the delivery of services such that family planning services targeted women and ignored men. Therefore, it is not surprising that couples would not discuss family planning and fertility strategy with one another.

An aspect of spousal communication is the age difference between couples. All things being equal, couples with ages close together are more likely to communicate on a wide range of issues, including those on fertility regulation and number of children. As observed from the Ghana Fertility Survey, the mean difference in age between spouses in Ghana was nine years (Casterline et. al., 1986). In situations where husbands are much older than their wives, as the case is in several African societies (see e.g., CBS, 1983; Casterline, et al., 1986; GSS & IRD, 1989), undue fear and intimidation, and respect for authority--vested in age--may prevent wives from freely exchanging ideas with their spouses. And even where differences exist between the wife and husband over attitudes and practice with regard to family planning, the husband's preference often dominates (Chaudhury, 1982; Cain, 1984). Among couples with higher education there seems to be high levels of spousal communication due in part to close proximity in age (see Nzioka, 1998).

In the GFAMS, respondents were asked to indicate whether they engage in selected activities together as couples. Couples were also asked if they ever discuss a diverse range of issues including fertility-related matters, and the frequency with which they, as couples, discuss the issues. In this section, we report on communication and discussion among couples on matters related to household, contraception, and fertility. Specifically on pregnancy prevention, respondents were asked to give reasons why the issue had not been discussed, and if they have been discussing it, who usually brings up the topic for discussion.

Table 5.1 presents the percent distribution of couples' conjugal relations. The results clearly indicate that most urban and rural couples did things together such as visiting relations, visiting hometown, attending funerals and other social functions. But regardless of residence, fewer couples in the study indicated that they attend religious services together. However, while over two-thirds of urban couples sat at the table to eat together, only about half of rural couples did so.

**Table 5.1**    Percentage Distribution of Couples' Conjugal Relations in Selected Household
Activities, According to Residence, GFAMS, 1992/93

| | DO ACTIVITIES TOGETHER | | | |
| | URBAN | | RURAL | |
| ACTIVITY | Wife | Husband | Wife | Husband |
|---|---|---|---|---|
| Sit at table to eat | 74.4 | 76.9 | 47.9 | 56.2 |
| Visit wife's relations | 74.6 | 76.4 | 74.2 | 82.7 |
| Visit husband's relations | 75.1 | 75.0 | 74.4 | 73.0 |
| Visit wife's hometown* | 64.4 | 64.7 | 67.6 | 69.1 |
| Visit husband's hometown* | 65.4 | 68.4 | 67.1 | 71.2 |
| Attend religious services | 46.7 | 58.3 | 49.9 | 60.1 |
| Attend funerals | 77.8 | 72.4 | 60.8 | 66.6 |
| Attend other social functions | 66.3 | 72.2 | 60.2 | 64.3 |
| Do other activities together | 80.0 | 78.0 | 59.4 | 72.4 |

**Note:** *Question applicable to only those living outside their hometown

Using the extent to which couples engage in activities together as a measure
of level of conjugality, we found variations in conjugal relations according to
education, age at first marriage, occupation, type of marriage, and residential status
as reported in Table 5.2. For instance, the results show that for both husbands and
wives, conjugal relations increased with increasing education. Most couples who
worked in professional and service occupations had strong conjugal relationships.
However, a disparity exists in the reporting of conjugal levels among couples who
were farmers and fishermen. In this occupational category, the men felt that they had
strong conjugality, whereas the women felt they only had moderate conjugality.

In terms of the relationship between choice of partner and conjugality, the data
indicate that when marriages were not arranged, couples had the tendency to report
stronger conjugality than when the marriages were arranged. Also, couples who had
contracted their marriages under the Ordinance or Church were more likely to have
stronger conjugality than their counterparts in Islamic or consensual marriages.
Likewise, co-residence living seems to be associated with strong conjugal relations.

**Table 5.2**    Percentage Distribution of Couples' Conjugal Relations, According to Selected Background Characteristics, GFAMS, 1992/93

| Background Characteristic | Strong Conjugality | | Moderate Conjugality | | Weak Conjugality | |
|---|---|---|---|---|---|---|
| | Wife | Hus. | Wife | Hus. | Wife | Hus. |
| **AGE** | | | | | | |
| Under 30 | 39.1 | 35.3 | 40.2 | 41.9 | 20.7 | 22.8 |
| 30-39 | 40.4 | 43.1 | 37.2 | 38.5 | 22.4 | 18.5 |
| 40+ | 34.8 | 43.5 | 37.6 | 34.7 | 27.6 | 21.9 |
| **RESIDENCE** | | | | | | |
| Urban | 40.1 | 44.2 | 38.9 | 35.2 | 21.0 | 20.6 |
| Rural | 35.9 | 38.8 | 38.1 | 41.1 | 26.1 | 20.1 |
| **LEVEL OF EDUC.** | | | | | | |
| No education | 25.2 | 32.5 | 41.7 | 32.5 | 33.1 | 35.0 |
| Elementary | 38.4 | 36.0 | 37.5 | 41.7 | 24.1 | 22.3 |
| Sec/tec/trg.college | 42.6 | 43.8 | 41.6 | 36.7 | 15.7 | 19.5 |
| Higher | 64.7 | 54.9 | 26.5 | 30.2 | 8.8 | 14.8 |
| **OCCUPATION** | | | | | | |
| Professional | 50.6 | 48.4 | 38.3 | 35.8 | 11.1 | 15.8 |
| Clerical | 54.5 | 47.9 | 34.5 | 34.4 | 10.9 | 17.7 |
| Sales | 40.2 | 51.4 | 42.4 | 37.1 | 17.4 | 11.4 |
| Service/transport | 53.2 | 36.1 | 40.4 | 42.6 | 6.4 | 21.3 |
| Farmer/fisherman | 25.0 | 40.0 | 50.0 | 28.6 | 25.0 | 31.4 |
| Craftsman | 45.1 | 41.7 | 27.4 | 33.3 | 27.4 | 25.0 |
| **CHOICE OF PARTNER** | | | | | | |
| Entirely by me | 38.2 | 41.8 | 40.8 | 37.5 | 21.0 | 20.7 |
| Help/consent of fam. | 40.3 | 44.0 | 33.3 | 38.2 | 26.3 | 17.8 |
| Arranged by family | 32.1 | 37.5 | 42.9 | 31.3 | 25.0 | 31.3 |
| Other | 41.7 | 27.3 | 33.3 | 45.5 | 25.0 | 27.3 |
| **TYPE OF MARRIAGE** | | | | | | |
| Customary | 37.9 | 41.5 | 41.8 | 40.3 | 20.3 | 18.2 |
| Ordinance/Church | 56.2 | 56.1 | 22.6 | 23.7 | 21.2 | 20.1 |
| Consensual | 23.5 | 27.5 | 36.1 | 38.2 | 40.3 | 34.3 |
| Islamic | 24.0 | 34.8 | 56.0 | 47.8 | 20.0 | 17.4 |
| **CO-RESIDENCE** | | | | | | |
| Yes | 39.6 | 42.7 | 39.1 | 37.4 | 21.3 | 19.9 |
| No | 28.0 | 36.6 | 34.4 | 39.6 | 37.6 | 23.8 |
| **TOTAL** | 38.5 | 42.1 | 38.6 | 37.5 | 23.0 | 20.4 |
| **NUMBER** | [348] | [381] | [349] | [340] | [208] | [185] |

As far as discussion of household issues are concerned, Table 5.3 points out that the majority of urban and rural couples discussed issues such as children's educational matters, current social affairs, acquisition of physical property, and acquisition of household items. It is interesting to note that while contraceptive method choice was the one issue which both urban and rural couples talked about the least, urban couples were more likely to discuss pregnancy prevention and method choice than their rural counterparts.

**Table 5.3**    Percentage Distribution of  Couples' Discussion of Selected Household Issues, GFAMS, 1992/93

| HOUSEHOLD ISSUE | DISCUSS ISSUE WITH SPOUSE | | | |
| | URBAN | | RURAL | |
| | Wife | Husband | Wife | Husband |
| --- | --- | --- | --- | --- |
| Children's education* | 86.7 | 89.1 | 82.5 | 83.8 |
| Current social affairs | 72.1 | 74.6 | 73.7 | 76.0 |
| Current political affairs | 67.9 | 69.1 | 65.9 | 74.4 |
| Purchase of household items | 90.1 | 90.5 | 84.4 | 91.3 |
| Purchase of physical property | 90.7 | 92.5 | 79.0 | 89.3 |
| Pregnancy prevention | 73.7 | 80.1 | 56.7 | 59.4 |
| Contraceptive method choice** | 57.5 | 58.2 | 31.4 | 32.2 |
| Other household issues | 72.0 | 85.7 | 82.2 | 86.0 |

**Note:**
* Question applicable to only those with children
**Question applicable to only ever/current users of modern contraceptive method

For urban and rural couples who did not discuss pregnancy prevention, Figures 5.1a & 5.1b illustrate that while about one-third wanted to give birth, another one-third did not think such discussions were necessary.  On conversations relating to pregnancy prevention, Table 5.4 indicates that overall 53 percent of wives reported that they were the ones who initiated discussions compared to 42 percent of husbands.    Regardless of background characteristic such as age, residence, educational level, occupation, choice of partner, type or form of marriage, and age at first marriage, wives perceived themselves as the primary initiators of the discussions, while husbands indicated that they were the ones who often initiated the discussions.

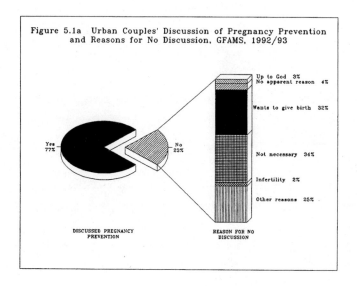

Figure 5.1a   Urban Couples' Discussion of Pregnancy Prevention and Reasons for No Discussion, GFAMS, 1992/93

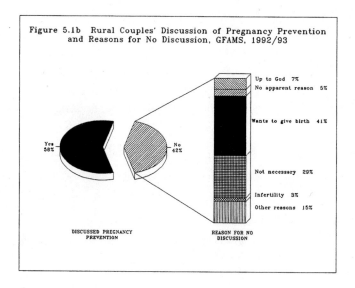

Figure 5.1b   Rural Couples' Discussion of Pregnancy Prevention and Reasons for No Discussion, GFAMS, 1992/93

**Table 5.4**   Percentage Distribution of Couples' by Their Initiation of Discussion on Pregnancy Prevention, According to Selected Background Characteristics, GFAMS, 1992/93

| | WHO INITIATES DISCUSSION | | | | | |
| | Wife Only | | Husband Only | | Wife or Husband | |
| Background Characteristic | Wife | Hus. | Wife | Hus. | Wife | Hus. |
|---|---|---|---|---|---|---|
| AGE | | | | | | |
| Under 30 | 49.6 | 21.0 | 25.2 | 59.0 | 25.2 | 20.0 |
| 30-39 | 48.6 | 31.8 | 24.7 | 45.5 | 26.6 | 22.7 |
| 40+ | 62.7 | 44.8 | 18.9 | 33.0 | 18.3 | 22.2 |
| | | | | | | |
| RESIDENCE | | | | | | |
| Urban | 52.7 | 39.0 | 21.9 | 40.9 | 25.5 | 20.0 |
| Rural | 52.1 | 28.6 | 26.9 | 45.0 | 21.0 | 26.4 |
| | | | | | | |
| LEVEL OF EDUC. | | | | | | |
| No education | 54.7 | 28.6 | 24.4 | 33.3 | 20.9 | 38.1 |
| Elementary | 47.3 | 25.3 | 27.4 | 54.4 | 25.3 | 20.3 |
| Sec/tec/trg.college | 60.6 | 39.9 | 18.3 | 41.9 | 21.1 | 18.2 |
| Higher | 72.4 | 48.3 | 0.0 | 23.8 | 27.6 | 28.0 |
| | | | | | | |
| OCCUPATION | | | | | | |
| Professional | 54.8 | 39.1 | 16.4 | 37.5 | 28.8 | 23.4 |
| Clerical | 51.1 | 51.2 | 20.0 | 34.9 | 28.9 | 14.0 |
| Sales | 52.1 | 40.0 | 20.8 | 40.0 | 27.1 | 20.0 |
| Service/transport | 55.3 | 27.3 | 21.1 | 48.9 | 23.7 | 23.9 |
| Farmer/fisherman | 66.6 | 25.0 | 11.1 | 37.5 | 22.2 | 37.5 |
| Craftsman | 56.8 | 28.0 | 12.6 | 48.4 | 30.5 | 23.6 |
| | | | | | | |
| CHOICE OF PARTNER | | | | | | |
| Entirely by me | 48.1 | 35.1 | 25.2 | 42.4 | 26.7 | 22.5 |
| Help/consent of fam. | 61.1 | 39.9 | 20.0 | 38.5 | 18.9 | 21.7 |
| Arranged by family | 52.9 | 9.1 | 17.6 | 72.7 | 29.4 | 18.2 |
| Other | 72.7 | 22.2 | 18.2 | 66.7 | 9.1 | 11.1 |
| | | | | | | |
| TYPE OF MARRIAGE | | | | | | |
| Customary | 51.4 | 32.6 | 22.0 | 43.4 | 26.6 | 24.0 |
| Ordinance/Church | 60.7 | 55.3 | 12.8 | 18.7 | 26.5 | 26.0 |
| Consensual | 47.9 | 22.9 | 41.5 | 71.1 | 10.6 | 6.0 |
| Islamic | 53.8 | 36.4 | 38.5 | 54.5 | 7.7 | 9.1 |
| | | | | | | |
| AGE AT 1ST MARRIAGE | | | | | | |
| Under 20 years | 48.4 | 7.7 | 27.0 | 69.2 | 24.5 | 23.1 |
| 20-25 years | 52.1 | 28.5 | 24.3 | 50.6 | 23.6 | 21.0 |
| 26+ | 59.3 | 40.6 | 17.1 | 36.3 | 23.6 | 23.1 |
| | | | | | | |
| TOTAL | 52.5 | 35.6 | 23.5 | 42.3 | 24.1 | 22.1 |
| NUMBER | [362] | [249] | [162] | [296] | [166] | [155] |

Despite this apparent disparity in the perceptions of wives and husbands, there are some noted differences that need to be mentioned. For instance, compared to younger women, those with less education, and those who married early, higher proportions of older women (aged 40+), women with secondary or higher education, and those who waited longer to get married reported that they were the primary initiators of discussions on pregnancy prevention.

A large number of couples in the GFAMS study discussed desired family size and birth spacing than postpartum sexual abstinence and breastfeeding as Figure 5.2 shows. While about 60 percent of both wives and husbands regularly discussed the size of their family and child spacing, only about one third regularly discussed breastfeeding and resumption of sexual intercourse after childbirth.

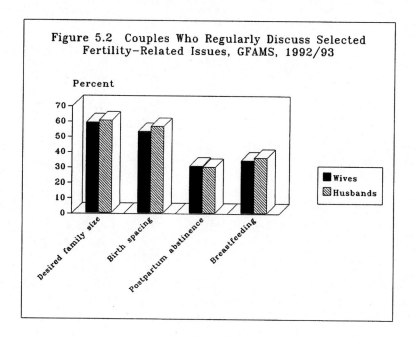

Figure 5.2   Couples Who Regularly Discuss Selected Fertility-Related Issues, GFAMS, 1992/93

**Table 5.5** Percentage Distribution of Couples' by Their Discussion of Selected Fertility-Related Issues, According to Reasons for the Frequency of the Discussion, GFAMS, 1992/93

| | HOW OFTEN ISSUE IS DISCUSSED | | | | | |
| | Not at all | | Seldom | | Often | |
| REASON FOR DISCUSSION OF: | Wife | Hus | Wife | Hus | Wife | Hus |
|---|---|---|---|---|---|---|
| **DESIRED FAMILY SIZE** | | | | | | |
| To be able to care for | 5.2 | 4.5 | 18.4 | 22.0 | 76.4 | 73.5 |
| We disagree on the issue | 29.0 | 24.1 | 35.5 | 31.0 | 35.5 | 44.8 |
| It's up to God | 66.7 | 53.8 | 22.2 | 15.4 | 11.1 | 30.8 |
| It's wife's decision | 66.7 | 57.1 | 16.7 | 21.4 | 16.7 | 21.4 |
| It's husband's decision | 66.7 | 62.5 | 8.3 | 31.3 | 25.0 | 6.3 |
| Other reasons | 33.6 | 23.7 | 23.8 | 29.5 | 42.5 | 46.9 |
| **BIRTH SPACING** | | | | | | |
| To be able to care for | 7.5 | 5.5 | 21.7 | 23.0 | 70.0 | 71.5 |
| We disagree on the issue | 57.1 | 50.0 | 42.9 | 33.3 | 0.0 | 16.7 |
| It's up to God | 75.1 | 61.5 | 25.0 | 7.7 | 0.0 | 30.8 |
| It's wife's decision | 76.9 | 71.4 | 23.1 | 19.0 | 0.0 | 9.5 |
| It's husband's decision | 42.9 | 71.4 | 28.6 | 14.3 | 28.6 | 14.3 |
| Other reasons | 28.6 | 26.0 | 21.9 | 21.5 | 49.5 | 52.6 |
| **POSTPARTUM ABSTINENCE** | | | | | | |
| Healthy for mother/child | 15.7 | 12.0 | 19.4 | 21.3 | 64.8 | 66.7 |
| Avoid pregnancy | 6.2 | 6.1 | 24.6 | 28.8 | 69.2 | 65.2 |
| We disagree on the issue | 82.1 | 86.3 | 14.3 | 7.5 | 3.6 | 6.3 |
| It's wife's decision | 81.8 | 89.1 | 9.1 | 7.8 | 9.1 | 3.1 |
| It's husband's decision | 66.7 | 77.4 | 13.3 | 16.1 | 20.0 | 6.5 |
| Other reasons | 53.4 | 52.8 | 25.4 | 26.4 | 21.2 | 20.8 |
| **BREASTFEEDING** | | | | | | |
| Healthy for child | 3.5 | 2.6 | 15.9 | 11.4 | 80.0 | 86.0 |
| It's wife's decision | 76.0 | 77.8 | 17.5 | 15.2 | 6.5 | 7.0 |
| It's husband's decision | 50.0 | 64.7 | 28.6 | 22.1 | 21.4 | 13.2 |
| Not had a child yet | 96.4 | 96.3 | 0.0 | 0.0 | 3.6 | 3.7 |
| Other reasons | 43.8 | 47.7 | 27.7 | 33.0 | 28.6 | 19.3 |

For couples who frequently discussed desired family size and birth spacing, Table 5.5 indicates that they did so in order to be able to take care of the children. However, couples hardly ever discussed postpartum sexual abstinence because they either disagreed on the issue or felt that it ought to be decided by the wife only.

Similarly, for those who never discussed breastfeeding, most felt that it had to be the wife's decision. But to promote the health of mother and child and avoid unwanted pregnancy some couples regularly discussed issues related to breastfeeding and postpartum sexual abstinence.

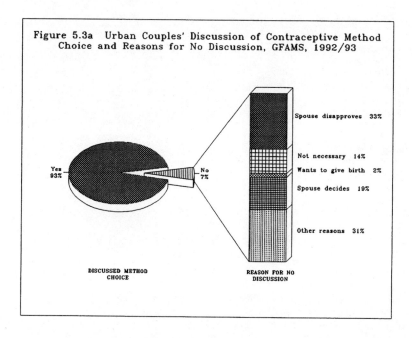

Figure 5.3a   Urban Couples' Discussion of Contraceptive Method Choice and Reasons for No Discussion, GFAMS, 1992/93

With regard to contraceptive method choice, Figures 5.3a & 5.3b indicate that the overwhelming majority (93 percent) of urban couples discussed it compared to 78 percent of rural couples. Nevertheless, for those couples who did not discuss a method choice, almost a third of both urban and rural couples indicated that the major reason they did not discuss was because of their spouse's disapproval. This finding, which may be explained by the issue of unequal power relations between couples in patriarchal societies, is similar to those reported in Table 4.6 above which shows that most wives discontinued using a modern contraceptive method because of their partners' disapproval.

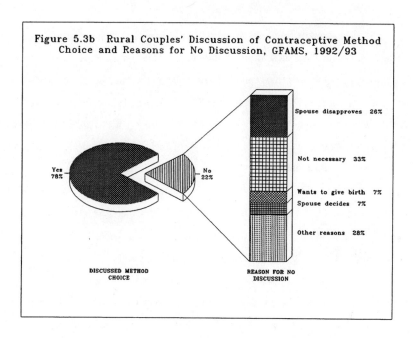

Figure 5.3b   Rural Couples' Discussion of Contraceptive Method
Choice and Reasons for No Discussion, GFAMS, 1992/93

To determine the percent distribution of the frequency of couples' discussion of desired family size, birth spacing, postpartum sexual abstinence, and breastfeeding according to background characteristics, further analyses were conducted. The results, (not reported here but available upon request from the authors), point out that couples were more likely to discuss the selected issues if they lived in urban areas, were educated, were monogamous, were in non-Islamic marriages, did not have arranged marriages, lived in the same household, and had stronger conjugal bonds than their counterparts who lived in rural areas, had no schooling, were in polygynous relationships, married under the Islamic law,  in marriages entirely arranged by family, do not live in the same household, and had weak conjugal relations.

## DECISION MAKING

Studies about demographic trends in sub-Saharan Africa have largely ignored the issue of power dynamics within relationships. This is in spite of the realization that couple intra-partner power relations affect socio-economic behaviors, including the use of contraceptives, desired or wanted family size, and child-spacing. Because of stratification of society (e.g., by class, caste, or gender), often based on access to resources and prestige, the behavior and actions of husbands tend to be quite different from wives and subsequently have impact on wives in several ways.

Caldwell (1982) has argued that economic and emotional nucleation within marriage is one of the pre-conditions for fertility decline. The rationale is that nucleation will promote inter-spousal communication, a factor that is important for decision making in all aspects of life, including those on fertility. In the social context in Ghana, couples and/or individuals hardly ever make decisions in isolation. Decisions are made with inputs from the wider socio-cultural system, such as from friends and in-laws. As pointed out earlier, marriage is between two individuals as well as other members of the extended family. In addition, there is a network of other people who influence decision making, such as friends and in-laws. The observations have led to the use of the social network theory to explain the nature of interactions that could also have implications for decision making on fertility (Pescosolido, 1992). As observed by Nzioka (1998), in the Siaya district of Kenya, "fertility decision-making were largely collective affairs" (p. 44).

A number of factors influence decision making. Social networks provide one of the structures for information and decision making in the Ghanaian system. Fertility decline can be achieved by utilising the network systems and identifying those who contribute to decision making on fertility, including contraceptive use. The first step will be identifying the significant others who contribute to the process. Evidence from South-East Asia and parts of Eastern and South Africa indicate that one need not achieve economic and emotional nucleation before fertility decline occurs (Dow et al., 1994).

While the previous section in this chapter dealt with communication between couples and the issues discussed, this section examines the processes involved in couple decision making on household and family-related issues so discussed. They are grouped into general issues (children's education, purchase of household items, and purchase of physical property), fertility-related issues (desired family size, birth spacing, breastfeeding, and postpartum sexual abstinence), and contraceptive-related issues (decision to use a method, method choice, change and discontinuation of a method). The approach was to find out whether the wife or husband made the decision alone on certain issues and jointly decided on others. In general, one would expect "domains" of major influence in decision making and areas of joint action.

**The Decision-Making Process**

Results from the GFAMS indicate that couples made joint decisions on most of the issues including desired family size, birth-spacing, and contraception as reported in Tables 5.6a & 5.6b. The only wife-dominated decision was in the area of breastfeeding. Although most of the decisions were reported to have been made jointly, some interesting patterns of decision making emerge from the data when analyzed according to socio-demographic background of respondents. Table 5.7 typifies these observed patterns. Among the findings were that the proportion of couples who reported joint decision making increased with increasing age at first marriage, urban living, education, and conjugal relations. Furthermore, the results show that couples were more likely to make joint decisions on fertility- and contraceptive-related issues if they had chosen their partners entirely by themselves or had married under the Ordinance/Church laws compared to those whose choice of partner was influenced by family members or had married under Customary or Islamic laws.

While most Ghanaian couples seem to be engaged in discussions and decision making on issues that affect their everyday lives, joint decision making was higher in our study for women who exhibited some autonomy through indicators such as

Table 5.6a   Percentage Distribution of Urban Couples by How Decisions are Arrived at on Selected Household Issues, GFAMS, 1992/93

| URBAN COUPLES' DECISION MAKING ON: | HUSBAND ALONE | | WIFE ALONE | | JOINT DECISION | | OTHERS | |
|---|---|---|---|---|---|---|---|---|
| | Wife | Hus. | Wife | Hus. | Wife | Hus. | Wife | Hus. |
| **GENERAL ISSUES** | | | | | | | | |
| Children's education | 16.1 | 17.8 | 3.8 | 2.2 | 79.7 | 79.2 | 0.4 | 0.8 |
| Purchase of household items | 9.7 | 11.9 | 11.4 | 6.4 | 78.9 | 81.7 | 0.0 | 0.0 |
| Purchase of physical property | 18.5 | 18.2 | 2.9 | 1.5 | 78.3 | 80.1 | 0.4 | 0.2 |
| **FERTILITY-RELATED ISSUES** | | | | | | | | |
| Desired family size | 8.8 | 12.7 | 8.2 | 2.5 | 82.7 | 84.1 | 0.4 | 0.8 |
| Birth spacing | 5.5 | 8.4 | 13.0 | 8.0 | 81.1 | 82.9 | 0.4 | 0.8 |
| Postpartum sexual abstinence | 12.5 | 15.3 | 28.8 | 25.9 | 58.3 | 58.6 | 0.4 | 0.2 |
| Breastfeeding | 2.0 | 4.2 | 53.3 | 51.0 | 44.1 | 44.4 | 0.6 | 0.4 |
| Other fertility-related issue | 20.0 | 8.7 | 10.0 | 17.4 | 70.0 | 73.9 | 0.0 | 0.0 |
| **CONTRACEPTION-RELATED ISSUE** | | | | | | | | |
| Whether to use a method | 11.8 | 15.5 | 10.7 | 6.0 | 74.9 | 75.7 | 2.6 | 2.9 |
| Choice of a method | 9.7 | 15.4 | 18.5 | 11.2 | 69.2 | 70.1 | 2.6 | 3.3 |
| Change of a method | 7.9 | 13.6 | 20.5 | 14.9 | 70.5 | 69.8 | 1.2 | 1.6 |
| Discontinue a method | 5.8 | 12.9 | 22.6 | 17.2 | 70.8 | 68.4 | 0.8 | 1.5 |
| Use of periodic abstinence | 9.9 | 12.5 | 29.1 | 26.8 | 61.1 | 60.7 | 0.0 | 0.0 |
| Other contraception-related issue | 45.5 | 38.5 | 45.5 | 38.5 | 9.1 | 23.1 | 0.0 | 0.0 |

WHO DECIDES ON ISSUE

**Table 5.6b** Percentage Distribution of Rural Couples by How Decisions are Arrived at on Selected Household Issues, GFAMS, 1992/93

| | WHO DECIDES ON ISSUE | | | | | | | |
| | Husband Alone | | Wife Alone | | Joint Alone | | Others Decision | |
| RURAL COUPLES' DECISION MAKING ON: | Wife | Hus. | Wife | Hus. | Wife | Hus. | Wife | Hus. |
|---|---|---|---|---|---|---|---|---|
| **GENERAL ISSUES** | | | | | | | | |
| Children's education | 14.3 | 20.0 | 4.7 | 1.5 | 80.1 | 78.2 | 0.9 | 0.3 |
| Purchase of household items | 14.1 | 16.5 | 7.0 | 2.8 | 78.0 | 80.4 | 0.8 | 0.3 |
| Purchase of physical property | 20.1 | 19.1 | 4.0 | 1.1 | 75.4 | 79.5 | 0.6 | 0.3 |
| **FERTILITY-RELATED ISSUES** | | | | | | | | |
| Desired family size | 10.3 | 24.6 | 14.6 | 2.6 | 71.7 | 71.4 | 3.4 | 1.4 |
| Birth spacing | 8.9 | 15.4 | 19.9 | 10.0 | 67.4 | 71.6 | 3.9 | 3.0 |
| Postpartum sexual abstinence | 16.3 | 18.6 | 17.5 | 14.4 | 63.6 | 64.0 | 2.7 | 3.0 |
| Breastfeeding | 3.5 | 6.1 | 59.7 | 50.3 | 35.8 | 42.0 | 1.0 | 1.5 |
| Other fertility-related issue | 12.5 | 11.1 | 37.5 | 11.1 | 50.0 | 77.8 | 0.0 | 0.0 |
| **CONTRACEPTION-RELATED ISSUE** | | | | | | | | |
| Whether to use a method | 11.4 | 20.1 | 17.1 | 6.7 | 66.8 | 69.1 | 4.7 | 4.1 |
| Choice of a method | 11.9 | 20.1 | 17.0 | 9.3 | 63.9 | 62.4 | 7.2 | 8.2 |
| Change of a method | 9.4 | 18.1 | 18.1 | 10.9 | 70.9 | 66.7 | 1.6 | 4.3 |
| Discontinue a method | 11.3 | 19.9 | 22.5 | 9.6 | 64.1 | 69.2 | 2.1 | 1.4 |
| Use of periodic abstinence | 21.9 | 25.2 | 12.3 | 5.3 | 64.2 | 68.0 | 1.6 | 1.5 |
| Other contraception-related issue | 16.7 | 75.0 | 0.0 | 8.3 | 83.3 | 16.7 | 0.0 | 0.0 |

**Table 5.7** Percentage Distribution of Couples by How Decisions are Arrived at on Whether to Use a Modern Contraceptive Method, According to Selected Background Characteristics, GFAMS, 1992/93

| | WHO DECIDES ON WHETHER TO USE A CONTRACEPTIVE METHOD | | | | | | | | | |
|---|---|---|---|---|---|---|---|---|---|---|
| | Husband Alone | | Wife Alone | | Joint Decision | | Total | | Number | |
| Characteristic | Wife | Hus. | Wife | Hus. | Wife | Hus. | Wife | Hus. | Wife | Hus |
| **AGE AT 1ST MARRIAGE** | | | | | | | | | | |
| Under 20 years | 19.4 | 40.0 | 15.3 | 0.0 | 65.3 | 60.0 | 100.0 | 100.0 | 124 | 10 |
| 20-25 years | 11.2 | 19.2 | 14.0 | 6.4 | 74.8 | 74.4 | 100.0 | 100.0 | 321 | 219 |
| 26+ years | 6.1 | 15.7 | 7.9 | 6.7 | 86.0 | 77.7 | 100.0 | 100.0 | 114 | 345 |
| **RESIDENCE** | | | | | | | | | | |
| Urban | 12.1 | 16.0 | 11.0 | 6.1 | 76.9 | 77.9 | 100.0 | 100.0 | 381 | 407 |
| Rural | 12.0 | 21.0 | 17.9 | 7.0 | 70.1 | 72.0 | 100.0 | 100.0 | 184 | 186 |
| **LEVEL OF EDUCATION** | | | | | | | | | | |
| No education | 29.0 | 40.0 | 20.3 | 10.0 | 50.0 | 50.0 | 100.0 | 100.0 | 64 | 10 |
| Elementary | 13.8 | 28.0 | 13.1 | 5.3 | 73.2 | 66.7 | 100.0 | 100.0 | 298 | 207 |
| Sec/tec/trg.college | 3.8 | 13.1 | 9.0 | 5.9 | 87.2 | 81.1 | 100.0 | 100.0 | 156 | 222 |
| Higher | 6.1 | 8.7 | 21.2 | 9.4 | 72.7 | 81.9 | 100.0 | 100.0 | 33 | 138 |
| **CHOICE OF PARTNER** | | | | | | | | | | |
| Entirely by me | 10.9 | 16.6 | 12.7 | 5.1 | 76.4 | 78.3 | 100.0 | 100.0 | 377 | 447 |
| Help/consent of fam. | 14.2 | 22.9 | 14.8 | 9.2 | 71.0 | 67.9 | 100.0 | 100.0 | 162 | 131 |
| Arranged by family | 9.1 | – | 18.2 | – | 72.7 | – | 100.0 | | 11 | – |
| **TYPE OF MARRIAGE** | | | | | | | | | | |
| Customary | 13.1 | 20.6 | 15.2 | 7.9 | 71.7 | 71.5 | 100.0 | 100.0 | 389 | 418 |
| Ordinance/Church | 1.9 | 3.6 | 5.7 | 1.8 | 92.5 | 94.6 | 100.0 | 100.0 | 106 | 112 |
| Consensual | 23.2 | 20.8 | 14.3 | 4.2 | 62.5 | 75.0 | 100.0 | 100.0 | 56 | 48 |
| Islamic | 16.7 | 27.3 | 16.7 | 9.1 | 66.7 | 63.6 | 100.0 | 100.0 | 12 | 11 |
| **CONJUGAL RELATIONS** | | | | | | | | | | |
| Strong conjugality | 9.2 | 15.0 | 12.7 | 6.7 | 78.2 | 78.3 | 100.0 | 100.0 | 229 | 267 |
| Moderate conjugality | 12.9 | 21.3 | 12.0 | 6.8 | 75.1 | 72.0 | 100.0 | 100.0 | 217 | 207 |
| Weak conjugality | 15.0 | 17.7 | 17.7 | 5.3 | 67.3 | 77.0 | 100.0 | 100.0 | 113 | 113 |

**Note:** – fewer than 10 cases

educational attainment, urbanization, and a "free hand" in their choice of partner. However, given the Ghanaian cultural context whereby in-laws are often considered significant members of the household, the nature of their influence in the couple decision-making process was assessed in the GFAMS sampled population.

## In-Law Influence in Decision Making[3]

By definition, the Ghanaian family might be a large social group of people all of who trace their descent from a common lineage directly through the mother line from a common female ancestress [matrilineal, e.g., Akans], or through a father line from a common male ancestor [patrilineal, e.g., the Ewe, Ga, Adangbe, Tallensi, Dagbon and the Lowiili] (Kuenyehia, 1978). The use of descent to define the family in Ghana, therefore, means that the family is typically more than the nuclear family of father, mother, and child(ren) as known in North America or Europe. The Ghanaian family, therefore, includes the larger extended family ("abusua") consisting of people such as in-laws, cousins, uncles, brothers, grandparents, and great-grandparents all of whom can influence decision making in conjugal relationships.

Although a much smaller unit of the nuclear family type is usually found in the urban areas and among the educated elite, the "nucleation" of the family in the city or elsewhere away from the ancestral home does not completely absorb individuals from extended family influence and obligations such as supporting parents financially (Oppong, 1974; Oppong, 1987). And since the lineage is responsible for burying its members, any shirk of lineage responsibilities may cause refusal of burial rites, the greatest shame that may befall someone (Bleek, 1987:139). Often, it is the case that stability in one's lineage takes precedence over stability in one's marriage. And whenever allegiance to the lineage is perceived as being weakened or threatened by a spouse, lineage members may instigate divorce or separation to disturb the conjugal

---

[3]This section benefitted from the generous contribution of Dr. John K. Anarfi of the Institute of Statistical, Social and Economic Research (ISSER), University of Ghana, Legon, Accra.

relationship (Bleek, 1987). By being the "watch dog" for clan/kinship interests, then, in-laws may become part of the conjugal decision-making process on matters that have implications for the larger family unit.

A related factor that influences the conjugal decision-making process is the type of residential arrangement of couples after marriage. Marital residences vary across matrilineal and patrilineal family systems in Ghana. The common forms of residence are viri-local, which absorbs the wife into the groom's family; duo-local, where a woman stays with her parental family; or neo-local, where the couple sets up their own residence separate from their respective families (Fiawoo, 1978b; Nukunya, 1978). As has been mentioned elsewhere in the chapter on marriage, residence of the wife with her matrikins is often preferred among the Akans of Ghana. The close kin relations often means that loyalties of the marriage partners remain with their respective lineages, an act that strengthens the woman's autonomy in her marital relationship (Bleek, 1987; Clark, 1994).

In the present study, respondents were asked to indicate the living or residential arrangements of their mother/father-in-laws and the influence, if any, that their in-laws have on their lives as married couples. The idea was to follow up questions on couple decision making to find out how others might also have input into some selected areas of family life. It is perceived that the closer the in-laws or other family relations, the higher the probability that they will influence the couples' decision-making process.

Table 5.8 indicates that while close to two-thirds of urban couples' in-laws lived outside of town, only about one-third of the in-laws of rural couples lived out of town. The remaining either lived in another part of town or the same area in town. Regardless of urban-rural residence, more wives lived in the same house with their in-laws than husbands, confirming the presence of duo-local residence.

**Table 5.8** Percentage Distribution of Where Couples' In-Laws Live, According to Residence, GFAMS,

| | RESIDENCE | | | |
| --- | --- | --- | --- | --- |
| | URBAN | | RURAL | |
| WHERE IN-LAWS LIVE | Wife | Husband | Wife | Husband |
| Same house as respondent | 13.9 | 4.0 | 15.8 | 9.0 |
| Same neighborhood as respondent | 3.7 | 4.6 | 17.5 | 20.2 |
| Another neighborhood in town | 19.6 | 22.6 | 28.7 | 35.7 |
| Another town | 59.9 | 65.9 | 37.0 | 34.3 |
| Deceased | 6.0 | 2.9 | 1.1 | 0.8 |
| TOTAL | 100.0 | 100.0 | 100.0 | 100.0 |
| NUMBER | [547] | [545] | [349] | [356] |

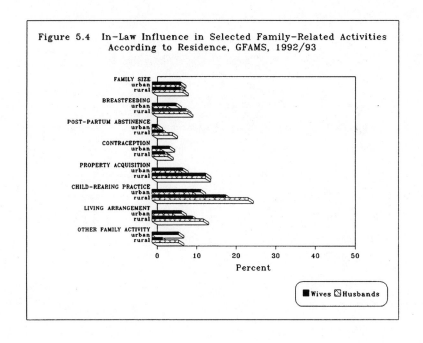

Figure 5.4  In-Law Influence in Selected Family-Related Activities According to Residence, GFAMS, 1992/93

On the influence of in-laws on family-related activities, Figure 5.4 shows some disparities between urban and rural couples. Among urban and rural couples, the single most important activity that in-laws had influence on was child-rearing practices. But with rural couples, in-laws' influence was felt in additional areas such as the acquisition of physical property (e.g., land and house) and living arrangements.

### In-law Influence by Background Characteristics

The extent of in-law influence according to selected background characteristics is shown in Table 5.9. Although most couples on the whole felt that the influence of their in-laws was weak, there are some variations that are worth reporting. For instance, couples living in rural areas, and those whose family had been involved with their partner choice felt stronger in-law influence than couples living in urban areas, and those who had chosen their partners entirely by themselves. Also, in-law influence appeared to be stronger for couples who had legitimized their marriages through Customary, Ordinance, Church, or Islamic laws than those in Consensual relationships.

The results further show that while husbands with no education were more likely to be strongly influenced by their in-laws than wives without education, wives with post-secondary or higher education perceived stronger in-law influence in their marriage than husbands with post-secondary or higher education. And as expected, if in-laws lived in the same area of town, they had stronger influence on couples than if they lived in another part of town or outside town. However, if in-laws lived in the same house as couples, they were more likely to have a stronger influence on husbands than wives.

In the Ghanaian society, as in many African societies, there are specific roles traditionally designed for women which they are socialized to play quite well. On the other hand, there appears to be no clear-cut roles for husbands apart from the recognition that they are the heads of the conjugal family. The feeling of strong in-law influence among educated wives in the decision making on family-related matters

**Table 5.9**   Percentage Distribution of Couples by the Extent of In-Law Influence, According to
Selected Background Characteristics, GFAMS, 1992/93

| | IN-LAW INFLUENCE | | | | | |
| | Strong Influence | | Moderate Influence | | Weak Influence | |
| Background Characteristic | Wife | Hus. | Wife | Hus. | Wife | Hus. |
|---|---|---|---|---|---|---|
| **AGE** | | | | | | |
| Under 30 | 10.1 | 8.1 | 16.4 | 11.0 | 73.5 | 80.9 |
| 30-39 | 10.5 | 9.9 | 11.4 | 11.7 | 78.1 | 78.3 |
| 40+ | 4.0 | 8.8 | 12.9 | 13.1 | 83.2 | 78.0 |
| | | | | | | |
| **RESIDENCE** | | | | | | |
| Urban | 7.7 | 6.2 | 11.3 | 9.3 | 81.0 | 84.5 |
| Rural | 10.8 | 13.7 | 17.3 | 16.8 | 72.0 | 69.5 |
| | | | | | | |
| **LEVEL OF EDUC.** | | | | | | |
| No education | 10.1 | 17.5 | 15.4 | 10.0 | 74.5 | 72.5 |
| Elementary | 8.5 | 10.6 | 13.1 | 10.1 | 78.5 | 79.4 |
| Sec/tec/trg.college | 7.7 | 7.8 | 14.4 | 12.5 | 77.9 | 79.7 |
| Higher | 12.1 | 6.8 | 6.1 | 18.6 | 81.8 | 74.5 |
| | | | | | | |
| **RELIGION** | | | | | | |
| Catholic | 13.3 | 10.6 | 12.0 | 15.3 | 74.7 | 74.1 |
| Protestant | 7.1 | 7.8 | 14.4 | 11.7 | 78.4 | 80.5 |
| Muslim | 5.1 | 7.1 | 12.8 | 7.1 | 82.1 | 85.7 |
| Traditionalist | 33.3 | 4.3 | 22.2 | 26.1 | 44.4 | 69.6 |
| Other religion | 13.3 | 18.3 | 11.7 | 10.0 | 75.0 | 71.7 |
| | | | | | | |
| **CHOICE OF PARTNER** | | | | | | |
| Entirely by me | 6.7 | 7.2 | 12.3 | 10.1 | 81.0 | 82.7 |
| Help/consent of fam. | 13.9 | 16.9 | 17.6 | 21.1 | 68.5 | 61.9 |
| Arranged by family | 14.8 | 6.3 | 14.8 | 0.0 | 70.4 | 93.8 |
| Other | 8.3 | 0.0 | 8.3 | 18.2 | 83.3 | 81.8 |
| | | | | | | |
| **TYPE OF MARRIAGE** | | | | | | |
| Customary | 9.1 | 10.5 | 14.3 | 12.1 | 76.5 | 77.4 |
| Ordinance/Church | 9.7 | 8.6 | 16.4 | 18.0 | 73.9 | 73.4 |
| Consensual | 7.6 | 2.0 | 6.8 | 5.9 | 85.6 | 92.2 |
| Islamic | 8.0 | 4.3 | 12.0 | 13.0 | 80.0 | 82.7 |
| | | | | | | |
| **IN-LAW'S RESIDENCE** | | | | | | |
| Same house | 9.9 | 24.1 | 21.4 | 13.0 | 68.7 | 63.0 |
| Same neighborhood | 17.5 | 19.6 | 18.8 | 17.5 | 63.8 | 62.9 |
| Another part of town | 7.8 | 9.2 | 16.7 | 12.4 | 75.5 | 78.4 |
| Another town | 7.7 | 5.2 | 9.6 | 11.6 | 82.7 | 83.2 |
| | | | | | | |
| **TOTAL** | 8.9 | 9.2 | 13.6 | 12.3 | 77.4 | 78.6 |
| **NUMBER** | [80] | [83] | [122] | [111] | [693] | [712] |

may stem from the fact that an educated woman wants to demonstrate her "emancipation" from traditional practices that recognize the man's authority in certain familial domains. In that respect, in-laws may want to put such a "domineering" wife (labeled as *Obaa akokonini* among the Akans--literally meaning a hen acting like a rooster) under check to protect the interests of the larger extended family unit.

Furthermore, the finding that couples in consensual unions feel less in-law influence in their relationship highlights the traditional attitude towards marriage. Tradition supports legitimacy; in the eyes of the family, a person in consensual union is not "known" and will, therefore, not be bothered. For example, people in consensual unions are not allowed to perform rituals normally expected from husbands/wives during the funeral of a father-/mother-in-law. Thus, family members may have a laissez-faire kind of attitude toward the decision-making process of consensual couples, particularly so if such relations do not appear to involve the "misappropriation" of economic resources and the transfer of property rights that are perceived as rightfully belonging to members of the extended family.

The results from the GFAMS confirm the fact that traditional beliefs and practices with regard to family communication and decision making still hold greater sway in rural than urban areas, and impacts more on women than men. However, the observed patterns also reflect a changing society where the influence of education as a militating factor strongly emerges in communication and decision making on household and fertility-related matters.

Among the objectives of female empowerment are to improve the women's self-esteem and their ability to make and implement decisions affecting their own lives and the lives of their family members. In contemporary Ghana, one such area of decision making is the involvement of paid activity and how independently earned income from work is disposed of, which is the focus of attention of the next chapter.

# 6

## CONTROL OF INCOME

As a significant strategic resource that increases women's marital power, income-earning capability, as well as the power to dispose of earnings, may help us in our attempt to understand female economic autonomy relative to men's. In many income-generating societies, disparities in the earning power between women and men have been clearly documented (see e.g., National Commission on Working Women, 1984; Chronicle of Higher Education, 1991; U.S. Department of Labor, 1991). Most of the disparities in the earning capacities have been part of institutional mechanisms that have systematically generated occupational segregation and men's situational advantage (Caldwell, 1980; Caldwell, et al., 1982; U.S. Bureau of the Census, 1991; Ferrante, 1998).

Despite the importance of income in demographic analysis, however, the income variable as a measure of "social well-being" is flawed due to its inability to capture those economic activities that do not attract monetary value (Estes, 1988:24). This concern becomes even more crucial in several developing countries such as Ghana, where the large informal sector of the economy makes it difficult to ascertain any accurate reporting on income. This chapter seeks to present and analyze information from the GFAMS on economic activities and utilization of resources by couples.

## DEFINITION AND PROBLEMS IN ELICITING
## INFORMATION ON INCOME

Generally, income is defined as money received over a given period of time. Such monetary returns can be in the form of salary, receipts from trade, and other forms of payment in kind. In most developing countries, however, data on income and income distribution are very difficult to obtain due to the problem of inclusion. Even when income data are available, they are subject to many limitations. Some of the major difficulties encountered when eliciting information on income are as follows:

### A.      The Problem of Definition of Income

The general experience in household surveys is that it is very difficult to capture all elements of income. It is therefore inevitable that in many such surveys income tends to be underestimated. For example, Kuznets (1966:196-97) indicates that income should be defined as payment received by individuals, including wages, salaries, and other compensation of employees, and entrepreneurial income and returns on property invested by households in the production process, but excluding income taxes. Ghana's Living Standard Survey 1991/92 measured income using a creation of six major components of income. The components include income from employment, household agriculture income, non-farm self employment income, rental income, income from remittances, and other income which includes scholarship, miscellaneous, and income from water sold (GSS, 1995).

The criteria for including variables in an income measure, in fact, varies from country to country. Ethiopia's Rural Household Income, Consumption, and Expenditure Survey of 1988 defined income as referring to domestic consumption of own crops and own livestock and livestock products, domestic consumption of goods and services purchased for resale or produced or processed in the household enterprise other than agriculture, wage and salaries, allowance, overtime, bonus, pension, commission, discounts (i.e., concessions obtained), computed rent of free housing (provided by employer), computed rent of employer subsidized housing (i.e., subsidized amount only), other employee benefit, interest received, profit and dividend received, computed rent of owner-occupied housing, remittance (regularly received), value of items obtained free, rent of personal possession, alimony, and other types of income (Central Statistical Authority, 1988).

**B.    Other Difficulties and Limitations of Income Data**

Besides the problem of definition, the following limitations have to be taken into account when dealing with income data from surveys: (1) *Lack of a sufficiently long term data*--a problem particularly common in Africa, where information based on time series is often limited, and (2) *Criteria for inclusion*. The question here is whether to use family units or the individual income recipient in household surveys. Each has its own merit, but the distribution of income by the individual normally reflects the disparities in income distribution that proceed from the pattern of production in a given economy.

Furthermore, income generated in the informal sector of the economy may come in small amounts, and may be used as it is made. Therefore, it is even difficult for respondents to assess what they earn in the first place and how the money is spent. Secondly, money earned may be spent on basic necessities such as food. Under such circumstances there will be no need to make decisions on how to spend what is earned (Desai & Jain, 1994 in Mason, 1995). Such is the situation of some of the rural women in the sample who are engaged in family activities of preparing fish brought by the men for sale. Profit earned is what is used as housekeeping ("chop") money. Some of the respondents, then, may be in situations where they spend their income immediately, as soon as it is earned. For such women, decision making on how money earned is spent is a luxury that does not occur. As a result, it is difficult to distinguish between money earned and money spent on the household. Thus, one needs to use caution in interpreting and comparing answers on income earned and spent.

In an attempt to circumvent some of the problems involved in the collection of income data in the country, we devised some unconventional means for income reporting. In the GFAMS, we asked respondents to indicate if they have an independent source of income outside the housekeeping (chop) money or other money from the spouse, and the main and supplementary source(s) of income. Respondents were then asked to provide an estimate of their income on a daily (boom days and sluggish days), weekly, monthly, or annual basis or any other duration which would be convenient for them. In addition, we explored the contribution of couples to household expenditures, including who determines how the respondent spends money (excluding the normal housekeeping money) that he/she earns in any economic activity. Thus, in this chapter, we are interested in married women's and men's income-earning capacity, their disposal of earnings, and their expenditure patterns.

## SOURCE(S) AND DISTRIBUTION OF INCOME

### Sources of Income

The overwhelming majority of wives and husbands have access to an independent source of income, irrespective of their areas of residence, age, level of education, occupation, religion or choice of marriage. In general, more husbands than wives, regardless of background characteristics, have access to an independent source of income, but the differences are not significant.

The distribution of the sources of income is shown in Table 6.1. In the urban areas, 82 percent of the wives and 85 percent of the husbands surveyed had a main source of income. The proportions were even higher in the rural areas where 87 percent of the wives and almost all the husbands (94 percent) had a major source of income. For urban couples, the main source of income was either wages, salaries or earnings from their occupation; 79 percent of wives and 84 percent of husbands specified occupation as the main source of income. The picture, however, was very different in the rural areas where the occupation was the main source of income for just a little over half of husbands and only a little over a third of wives. Thus, a significant amount of the income of the rural couples was derived from sources other than their main occupation.

**Table 6.1**   Percentage Distribution of Couples Who Have Independent Source(s) of Income by the Specific Source, According to Residence, GFAMS, 1992/93

| | RESIDENCE | | | |
| | URBAN | | RURAL | |
| SOURCE OF INCOME | Wife | Husband | Wife | Husband |
|---|---|---|---|---|
| MAIN SOURCE | | | | |
| Occupation | 78.5 | 83.9 | 37.1 | 53.0 |
| Spouse | 1.8 | 0.2 | 0.3 | 0.0 |
| Relations | 0.0 | 0.2 | 0.3 | 0.0 |
| Other | 19.7 | 15.7 | 62.3 | 46.7 |
| TOTAL | 100.0 | 100.0 | 100.0 | 100.0 |
| NUMBER | [452] | [466] | [310] | [338] |
| MINOR SOURCE | | | | |
| Occupation | 26.6 | 27.1 | 10.6 | 10.8 |
| Spouse | 7.6 | 0.8 | 0.0 | 0.4 |
| Relations | 0.8 | 1.1 | 0.0 | 0.0 |
| Other | 65.0 | 71.1 | 89.4 | 88.4 |
| TOTAL | 100.0 | 100.0 | 100.0 | 100.0 |
| NUMBER | [237] | [266] | [236] | [250] |

The apparent reason for this sharp difference is that in the rural areas, even those in any regular employment (e.g., as laborers, clerks, teachers, etc.) are likely to combine other activities such as food or cash crops farming, livestock rearing, and production of handicrafts with such employment. And it is not unusual to derive more income from these other activities than from the regular employment. This also seems to be the main explanation why for those who had a minor source of income, the greatest proportion of such income came from a variety of sources other than occupation or relations.

**Distribution of Income**

In terms of the income distribution, the data indicate that, on the whole, urban and rural husbands earned more money than their spouses, irrespective of how the income data had been reported. Individuals earning fixed income did not have trouble reporting their income levels since there was not much variation in what they earned over time. However, income earned on a daily basis could vary widely depending on whether it was a sluggish ("bad") day or a boom ("good") day in terms of business activity or turn-over. Income earned on a sluggish day and a boom day are presented in Table 6.2.

**Table 6.2**   Percentage Distribution of Income-Earning Couples by Income Levels, According to Residence, GFAMS, 1992/93

| | RESIDENCE | | | |
| | URBAN | | RURAL | |
| INCOME LEVEL | Wife | Husband | Wife | Husband |
|---|---|---|---|---|
| ON A SLUGGISH DAY | | | | |
| Under 10,000 cedis | 95.5 | 89.0 | 85.2 | 80.9 |
| 10,000-19,999 cedis | 2.8 | 4.2 | 4.4 | 8.2 |
| 20,000-49,999 cedis | 1.4 | 4.2 | 7.4 | 7.3 |
| 50,000-99,999 cedis | 0.3 | 2.5 | 2.2 | 3.6 |
| 100,000-199,999 cedis | 0.0 | 0.0 | 0.7 | 0.0 |
| 200,000-499,999 cedis | 0.0 | 0.0 | 0.0 | 0.0 |
| 500,000+ cedis | 0.0 | 0.0 | 0.0 | 0.0 |
| TOTAL | 100.0 | 100.0 | 100.0 | 100.0 |
| NUMBER | [286] | [118] | [164] | [110] |
| ON A BOOM DAY | | | | |
| Under 10,000 cedis | 64.4 | 43.8 | 79.9 | 58.2 |
| 10,000-19,999 cedis | 21.6 | 22.7 | 7.9 | 17.2 |
| 20,000-49,999 cedis | 11.3 | 16.4 | 6.1 | 14.9 |
| 50,000-99,999 cedis | 2.7 | 7.8 | 4.3 | 7.5 |
| 100,000-199,999 cedis | 0.0 | 5.5 | 1.8 | 2.2 |
| 200,000-499,999 cedis | 0.0 | 3.1 | 0.0 | 0.0 |
| 500,000+ cedis | 0.0 | 0.8 | 0.0 | 0.0 |
| TOTAL | 100.0 | 100.0 | 100.0 | 100.0 |
| NUMBER | [292] | [128] | [164] | [134] |

**Note:** Exchange rate as at Dec. 1992 was $US 1.00 = 500 cedis

As the data show, most respondents (80-90 percent of categories of respondents) claimed they earned under 10,000 cedis on a sluggish day, with only small proportions earning significantly more than this amount on a sluggish day. But even on a boom day, the vast majority still earned less than 10,000 cedis, except for urban husbands where a majority (56 percent) earned more than 10,000 cedis. The income disparities between urban-rural and men-women persisted on a monthly basis as illustrated in Figure 6.1.

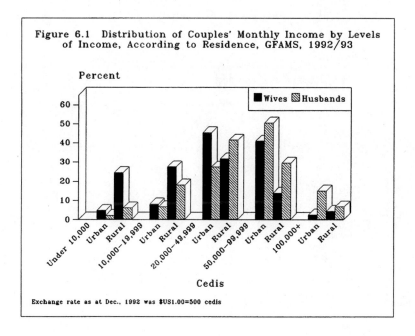

Figure 6.1   Distribution of Couples' Monthly Income by Levels of Income, According to Residence, GFAMS, 1992/93

Generally, couples' monthly income seemed to be on the low side, especially in the rural areas as the data show. Only 14 percent of wives in the rural areas earned between 50, 000 and 100,000 cedis, while in the urban areas 41 percent of all wives earned that amount. Similarly, while half of urban husbands also earned 50,000-100,000 cedis, only 29 percent of rural husbands earned that amount.

Since there were fewer respondents in the sample (particularly non-wage earners) who reported income on a monthly basis than daily, however, one should treat these findings with some caution. On the whole, though, the income distribution from the GFAMS, whether reported on a daily or a monthly basis, points to a clear pattern of low levels of reported income and gender differentials, as well as rural-urban differences among our sampled population.

## AUTONOMOUS DECISION ON DISPOSAL OF INCOME

It seems that irrespective of one's background characteristic (e.g., sex, age, level of education, religion, occupation, etc.), the vast majority of couples decided on their own how their incomes were to be disposed of. For both husbands and wives, the proportion of respondents who decided independently on how to spend their incomes was generally over 80 percent, with only slight or minor exceptions.

As can be seen in Table 6.3, husbands generally disposed of their incomes more independently than wives (90 percent as against 81 percent), but the difference is not large. Differences by economic background characteristics were consistent with data from GDHS of 1988 which indicated that in all occupations, a significant majority of women in Ghana were economically independent in the sense that they alone decided how all the money they earned from their productive work will be used. The percentages reported from the GDHS ranged from 84 among agricultural workers to about 94 for modern cash workers, which include professionals, administrative, managerial, technical, and related workers (Blanc & Lloyd, 1990).

In the present study, some of the differences by background characteristics are, however, worthy of note as they may be significant pointers to some of the changes slowly taking place within the family or household. For example, within "type of marriage" independent decision making was lowest for wives in Ordinance/Church marriage (66 percent) and highest for Islamic and consensual unions (100 percent). As Ordinance/Church marriages are more characteristic of the elite or highly educated, the lower proportion of independent decision making may

**Table 6.3** Percentage Distribution of Couples by Whether They Decide on Their Own to Dispose of Their Independently-Earned Money, According to Selected Background Characteristics, GFAMS, 1992/93

| Background Characteristic | OWN DECISION TO SPEND MONEY | | | |
| | Wife | | Husband | |
| | Percent | Number | Percent | Number |
|---|---|---|---|---|
| AGE | | | | |
| Under 30 | 82.0 | 214 | 86.6 | 103 |
| 30-39 | 85.6 | 255 | 88.7 | 299 |
| 40+ | 72.8 | 131 | 92.2 | 306 |
| RESIDENCE | | | | |
| Urban | 82.4 | 357 | 95.2 | 435 |
| Rural | 79.5 | 244 | 82.7 | 278 |
| LEVEL OF EDUCATION | | | | |
| No education | 86.3 | 107 | 75.0 | 27 |
| Elementary | 84.9 | 348 | 90.1 | 308 |
| Sec/tec/trg.college | 68.3 | 110 | 93.4 | 241 |
| Higher | 79.3 | 23 | 89.3 | 125 |
| OCCUPATION | | | | |
| Professional | 80.0 | 60 | 87.4 | 181 |
| Clerical | 73.3 | 33 | 96.2 | 75 |
| Sales | 86.0 | 153 | 94.3 | 33 |
| Service/transport | 71.8 | 28 | 96.9 | 94 |
| Farmer/fisherman | ** | ** | 65.6 | 21 |
| Craftsman | 68.9 | 71 | 92.7 | 152 |
| RELIGION | | | | |
| Catholic | 78.4 | 105 | 88.3 | 143 |
| Protestant | 80.0 | 401 | 90.2 | 433 |
| Muslim | 92.6 | 25 | 94.3 | 33 |
| Traditionalist | ** | ** | 90.0 | 18 |
| Other religion | 90.0 | 45 | 94.3 | 50 |
| No religion | 84.2 | 16 | 82.1 | 32 |
| CHOICE OF PARTNER | | | | |
| Entirely by me | 85.4 | 409 | 92.5 | 546 |
| Help/consent of family | 70.2 | 151 | 82.7 | 143 |
| Arranged by family | 95.5 | 21 | 84.6 | 11 |
| TYPE OF MARRIAGE | | | | |
| Customary | 81.0 | 425 | 90.6 | 500 |
| Ordinance/Church | 65.5 | 74 | 82.9 | 107 |
| Consensual | 100.0 | 81 | 96.7 | 88 |
| Islamic | 100.0 | 18 | 100.0 | 17 |
| CO-RESIDENCE | | | | |
| Yes | 79.8 | 522 | 89.7 | 627 |
| No | 92.7 | 76 | 92.4 | 85 |
| NO. OF CHN LIVING | | | | |
| No child | 76.1 | 35 | 80.5 | 33 |
| 1-2 children | 83.4 | 196 | 88.9 | 208 |
| 3-4 children | 75.0 | 207 | 89.5 | 265 |
| 5+ children | 88.8 | 158 | 93.5 | 201 |
| TOTAL | 81.2 | 601 | 89.9 | 713 |

**Note:** ** Fewer than 10 cases

be a reflection of a move towards jointness in decision-making among such couples. The data on income decision making by level of education partially seem to confirm this particular influence. Although the highly educated did not appear to behave very differently from the others, wives in particular were slightly less likely to dispose of their independently-earned income on their own if they had secondary or higher education than their counterparts with low or no education.

Quite clearly, co-residence was an important factor in decision making on income disposal. Couples who lived in separate houses were more likely to make independent decisions than those who lived in the same house; but again the differences were not very pronounced. Similarly, couples with children reported independent decision making than couples with no children; and as the number of children increased so did the proportions of couples who made independent monetary decisions. Figures 6.2a & 6.2b illustrate who else influenced monetary decisions.

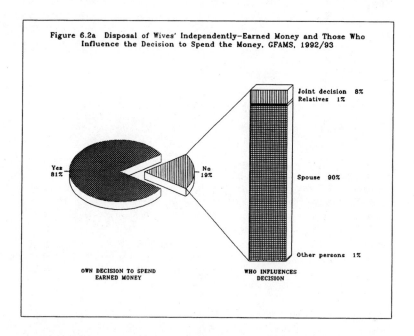

Figure 6.2a  Disposal of Wives' Independently-Earned Money and Those Who Influence the Decision to Spend the Money, GFAMS, 1992/93

Joint decision  8%
Relatives  1%

Yes 81%

No 19%

Spouse  90%

Other persons  1%

OWN DECISION TO SPEND
EARNED MONEY

WHO INFLUENCES
DECISION

The data show that, of the approximately 20 percent of wives who did not control the disposal of their own income, 90 percent of them said their spouse made the decision for them, while of the 10 percent of husbands who did not decide on their own to spend earned money, their wives influenced their decisions about 80 percent of the time.

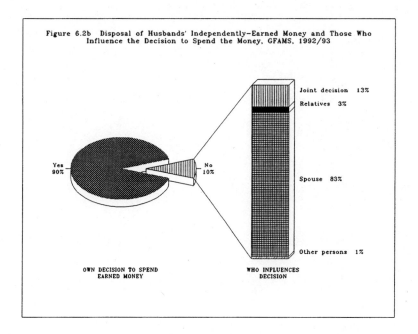

Figure 6.2b Disposal of Husbands' Independently-Earned Money and Those Who Influence the Decision to Spend the Money, GFAMS, 1992/93

## Monetary Contribution to Selected Household Expenditures

The data in Table 6.4 show that husbands' perceptions or assessment of their contributions to household expenditure did not necessarily correspond with those of their wives. On all major items of expenditure, husbands' responses differed from those of their wives as to who pays for what item. In spite of these apparent contradictions, some very general patterns can be discerned.

For urban couples, there was a high degree of consensus among both husbands and wives that husbands were mainly responsible for rent or making house

**Table 6.4**   Percentage Distribution of Couples by Their Monetary Contribution to Selected Household Expenditures, GFAMS, 1992/93

| | LEVEL OF MONETARY CONTRIBUTION | | | | | | | |
|---|---|---|---|---|---|---|---|---|
| | Husband Alone | | Wife Alone | | Joint Decision | | Others' Distribution | |
| URBAN COUPLES' CONTRIBUTION TO: | Wife | Hus. | Wife | Hus. | Wife | Hus. | Wife | Hus. |
| Household meals | 55.7 | 67.6 | 6.0 | 2.9 | 38.1 | 29.0 | 0.2 | 0.4 |
| House payment/rent | 84.8 | 85.9 | 6.1 | 4.1 | 2.9 | 3.6 | 6.1 | 6.5 |
| Utility bills | 74.8 | 80.6 | 7.4 | 3.4 | 16.7 | 14.2 | 1.1 | 1.9 |
| Children's school fees* | 71.6 | 76.9 | 6.5 | 2.2 | 18.0 | 17.0 | 3.9 | 3.9 |
| Children's clothing* | 19.8 | 32.7 | 8.0 | 1.7 | 70.3 | 63.2 | 1.9 | 2.3 |
| Own clothing | 11.2 | 89.3 | 42.8 | 1.3 | 45.5 | 9.2 | 0.5 | 0.2 |
| Own transportation needs | 19.5 | 86.4 | 61.0 | 1.5 | 18.8 | 11.9 | 0.7 | 0.2 |
| Family car expenses* | 63.9 | 61.3 | 4.2 | 2.9 | 4.2 | 8.0 | 27.7 | 27.7 |
| Donations, funeral expenses, etc. | 34.9 | 53.9 | 13.7 | 2.1 | 50.5 | 43.9 | 0.9 | 0.2 |
| | | | | | | | | |
| RURAL COUPLES' CONTRIBUTION TO: | Wife | Hus. | Wife | Hus. | Wife | Hus. | Wife | Hus. |
| Household meals | 52.1 | 51.1 | 14.9 | 3.4 | 32.1 | 44.9 | 0.8 | 0.6 |
| House payment/rent | 61.4 | 80.0 | 15.2 | 2.9 | 21.0 | 13.7 | 2.4 | 3.4 |
| Utility bills | 44.9 | 62.5 | 18.8 | 7.1 | 33.7 | 27.6 | 2.6 | 2.9 |
| Children's school fees* | 46.6 | 68.9 | 18.8 | 4.8 | 32.4 | 25.1 | 2.3 | 1.3 |
| Children's clothing* | 20.5 | 43.7 | 16.1 | 6.2 | 62.2 | 49.9 | 1.2 | 0.6 |
| Own clothing | 13.9 | 80.1 | 36.3 | 2.3 | 49.9 | 17.3 | 0.5 | 0.3 |
| Own transportation needs | 18.7 | 76.4 | 44.3 | 2.0 | 36.7 | 21.0 | 0.3 | 0.6 |
| Family car expenses* | 40.0 | 71.2 | 20.0 | 3.8 | 30.0 | 21.2 | 10.0 | 3.8 |
| Donations, funeral expenses, etc. | 17.6 | 48.6 | 29.3 | 2.4 | 52.8 | 47.7 | 0.3 | 1.2 |

**Note:** *Only if applicable

payments, utility bills (i.e., payment for appropriate household items such as water, electricity, kerosene, firewood, charcoal, or gas for cooking), children's school fees, transportation needs and/or the maintenance of the family car. For the payment of rent and utility bills, for example, over 75 percent of wives and husbands agreed that the husband alone was responsible for these household expenditures. The wives' contribution in these areas were clearly low, although some jointness (e.g., between 14 to 18 percent for utility bills) was also reported.

With regard to other expenditure patterns the results of our analysis show that more couples reported joint responsibility for expenditures on children's clothing, donations, and funeral expenses. The data also show that a significant majority of couples claimed sole responsibility for their transportation. But while higher proportions of husbands reported that they were solely responsible for their own personal clothing, wives asserted that expenditures on personal clothing was done largely on a joint basis, thus assigning a role for husbands as well.

The pattern of income disposal in the rural areas differs in many ways from that in the urban areas for some obvious reasons. Not only are rural wages or incomes considerably lower than urban ones as reported earlier on in this chapter, but the major items of expenditure also vary in importance. Very few rural households are likely to pay any expensive rents or utility bills because such modern amenities as electricity, gas for cooking, pipe water, etc. are likely to be unavailable, although rural residents are likely to spend money on kerosene, firewood, or charcoal regularly for household use. Also, houses in the rural areas are easily constructed using less expensive locally-acquired building materials. Moreover, there is the tendency for rural husbands and/or wives to live in family houses where rent will not be charged and utility bills may be the responsibility of the family/clan head.

In the next section, we focus on couples' monetary contributions in the following three general areas: (1) household meals, (2) house payment or rent, (3) children's school fees. Special attention is given to these three areas because of their centrality in the family's day-to-day survival and well-being.

*Payment for Household Meals*:

It is traditional in Ghanaian society for a man, as befits his role as the head of the household, to give out money "chop-money" as it is called, either on a daily or monthly basis to the wife for preparing meals for the family. Failure or inability to do this is looked upon with a great deal of scorn and contempt by the society. The sharp rise in the cost of living in recent years has increasingly undermined the husband's ability to perform this duty satisfactorily. Data from a recent National Living Standards Survey indicate that average household expenditures exceed income by some 63 percent. This means that the average housewife has to find some extra money to supplement whatever she receives from her husband for preparing food (see e.g., Lloyd & Gage-Brandon, 1993).

Indeed, data from Table 6.4 confirm that monetary contribution for household meals in the urban areas may be moving from husband-only to joint contribution; 38 percent of wives and 29 percent of husbands in the survey admitted as much, that this is becoming the pattern, although the husband's role was still widely acknowledged by 56 percent of wives and 68 percent of husbands. Responsibility for household meals seems to becoming a joint responsibility even in the rural areas. Almost 45 percent of husbands and 32 percent of wives stated that both were jointly responsible for this expenditure. However, about half of each category still asserted that it was the husband's sole responsibility.

Though there were only minor differences in terms of contributions to household meals by background characteristics of respondents, Table 6.5a shows that level of education, co-residential status, and family size appear to have significant effects on couples' perceptions as to who pays for household meals.

One's education seemed to have a strong influence on one's perception of joint contribution to the household meals. For both wives and husbands, there was an inverse correlation between education and perception of joint responsibility. The lower the level of education, the greater the proportion of couples, particularly husbands, who assigned joint responsibility for the payment of household meals.

Table 6.5a  Percentage Distribution of Couples by Their Monetary Contribution to Household Meals, According to Selected Background Characteristics, GFAMS, 1992/93

| Background Characteristic | LEVEL OF CONTRIBUTION | | | | | |
| | Husband Alone | | Wife Alone | | Joint Contribution | |
| | Wife | Hus. | Wife | Hus. | Wife | Hus |
|---|---|---|---|---|---|---|
| RESIDENCE | | | | | | |
| Urban | 55.8 | 67.9 | 6.0 | 3.0 | 38.2 | 29.2 |
| Rural | 32.4 | 51.4 | 15.1 | 3.4 | 52.6 | 45.2 |
| | | | | | | |
| LEVEL OF EDUCATION | | | | | | |
| No education | 30.9 | 56.4 | 14.1 | 0.0 | 55.0 | 43.6 |
| Elementary | 45.6 | 57.2 | 11.2 | 2.6 | 43.2 | 40.2 |
| Sec/tec/trg.college | 59.4 | 63.9 | 3.6 | 3.7 | 37.1 | 32.3 |
| Higher | 47.1 | 68.9 | 0.0 | 4.3 | 52.9 | 26.7 |
| | | | | | | |
| OCCUPATION | | | | | | |
| Professional | 37.0 | 69.6 | 3.7 | 1.4 | 59.3 | 29.0 |
| Clerical | 47.3 | 70.8 | 1.8 | 3.1 | 50.9 | 26.0 |
| Sales | 44.8 | 60.0 | 8.2 | 0.0 | 47.0 | 40.0 |
| Service/transport | 42.6 | 61.3 | 4.3 | 2.5 | 53.2 | 36.1 |
| Farmer/fisherman | 30.8 | 42.9 | 7.7 | 0.0 | 61.5 | 57.1 |
| Craftsman | 50.4 | 63.9 | 8.8 | 1.0 | 40.7 | 35.1 |
| | | | | | | |
| CHOICE OF PARTNER | | | | | | |
| Entirely by me | 47.7 | 61.7 | 8.0 | 3.4 | 44.4 | 34.9 |
| Help/consent of family | 40.7 | 57.8 | 12.4 | 2.1 | 46.9 | 40.1 |
| Arranged by family | 55.6 | 66.7 | 18.5 | 6.7 | 25.9 | 26.7 |
| Other | 75.0 | 72.7 | 8.3 | 0.0 | 16.7 | 27.3 |
| | | | | | | |
| TYPE OF MARRIAGE | | | | | | |
| Customary | 43.5 | 57.3 | 10.8 | 3.3 | 45.7 | 39.3 |
| Ordinance/Church | 57.4 | 65.2 | 5.1 | 3.6 | 37.5 | 31.2 |
| Consensual | 51.3 | 82.2 | 8.5 | 2.0 | 40.2 | 15.8 |
| Islamic | 43.5 | 55.0 | 4.3 | 0.0 | 52.2 | 45.0 |
| | | | | | | |
| CO-RESIDENCE | | | | | | |
| Yes | 48.1 | 63.3 | 8.7 | 3.0 | 43.2 | 33.7 |
| No | 31.9 | 45.5 | 17.6 | 4.0 | 50.5 | 50.5 |
| | | | | | | |
| NO. OF CHN LIVING | | | | | | |
| No child | 43.3 | 62.3 | 11.9 | 7.5 | 44.8 | 30.2 |
| 1-2 children | 48.7 | 64.3 | 9.4 | 2.7 | 41.9 | 33.0 |
| 3-4 children | 50.5 | 62.5 | 7.6 | 2.3 | 41.9 | 35.2 |
| 5+ children | 36.3 | 55.7 | 12.7 | 3.9 | 51.0 | 40.4 |
| | | | | | | |
| TOTAL | 46.6 | 61.4 | 9.6 | 3.1 | 43.8 | 35.5 |
| NUMBER | [419] | [550] | [86] | [28] | [394] | [318] |

For couples who did not live in the same house, the wife was more likely to see herself as a joint contributor to the expenditure on household meals than the wife who lived in the same house as the husband (51 percent as against 43 percent). Similarly, a greater degree of jointness in payment for household meals was also reported by wives with 5 or more children (51 percent). This is understandable since most husbands are not likely to adjust their allocation for household expenditures on a child by child basis but rather as a fixed proportion of their income, thus compelling the wives to increasingly draw on their own resources to make up for the shortfall.

*Payment for House or Rent:*

With the exception of two factors, namely urban-rural residence and co-residence, background characteristics did not seem to exhibit any unusual pattern for house or rent payment. For reasons explained earlier, a smaller proportion of wives in the rural areas than urban wives agreed that it is the husband's sole responsibility to provide housing. Whereas 90 percent of urban wives agreed, only 63 percent of rural wives accepted this as the results in Table 6.5b show.

As expected, there was less unanimity in the rural areas as was expressed in the urban areas as to which partner was responsible for housing expenses as seen in Table 6.5b. In the urban sample, 90 percent of wives agreed that these were solely the husband's responsibility, whereas only 63 percent of wives in the rural sample agreed that husbands should solely contribute to housing expenses. For couples who lived in the same house, over 80 percent agreed that the man paid for housing, while for those who did not live in the same house with their husbands, only 55 percent of wives and almost 80 percent of husbands agreed that the man was solely responsible for the rent. In fact, over twice as many wives as well as husbands who did not reside in the same house reported joint contribution on housing expenses. Similarly, couples who reported stronger conjugal relations were more likely to contribute jointly to house or rent payment than those with weak conjugal bonds.

**Table 6.5b** Percentage Distribution of Couples by Their Monetary Contribution to House
Payment/Rent, According to Selected Background Characteristics,
GFAMS, 1992/93

| | LEVEL OF CONTRIBUTION | | | | | |
| | Husband Alone | | Wife Alone | | Joint Contribution | |
| Background Characteristic | Wife | Hus. | Wife | Hus. | Wife | Hus |
|---|---|---|---|---|---|---|
| RESIDENCE | | | | | | |
| Urban | 90.4 | 91.8 | 6.5 | 4.4 | 3.1 | 3.8 |
| Rural | 62.9 | 82.8 | 15.6 | 3.0 | 21.5 | 14.1 |
| LEVEL OF EDUCATION | | | | | | |
| No education | 74.2 | 68.0 | 13.5 | 0.0 | 12.4 | 32.0 |
| Elementary | 76.3 | 89.9 | 12.8 | 3.7 | 10.9 | 6.4 |
| Sec/tec/trg.college | 91.7 | 90.2 | 2.6 | 3.9 | 5.8 | 5.9 |
| Higher | 82.1 | 87.5 | 7.1 | 5.5 | 10.7 | 7.0 |
| OCCUPATION | | | | | | |
| Professional | 76.1 | 92.6 | 7.5 | 1.8 | 16.4 | 5.5 |
| Clerical | 88.9 | 91.2 | 4.4 | 5.9 | 6.7 | 2.9 |
| Sales | 83.8 | 100.0 | 12.8 | 0.0 | 3.4 | 0.0 |
| Service/transport | 85.7 | 87.8 | 8.6 | 6.1 | 5.7 | 6.1 |
| Farmer/fisherman | ** | 73.9 | ** | 4.3 | ** | 21.7 |
| Craftsman | 85.7 | 92.2 | 6.0 | 3.1 | 8.3 | 4.7 |
| CHOICE OF PARTNER | | | | | | |
| Entirely by me | 84.5 | 89.7 | 8.3 | 4.1 | 7.3 | 6.2 |
| Help/consent of family | 70.8 | 83.5 | 13.2 | 3.9 | 16.0 | 12.6 |
| Arranged by family | 71.4 | ** | 14.3 | ** | 14.3 | ** |
| Other | ** | ** | ** | ** | ** | ** |
| TYPE OF MARRIAGE | | | | | | |
| Customary | 76.3 | 87.9 | 11.7 | 3.5 | 12.0 | 8.5 |
| Ordinance/Church | 90.1 | 88.3 | 3.0 | 5.8 | 6.9 | 5.8 |
| Consensual | 90.5 | 95.6 | 8.1 | 2.9 | 1.4 | 1.5 |
| Islamic | 88.9 | 82.4 | 5.6 | 5.9 | 5.6 | 11.8 |
| CO-RESIDENCE | | | | | | |
| Yes | 82.7 | 89.8 | 8.6 | 3.8 | 8.6 | 6.4 |
| No | 54.8 | 79.7 | 23.8 | 5.1 | 21.4 | 15.3 |
| CONJUGAL RELATIONS | | | | | | |
| Strong conjugality | 77.6 | 86.9 | 8.9 | 3.5 | 13.4 | 9.6 |
| Moderate conjugality | 83.0 | 86.5 | 10.6 | 5.8 | 6.4 | 7.7 |
| Weak conjugality | 82.9 | 96.6 | 9.8 | 1.7 | 7.3 | 1.7 |
| TOTAL | 80.8 | 88.8 | 9.7 | 3.9 | 9.5 | 7.3 |
| NUMBER | [476] | [522] | [57] | [23] | [56] | [43] |

**Note:** ** Fewer than 10 cases

**Control of Income**

**Table 6.5c** Percentage Distribution of Couples by Their Monetary Contribution to Children's School Fees, According to Selected Background Characteristics, GFAMS, 1992/93

| Background Characteristic | LEVEL OF CONTRIBUTION | | | | | |
|---|---|---|---|---|---|---|
| | Husband Alone | | Wife Alone | | Joint Contribution | |
| | Wife | Hus. | Wife | Hus. | Wife | Hus |
| RESIDENCE | | | | | | |
| Urban | 74.5 | 80.0 | 6.8 | 2.3 | 18.7 | 17.7 |
| Rural | 47.7 | 69.8 | ` 19.2 | 4.8 | 33.1 | 25.4 |
| | | | | | | |
| LEVEL OF EDUCATION | | | | | | |
| No education | 46.6 | 69.4 | 15.3 | 0.0 | 38.2 | 30.6 |
| Elementary | 62.0 | 76.2 | 14.3 | 3.1 | 23.7 | 20.7 |
| Sec/tec/trg.college | 80.4 | 76.4 | 3.0 | 3.9 | 16.7 | 19.7 |
| Higher | 71.4 | 76.6 | 3.6 | 4.1 | 25.0 | 19.3 |
| | | | | | | |
| OCCUPATION | | | | | | |
| Professional | 67.2 | 82.8 | 7.8 | 2.1 | 25.0 | 15.1 |
| Clerical | 71.7 | 77.3 | 4.3 | 1.1 | 23.9 | 21.6 |
| Sales | 67.3 | 93.3 | 10.9 | 0.0 | 21.8 | 6.7 |
| Service/transport | 73.8 | 77.6 | 4.8 | 5.6 | 21.4 | 16.8 |
| Farmer/fisherman | 54.5 | 64.5 | 9.1 | 0.0 | 36.4 | 35.5 |
| Craftsman | 60.8 | 77.5 | 8.8 | 0.6 | 30.4 | 21.9 |
| | | | | | | |
| CHOICE OF PARTNER | | | | | | |
| Entirely by me | 68.3 | 77.1 | 9.3 | 3.3 | 22.4 | 19.7 |
| Help/consent of family | 53.2 | 73.4 | 17.7 | 4.0 | 29.1 | 22.5 |
| Arranged by family | 63.6 | 57.1 | 4.5 | 0.0 | 31.8 | 42.9 |
| Other | ** | ** | ** | ** | ** | ** |
| | | | | | | |
| TYPE OF MARRIAGE | | | | | | |
| Customary | 60.8 | 73.7 | 13.2 | 3.5 | 26.0 | 22.8 |
| Ordinance/Church | 75.0 | 76.7 | 6.7 | 4.7 | 18.3 | 18.6 |
| Consensual | 72.5 | 93.8 | 8.8 | 0.0 | 18.8 | 6.3 |
| Islamic | 54.5 | 78.9 | 9.1 | 0.0 | 36.4 | 21.1 |
| | | | | | | |
| CO-RESIDENCE | | | | | | |
| Yes | 65.0 | 76.8 | 10.9 | 3.0 | 24.0 | 20.2 |
| No | 52.7 | 68.2 | 18.9 | 5.9 | 28.4 | 25.9 |
| | | | | | | |
| NO. OF CHN LIVING | | | | | | |
| No child | – | – | – | – | – | – |
| 1-2 children | 68.4 | 78.9 | 12.3 | 3.4 | 19.3 | 17.7 |
| 3-4 children | 66.2 | 74.4 | 9.5 | 3.3 | 24.3 | 22.3 |
| 5+ children | 54.2 | 75.3 | 15.0 | 3.0 | 30.7 | 21.7 |
| | | | | | | |
| TOTAL | 64.0 | 75.9 | 11.7 | 3.3 | 24.4 | 20.7 |
| NUMBER | [494] | [593] | [90] | [26] | [188] | [162] |

Note: ** Fewer than 10 cases     – Question not applicable

*Payment of Children's School Fees*:

Rural-urban residence, co-residence and number of children in the family again stand out clearly as three background characteristics which influence responsibility for payment of children's school fees. Payment for school fees was more of a joint responsibility in the rural areas than in the urban areas. Table 8.6c indicates that wives in rural areas were more likely to see payment of fees as a joint responsibility (33 percent) than wives in the urban areas (19 percent). The proportion of wives in rural areas who claimed sole responsibility for paying fees was also substantial (19 percent) compared to only 7 percent in urban areas. A possible explanation for this is the fact that rural wives do not see such payments as burdensome since fees are likely to be very low at the basic level of the educational system where most rural kids end up.

Wives who did not live in the same houses with their husbands also saw themselves as playing a greater role in payment of their children's school fees either jointly with their husbands or on their own (28 and 19 percent respectively) as data in Table 6.5c show. Again, the more children a couple had, the greater the degree of jointness in paying for children's school fees and a corresponding decline in the husband's sole responsibility for such payments.

On the whole, it appears that wives' and husbands' contributions to various household expenditures are patterned along traditional lines of spousal obligations. For instance, it has been a long standing tradition for Ghanaian husbands to provide the housekeeping (chop) money for the family. However, anecdotal evidence seems to suggest that, although a husband may not be in a position to adequately provide the finances for his family's maintenance, it is quite possible that some wives may give him undue credit for being the sole provider in order to protect the family image. It is usually the case that inadequate housekeeping money provided by the husband may mean that the wife on her own would have to cover the expenses of such basic household items as soap, tooth paste, detergent, and water. Thus, caution must be exercised in interpreting the data on contribution to some household expenditures.

Generally, though, the GFAMS data suggest that women and men from the sampled areas had independent sources of income, exhibited some control over how the money they earned should be disposed of, and contributed to various domains of household expenditure. It can be said that the patterns of monetary contributions to household expenditures were manifestations of wives' and husbands' perceptions of their roles, responsibilities and obligations within the social context. With that in mind, gender roles and responsibilities in Ghana will be examined next.

7
_____

# GENDER ROLES AND LEADERSHIP

## GENDER ROLES

Society's expectations of the proper behavior, activities, and responsibilities of females and males constitute gender roles. Through a lifelong process of socialization, each society defines and reinforces its notions of roles "appropriate" for the sexes, and conditions women and men to assume these as they are growing up (Miller, 1995; 1998, Adler et al., 1992, Disch, 1997). Although there are cross-cultural variations in gender expectations, most societies have traditionally associated "tenderness" with women and "toughness" with men. These labels are interpreted to carry nurturing and subservient roles for women, while for men they carry aggressive and controlling roles (Schaefer, 1998).

To attempt to explain why women and men are assigned to different roles, functionalist theorists maintain that instituting gender roles is a form of division of labor that lead to efficiency and social stability (see e.g., Parsons & Bales, 1955). Conflict theorists, on the other hand, argue that traditional gender roles have been built on unequal power relationships in a hierarchy with men generally being the beneficiaries of such arrangements that assign women to less valuable roles that affect their life chances and opportunities (Miller & Garrison, 1982; Ferree & Hall, 1996; Schaefer & Lamm, 1998).

Oppong and Abu's (1984) seven roles model provides a framework for examining gender roles in Ghana. Originally developed for the study of female roles, the concept can be applied to both sexes. According to the model, a person performs seven overlapping roles in the society. These are individual, conjugal, parental, domestic, kin, community, and occupational roles. Each of these roles has its prescribed obligations and responsibilities some of which are age-sex dependent. There are also the prescribed rewards and sanctions for adherence to the gender role expectations. In the Ghanaian traditional system one of the immediate sanctions for a violator of societal norms was ridicule in the form of sing-songs, proverbs, stories, or riddles.

To a large extent the traditional role expectations with division of labor along gender and/or age lines continue to influence behavior in Ghanaian households. While the mother is responsible for the provision of the basic household needs involving cleaning, washing, cooking, fetching water, and taking care of dependents, the father is expected to head the household and provide shelter and financial support for the maintenance of the household. With co-residence of spouses, and social mobility by way of formal education and urbanization, men tend to shoulder some parenting responsibility and give moderate levels of support to conjugal roles, joint housing interests, and shared domestic tasks (Oppong, 1970; Caldwell, 1982; Oppong, 1982; Bleek, 1987; Oppong, 1987).

But although couples in Ghana may contribute to a common cause such as upkeep of their children, they hardly ever pool their financial resources and property together because of their role expectations that go beyond the "nuclear" family (Oppong, 1982; Bleek, 1987). Women and men may keep most of their financial and other resources to themselves to enable them to effectively play their segregated roles and responsibilities to the household as well as to extended family and community members. For instance, an important role expectation for the individual includes providing for most of the needs of parents in old age.[4] This may account for the lack of economic nucleation between couples since the extended family obligations can not be fully met with joint economic accounting (see, e.g., Oppong, 1974). Thus any discussion on roles and responsibilities, economic and emotional nucleation needs to be situated in the socio-cultural context in which they occur.

The role of the Ghanaian woman also extends to the community, with the nature of involvement varying by ethnic affiliation. In most ethnic groups, women can serve as traditional healers, priestess, herbalists, medical practitioners, and birth attendants (Fiawoo, 1978b; ROG & UNICEF, 1990). The older women play a special role in assisting the young in childbirth and infant/child care. For those reasons, it is expected of grandparents in many Ghanaian ethnic groups to cease childbearing once their own daughters start having babies of their own (Hagan, 1983).

In the GFAMS, questions were asked to explore the attitudes of the respondents toward the roles and responsibilities perceived to be "appropriate" for females and males. Additionally, respondents were asked to indicate what they considered to be the ideal occupations for females and males, and the extent to which females and males should be educated and why.

## Appropriate Household Chores For Wives And Husbands

Household chores considered appropriate for wives include cooking meals, cleaning house, washing clothes and dishes, fetching water, caring for children, ironing clothes, and every other household chore. Data from Table 7.1 clearly show that about one-third of the couples in urban and rural areas said the cooking of meals is the appropriate household chore for wives. In the same vein, regardless of residence, over a quarter of women and men in the sample indicated cleaning of the

---

[4]There is an Akan proverb which says that *"Se obi boa wo ma wo fifiri esee a, wo nso wo boa no ma otutu esee"* literally translated to mean that if your parents help you to grow your teeth, it is your responsibility to help them to lose theirs.

house as an appropriate household chore for wives, with similar proportions selecting
washing dishes and clothes as appropriate for women.

**Table 7.1**    Percentage Distribution of Couples' Views on Appropriate Household Chores for
Wives and Husbands, According to Residence, GFAMS, 1992/93

|  | URBAN | | RURAL | |
|---|---|---|---|---|
| CHORES FOR WIVES | Wife | Husband | Wife | Husband |
| Cook meals | 32.9 | 32.6 | 31.4 | 30.3 |
| Clean house | 29.1 | 27.8 | 27.6 | 26.3 |
| Wash clothes & dishes | 28.9 | 28.7 | 23.0 | 22.5 |
| Fetch water | 1.5 | 1.8 | 5.5 | 5.8 |
| Care for children | 3.2 | 4.5 | 3.6 | 4.9 |
| Iron clothing | 1.0 | 0.9 | 0.3 | 0.4 |
| All household chores | 1.2 | 0.7 | 7.1 | 7.7 |
| Other chores | 2.2 | 2.9 | 1.5 | 2.1 |
| TOTAL | 100.0 | 100.0 | 100.0 | 100.0 |
| | | | | |
| CHORES FOR HUSBANDS | | | | |
| Iron clothing | 19.3 | 18.7 | 10.2 | 7.7 |
| Help care for children | 11.9 | 10.4 | 16.0 | 21.5 |
| Help wife when needed | 10.4 | 9.9 | 12.8 | 13.0 |
| Help wife cook meals | 8.3 | 7.9 | 8.1 | 9.9 |
| Repair physical damage to house | 3.7 | 5.7 | 10.4 | 10.8 |
| Clean around house | 4.8 | 4.6 | 2.5 | 3.9 |
| No chores for men | 2.6 | 1.0 | 11.4 | 9.4 |
| Other chores | 39.0 | 41.8 | 28.6 | 23.9 |
| TOTAL | 100.0 | 100.0 | 100.0 | 100.0 |

With respect to fetching water in the house, two percent each of wives and
husbands in the urban areas felt it was a household chore for wives compared to six
percent each for their rural counterparts. The relatively higher proportion in rural
areas may be due to the presence of pipe-borne water in most homes in the urban
areas, hence making the fetching of water not as demanding a household chore in the
urban centers as in the rural areas where most of the inhabitants still rely on ponds,

streams, and wells for their domestic water needs. While a mere one percent of urban couples indicated that all household chores were the responsibility of the wife, about 7 percent of couples in the rural areas held that opinion.

The household chores appropriate for husbands which were enumerated include: iron clothing, help care for children, help wife when needed, help wife to cook, repair physical damage, weed around house, as well as the idea of no chores for men. A feature of most of the chores specified for husbands was that they were only expected to help wives do the work such as cooking or caring for children. In other words, the chores in question were implicitly considered as being for wives, thus husbands just lend a helping hand when called upon or when they feel like it.

Since fertility rates are higher in the rural areas than the urban areas, it is not surprising for rural wives and husbands alike to feel that helping to take care of the children was an appropriate chore for husbands. While about 12 percent of urban wives and 10 percent of urban husbands thought it was appropriate for husbands to help care for children, more rural couples (16 percent of wives; 22 percent husbands) felt so.

It appears that rural couples have more relaxed attitudes about many household chores for husbands than their urban counterparts. For example, while only 1-3 percent of urban couples thought that no household chores were appropriate for husbands, this opinion was held by 9 percent of rural wives and 11 percent of their husbands. This situation might be a reflection of the fact that more rural households than urban households get much of the help they need in performing household tasks from neighbors or relatives who often live close by.

## Appropriate Family Responsibilities For Wives And Husbands

In terms of family responsibilities, the data in Table 7.2 indicate that while wives were expected to be primarily responsible for rearing the children, feeding the family and keeping the house clean, they were also expected to be responsible for supplementing their husband's income and ensuring peace and harmony in the family.

It is interesting to observe that regardless of residence, a sizable proportion of both wives and husbands reported that the wife had a responsibility to add to the spouse's income. Again, this confirms the findings (discussed in Chapter 6) that perhaps given the rising cost of living in the country in recent years, monetary contribution for household meals in both the urban and rural areas may be moving from husband-only to joint contribution, as up to 15 percent of couples acknowledge in Table 7.2.

**Table 7.2**   Percentage Distribution of Couples' Views on Appropriate Family Responsibilities for Wives and Husbands, According to Residence, GFAMS, 1992/93

|  | URBAN | | RURAL | |
|---|---|---|---|---|
| RESPONSIBILITY FOR WIVES | Wife | Husband | Wife | Husband |
| Rear children | 19.5 | 20.5 | 19.8 | 22.2 |
| Feed the family | 18.3 | 18.6 | 22.9 | 23.3 |
| Add to spouse's income | 12.1 | 13.1 | 14.5 | 14.4 |
| Keep house clean | 13.5 | 14.1 | 9.5 | 8.1 |
| Ensure peace and harmony | 7.8 | 9.3 | 15.4 | 15.2 |
| Help spouse in everything | 3.4 | 3.5 | 7.8 | 8.9 |
| Entertain visitors | 2.7 | 2.4 | 2.9 | 2.1 |
| Other responsibilities | 22.6 | 18.5 | 7.2 | 5.8 |
| TOTAL | 100.0 | 100.0 | 100.0 | 100.0 |
| RESPONSIBILITY FOR HUSBANDS | | | | |
| Provide family needs | 32.7 | 35.1 | 40.6 | 40.1 |
| Pay children's school fees | 24.3 | 23.9 | 20.1 | 21.6 |
| Manage the family | 8.6 | 8.9 | 11.4 | 10.9 |
| Control/discipline children | 9.0 | 8.8 | 9.6 | 7.7 |
| Provide security for family | 4.8 | 5.7 | 10.7 | 11.3 |
| Keep spouse company | 2.2 | 0.9 | 0.9 | 1.0 |
| Other responsibilities | 18.4 | 16.7 | 6.6 | 7.3 |
| TOTAL | 100.0 | 100.0 | 100.0 | 100.0 |

It is not new for most Ghanaian wives to be making financial contributions to their household expenditures out of their own income-generating activities such as trading, fish-mongering, sale of agricultural products, and arts and crafts. However, since Ghana, like a number of African countries, embarked on structural adjustment programs in the 1980s as a fix for its ailing economy, there has been an increased burden on women to do more to sustain their households.

The adjustment program in Ghana, called the Economic Recovery Program (ERP) which began in 1983, emphasized, among other things, price controls, removal of government subsidies on consumer goods and services, devaluing the local currency, downsizing the state bureaucracy through layoffs of civil servants, and privatization of government-owned enterprises (Cornia, et al., 1987; Jonah, 1989; Schatz, 1994; Ho-Won, 1995). Therefore, although the structural adjustment program might have benefitted the export sector of the Ghanaian economy and trimmed down the size of government, average urban workers, the rural poor, small food-crop farmers and landless wage farmers suffered the most. Cuts in subsidies created higher food prices and the introduction of user fees for basic services such as education and health care. And as incomes shrunk and families saw their standards of living declining, both wives and husbands increased their expectation that the wife should make more financial contribution to the household budget.

The family responsibilities listed for husbands in the GFAMS comprise providing family needs (such as shelter, clothing, and "chop-money"), paying school fees for the children, managing the family, controlling and disciplining the children, providing security for the family, and keeping the wife company, among others things. Regardless of residence, over one-third of couples reported that the most important family responsibility for the husband was still to provide for the needs of the family, with over another 20 percent assigning to the husband the responsibility of paying for children's school fees.

Not surprisingly, results from the present study confirm the gender division of household chores and family responsibilities. Most urban and rural couples felt that the appropriate household chores for women were to cook the meals, clean the house, wash the clothes and dishes. These same couples felt that the chores for men in the society should include ironing the clothes, helping to care for the children, helping the wife when needed, and repairing physical damage to property. Despite what appears to be the similarities in the perceptions of urban and rural couples on household chores, significantly more rural couples than urban couples indicated that men should not perform any chores in the home.

Family responsibilities were similarly assigned on traditional gender role lines with the husband being the provider, and the wife responsible for the daily responsibilities of cooking, cleaning and child-care. Additionally, wives were openly called upon to supplement monetary expenditures in the household, a changing dynamic which might be attributed to the economic situation in the country.

**Ideal Occupation For Women And Men**

The responses to the questions on ideal occupation appropriate for women and men in the society were similarly consistent with our expectations as shown in Table 7.3. Irrespective of residence, most women and men felt that trading, hairdressing, seamstress, public school teaching, and nursing/midwifery were ideal occupations for women. According to views gathered from wives, 19-21 percent said that the ideal occupation for women was trading while about 15-20 percent said it was either dressmaking or hairdressing, with another 8-11 percent indicating public school teaching or nursing/midwifery as ideal occupations for women. However, while more urban couples (8-9 percent) than rural couples (4-5 percent) mentioned secretarial work for women, more rural couples (7-10 percent) than urban couples (2-3 percent) believed that being a farmer was appropriate for women.

Some of the ideal occupations mentioned for men include artisans, engineering, medicine, driving, law, business, farming/fishing, teaching, public service, and university teaching. The occupation that most rural and urban couples agreed was appropriate for men was artisan, agreed to by 15 percent of urban couples as well as 19 percent of rural couples. For the purposes of this study, "artisan" is a generic term for several occupations such as welding, woodworking, brick-laying, and auto-mechanic. Beyond being an artisan, more urban couples (12-13 percent) than rural couples (7 percent) mentioned engineering as ideal for men. Also, significantly more

**Table 7.3**    Percentage Distribution of Couples' Views on Ideal Occupation for Women and Men, According to Residence, GFAMS, 1992/93

| IDEAL OCCUPATION FOR WOMEN | URBAN | | RURAL | |
| --- | --- | --- | --- | --- |
| | Wife | Husband | Wife | Husband |
| Trader | 19.9 | 18.8 | 21.3 | 17.4 |
| Hairdresser/seamstress | 15.4 | 14.2 | 19.8 | 19.4 |
| Public school teacher | 11.0 | 11.4 | 7.5 | 9.9 |
| Nurse/midwife | 10.4 | 9.9 | 7.8 | 8.7 |
| Secretarial work | 8.0 | 9.4 | 3.6 | 5.3 |
| University professor | 5.9 | 5.3 | 5.1 | 2.8 |
| Medical doctor | 5.0 | 5.6 | 0.3 | 1.0 |
| Caterer/baker/matron | 5.0 | 5.3 | 7.3 | 8.4 |
| Lawyer | 2.6 | 3.5 | 0.6 | 1.5 |
| Farmer | 2.2 | 3.0 | 6.5 | 9.4 |
| Cashier/bank teller | 1.4 | 1.1 | 0.1 | 0.2 |
| Domestic servant | 0.4 | 0.4 | 0.1 | 2.3 |
| Pharmacist | 0.3 | 0.6 | 0.1 | 0.5 |
| Fish processer/monger | 0.2 | 0.2 | 4.1 | 1.1 |
| Homemaker | 0.2 | 0.7 | 0.5 | 0.7 |
| Liquor distiller | 0.0 | 0.0 | 1.4 | 0.8 |
| Any occupation | 0.2 | 0.5 | 9.4 | 6.2 |
| Other occupations | 11.6 | 10.1 | 4.5 | 4.4 |
| TOTAL | 100.0 | 100.0 | 100.0 | 100.0 |

| IDEAL OCCUPATION FOR MEN | | | | |
| --- | --- | --- | --- | --- |
| Artisan | 15.3 | 13.9 | 18.5 | 19.2 |
| Engineer | 12.0 | 13.3 | 6.9 | 6.5 |
| Medical doctor | 11.5 | 10.7 | 3.1 | 4.2 |
| Businessman | 6.2 | 5.4 | 3.0 | 2.6 |
| Driver | 5.9 | 5.2 | 9.3 | 8.0 |
| Lawyer | 5.9 | 5.9 | 2.7 | 3.3 |
| Farmer | 5.3 | 5.9 | 12.5 | 13.0 |
| Armed force | 4.7 | 4.3 | 2.3 | 2.2 |
| Public school teacher | 3.7 | 5.1 | 4.5 | 4.3 |
| Road/building contractor | 3.2 | 4.3 | 3.2 | 4.3 |
| Accountant | 2.2 | 3.4 | 2.1 | 3.0 |
| Public/civil servant | 2.0 | 1.8 | 4.4 | 5.2 |
| University professor | 1.7 | 1.8 | 2.8 | 2.8 |
| Fisherman | 1.6 | 1.8 | 6.4 | 4.5 |
| Pharmacist | 0.7 | 1.3 | 0.7 | 1.0 |
| Liquor distiller | 0.0 | 0.1 | 1.0 | 0.2 |
| Any occupation | 0.3 | 0.8 | 5.3 | 5.1 |
| Other occupations | 17.8 | 14.9 | 11.4 | 10.6 |
| TOTAL | 100.0 | 100.0 | 100.0 | 100.0 |

urban couples selected the study of medicine as ideal occupation for men than their rural counterparts. On the contrary, more rural couples than urban couples cited farming, fishing, driving, and public service as ideal occupation for men.

Both women and men in Ghana are expected to work to earn a living according to the results of the GFAMS. Nevertheless, they are expected to be in different types of occupations, patterned along the traditional notions of what activities the sexes have always done in the society; for women--nurturing, health care providers, beauticians, and informal sector employees, and for men--professionals, mechanics, and activities involving physical labor. We believe that it is against this background that "appropriate" levels of education for women and men were envisioned.

## Ideal Level of Formal Education For Women And Men

Table 7.4 presents information on couples' views on the highest level of formal education appropriate for both sexes. The data generally show that wives in both rural and urban areas expected lower levels of education for women than men. However, the urban residents aspired for higher levels of education for both men and women, compared to their rural counterparts. For instance, while only 4 percent of urban couples expected the highest level of education appropriate for women to be basic or elementary school education, twice as many (7-9 percent) rural couples did.

It is, however, worth mentioning that over 28 percent of the urban wives and 20 percent of urban husbands said women can go as far as the secondary school level. The proportion of rural couples who gave this level was about 15 percent. Also, about two-thirds of urban couples and about half of rural couples recognized university and advanced levels as the highest level of education appropriate for women. Although this is commendable, bearing in mind the impact of education in socio-economic development and fertility reduction, this ideal of higher education for all has not been widely translated into reality in many Ghanaian households. We examine some of the common reasons in the next section.

**Table 7.4**    Percentage Distribution of Couples' Views on the Highest Level of Education Appropriate for Women and Men, According to Residence, GFAMS, 1992/93

| APPROPRIATE EDUC. FOR WOMEN | URBAN | | RURAL | |
|---|---|---|---|---|
| | Wife | Husband | Wife | Husband |
| Basic/elementary education | 3.8 | 4.2 | 9.2 | 7.4 |
| Technical/commercial education | 1.5 | 2.6 | 4.3 | 5.4 |
| Teacher-/nursing training | 0.2 | 0.4 | 4.6 | 5.1 |
| Secondary school education | 28.4 | 19.5 | 15.3 | 14.6 |
| Polytechnic education | 2.2 | 2.0 | 4.3 | 1.1 |
| University education | 60.5 | 66.1 | 49.1 | 53.4 |
| Any educational level by ability | 3.1 | 4.9 | 9.2 | 11.4 |
| No opinion | 0.4 | 0.4 | 3.8 | 1.4 |
| TOTAL | 100.0 | 100.0 | 100.0 | 100.0 |

| APPROPRIATE EDUC. FOR MEN | | | | |
|---|---|---|---|---|
| Basic/elementary education | 2.0 | 1.3 | 2.6 | 1.4 |
| Technical/commercial education | 0.9 | 1.8 | 0.9 | 2.3 |
| Teacher-/nursing training | 0.0 | 0.0 | 2.6 | 1.7 |
| Secondary school education | 13.5 | 6.5 | 8.0 | 5.1 |
| Polytechnic education | 0.9 | 1.5 | 2.0 | 2.0 |
| University education | 78.9 | 83.1 | 70.9 | 74.6 |
| Any educational level by ability | 3.6 | 5.8 | 9.7 | 11.3 |
| No opinion | 0.2 | 0.0 | 3.4 | 1.7 |
| TOTAL | 100.0 | 100.0 | 100.0 | 100.0 |

## *Reasons for the Appropriateness of Secondary and University Education*

Secondary school and university levels of education were selected by most of the couples as the highest appropriate levels of education for both Ghanaian women and men. Reasons were therefore sought from them as to why they felt these two levels of education should be the appropriate highest levels. The dominant reason for university or advanced education for women and men was to enable them to obtain well-paid jobs as shown in Figures 7.1a & 7.1b. Other popular reasons included to be comfortable and respected in life, and to acquire knowledge. Similar reasons were given by about 20 percent of couples who felt that the highest level of education appropriate for women and men was secondary education.

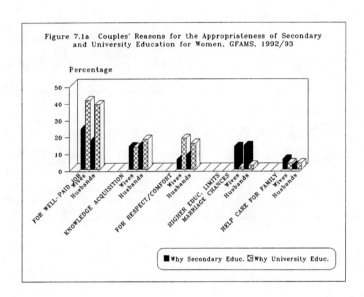

Figure 7.1a  Couples' Reasons for the Appropriateness of Secondary and University Education for Women. GFAMS, 1992/93

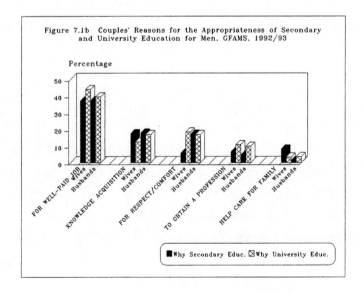

Figure 7.1b  Couples' Reasons for the Appropriateness of Secondary and University Education for Men. GFAMS, 1992/93

However, an additional reason why secondary education was mentioned as enough for women was that higher education limits a woman's marriage chances and her reproductive capabilities. It is interesting to note that this view was held by about 14 percent of both wives and husbands who chose that level of education as the highest appropriate for women. This is not totally surprising in a society where marriage occurs early (especially for females) and is near universal; such is the case in Ghana that women, in particular, are not encouraged to spend too many years seeking higher education as their biological clocks may be running out and hence may not be able to secure good husbands. After all, it is a well documented fact that most "....African women take their reproductive tasks seriously, celebrate their ability to give birth, and refuse to subordinate their biological roles to other roles within society..." (Mikell, 1997:8).

As formal education in Ghana and much of Africa has traditionally targeted men over women, it is no accident that men dominate in the administrative, managerial, professional, and technical areas of the economy, with the majority of women typically engaged in trading, service, and agricultural-related work. This occupational division not only creates administrative practices that are discriminatory for women, but also excludes them from governance and decision making positions. The next section of this chapter examines some leadership positions for African women in the traditional society as well as contemporary affairs of the modern state.

## WOMEN IN LEADERSHIP POSITIONS

The performance of the productive and reproductive roles of both women and men in several African societies has been carried out through membership in lineages and family groups. Although these roles have traditionally included the right to political participation and occupation of public leadership roles, only high-status lineages or family groups have been given the privilege of leadership positions, and the privileges have been greater for males than females. Nevertheless, there is abundant literature that documents the leadership roles that women have taken in their communities throughout the history of the African continent as queens, queenmothers, priestesses, guardians of traditions and the social order, and even in some cases as warriors protesting against colonial rule (Rattray, 1923; Fortes, 1950; Aidoo, 1994; Ekechi, 1996; Mikell, 1997).

Some noted examples of African women's leadership prowess in the public arena in recent times include the role of the female prophetess Nehanda of Zimbabwe who led her people in 1863 to resist the expansion of Cecil Rhodes' imperialist agenda; the role of Empress Taytu in the Ethiopian-Italian War of 1895-1896 resisting Italian territorial claims; the Asante queenmother, Yaa Asantewaah, who rallied and led the Asantes of Ghana to war against the British colonial authority in the Yaa Asantewaah War of 1900 to preserve the *Golden Stool*, a symbol of cultural identity; the Kikuyu Women in 1922 protesting against taxation and the use of forced labor under colonial rule in Kenya; and the Women's War in Nigeria in 1929 challenging indirect rule and taxation by colonial authorities and their cronies (Lebeuf, 1963; Aidoo, 1994; Ekechi, 1996).

The Ghanaian society has always provided some opportunities for older adults to participate in some aspects of community life. For both sexes, middle and old age people are highly esteemed although there is a clear division of labor between the sexes in what they do. Men are more likely to control the executive branch of government in the towns and villages in Ghana. Older and middle aged men, for the most part, form the bulk of the legislative and executive members ("elders") in the traditional political structures. They also control the judiciary apparatus in many of the towns and villages in the country.

However, women, by virtue of age, join the group of "elders" and opinion leaders in their local communities. After menopause, women qualify for different positions which were closed to them during the period of childbearing. For instance, among the Akans, women hold positions as queenmothers in charge of women's affairs and responsible for choosing the successor to the throne ("omanhene," "ohene," or "odikro"). It should be noted, however, that the queenmother positions are only available to women of royal birth or to older women freed from reproductive and related duties (Nukunya, 1978; ROG & UNICEF, 1990:70). On the other hand, among the patriachial societies of northern Ghana including the Mole-Dagbani, Grussi, Gurma, and Gonja, and the Ewes of the Volta region, women do not have political positions, and therefore, have less of a role to play in community affairs.

Thus, although some African women might have exhibited successful political or public activity, their participation cannot be taken an index of widespread female participation in public life. Even the limited roles that women played in administrative and community affairs began to erode in modern African states born out of the legacies of colonialism. With the shift of the economic structure from a familial to a market economy, and disruption of the traditional structures of governance which vested power and authority in indigenous leaders of both sexes, colonially-constructed bureaucracies, courts, and political structures that focus on men became the norm in several African societies. Thus, many women were not only alienated from the administrative processes of national and community affairs, they also experienced pre-entry discrimination in the labor force, worked in feminized occupations, and received minimum benefits from the enlarged bureaucracies and occupational opportunities in the modern economy (Hart, 1973; Date-Bah, 1982; Akuffo, 1990; Mikell, 1997).

Undoubtedly, the disparity between the sexes in the formal versus informal sectors of the economy and the public arena, a feature common throughout much of sub-Saharan Africa, seems to lower the aspirations of women themselves to work hard to attain higher education. And without higher education it is impossible to seek high administrative or political office in the modern state. The consequences are that men dominate and legislate in the new "public" domain and in the "rationalized" cash transaction markets of bureaucratic capitalism (Dormor, 1994:18).

In the GFAMS, respondents were asked to indicate the extent to which they agreed to having women in selected leadership positions in the country, such as bosses at the work place, district assembly members, parliamentary candidates, cabinet ministers, and presidential candidates. Also, reasons were sought as to why women should or should not occupy the above-mentioned leadership positions. Figure 7.2 presents the distribution of urban and rural couples' views respectively on leadership positions for Ghanaian women.

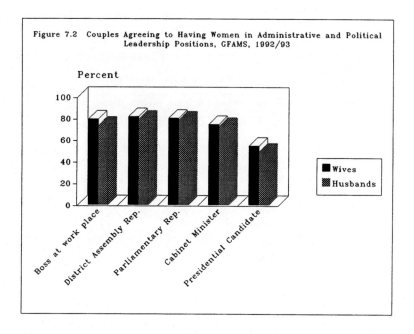

Figure 7.2  Couples Agreeing to Having Women in Administrative and Political Leadership Positions, GFAMS, 1992/93

On the whole, the results indicate that the overwhelming majority of couples felt that Ghanaian women should be allowed to hold leadership positions as bosses at the work place, members of the district assembly, parliamentarians, and cabinet ministers. The patterns of response in each of the four positions mentioned above looks very similar, and thus will be discussed together. The only contention arose over the issue of women as presidential candidates, which was agreed to by only about half of the couples in the sample. The issue of the presidency, therefore, will be examined in a separate section.

**Views on Women in Administrative and Non-Presidential Leadership Positions**

The most dominant reason couples gave for agreeing to women in each of the positions mentioned was that if equally qualified they should be allowed to partake in decision making. Figure 7.3 shows a typical pattern of responses illustrating our sampled population's views on women as heads of administrative positions or political positions other than the presidency.

Indeed, almost half of all couples agreed that qualified women should not be bypassed in favor of men for the selected leadership positions. Additionally, a sizable proportion of couples felt that women can perform as creditably as men in all the positions under discussion. Also, some couples indicated that giving women a chance in leadership positions will ensure gender equity and better representation of women's interests in the country.

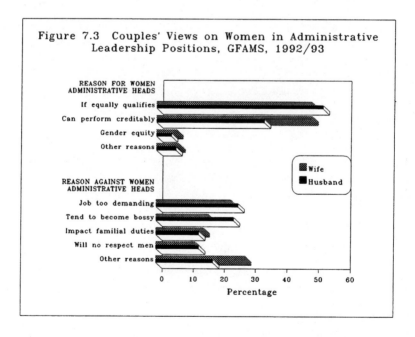

Figure 7.3   Couples' Views on Women in Administrative Leadership Positions, GFAMS, 1992/93

For couples who did not accept that women should be in leadership positions in the selected areas, the major concern was that the jobs will be too demanding for women. It is interesting to note that relatively more wives than husbands in the study were not in favor of women as political leaders because of the view that the job will be too demanding on women. Another reason why couples, but men in particular, opposed women in leadership positions was related to their concern about the fact that women might become bossy and would not respect men if they were put in higher positions. This reaction is expected since Ghanaian men for far too long have been in leadership positions and have felt comfortable in the public sphere of the modern state. Women in the public arena, then, could be seen as an "encroachment" on men's territory; an act that may accord more women the power base to challenge men's authority in those domains.

Generally, only about 15 percent of both sexes believed that leadership positions outside the home would have negative impact on women's familial responsibilities. Given the emphasis the Ghanaian society put on familial roles and responsibilities, and the dominant role of women in the home in fulfilling the household tasks, it is expected that leadership positions that are perceived as taking women away from the home may not be favored even among women.

Table 7.5 presents the distribution of couples' views on women in administrative leadership positions by background characteristics. The data show that for almost all of the background variables, the proportion of wives that agreed to having women in leadership positions was higher than husbands. However, there were some disparities worth noting.

For example, there was a positive relationship between the level of education and approving of women's leadership. The general pattern shown by both wives and husbands is that the higher the level of education, the higher the proportion of respondents who agreed to women being in higher administrative leadership positions. However at each respective level of education, the proportion of wives agreeing was greater than that of husbands. Up to 97 percent of wives with university or advanced

**Table 7.5** Percentage Distribution of Couples Who Agree to Having Women as Administrative Heads, According to Selected Background Characteristics, GFAMS, 1992/93

| | WOMEN IN ADMINISTRATIVE LEADERSHIP POSITIONS | | | | |
|---|---|---|---|---|---|
| | Wife | | | Husband | |
| Background Characteristic | Percent | Number | | Percent | Number |
| **AGE** | | | | | |
| Under 30 | 83.6 | 335 | | 64.7 | 133 |
| 30-39 | 83.8 | 334 | | 73.7 | 384 |
| 40+ | 79.7 | 202 | | 80.1 | 367 |
| **RESIDENCE** | | | | | |
| Urban | 84.0 | 526 | | 77.6 | 541 |
| Rural | 80.5 | 348 | | 71.2 | 347 |
| **LEVEL OF EDUCATION** | | | | | |
| No education | 75.0 | 144 | | 67.6 | 37 |
| Elementary | 81.7 | 486 | | 68.8 | 384 |
| Sec/tec/trg.college | 87.0 | 192 | | 79.0 | 291 |
| Higher | 96.9 | 32 | | 85.9 | 156 |
| **OCCUPATION** | | | | | |
| Professional | 92.1 | 76 | | 87.3 | 213 |
| Clerical | 94.4 | 54 | | 76.6 | 94 |
| Sales | 83.5 | 176 | | 76.5 | 34 |
| Service/transport | 97.8 | 45 | | 71.7 | 120 |
| Farmer/fisherman | 83.3 | 12 | | 83.3 | 30 |
| Craftsman | 75.5 | 110 | | 71.8 | 188 |
| **RELIGION** | | | | | |
| Catholic | 86.4 | 154 | | 79.4 | 165 |
| Protestant | 83.6 | 592 | | 75.9 | 555 |
| Muslim | 67.6 | 37 | | 65.9 | 41 |
| Traditionalist | ** | ** | | 52.4 | 21 |
| Other religion | 69.0 | 58 | | 72.9 | 59 |
| No religion | 90.5 | 21 | | 70.7 | 41 |
| **CHOICE OF PARTNER** | | | | | |
| Entirely by me | 82.2 | 583 | | 75.5 | 670 |
| Help/consent of family | 85.4 | 233 | | 72.7 | 187 |
| Arranged by family | 71.4 | 28 | | 66.7 | 15 |
| **TYPE OF MARRIAGE** | | | | | |
| Customary | 84.5 | 599 | | 74.4 | 629 |
| Ordinance/Church | 80.6 | 134 | | 83.0 | 135 |
| Consensual | 79.8 | 98 | | 70.4 | 98 |
| Islamic | 60.9 | 22 | | 63.6 | 22 |
| **FORM OF MARRIAGE** | | | | | |
| Monogamous couple | 83.3 | 767 | | 76.5 | 787 |
| Polygynous husband | – | – | | 65.3 | 95 |
| Polygynous wife | | | | | |
| 1st ranked wife | 77.3 | 44 | | – | – |
| 2nd ranked wife | 76.8 | 56 | | – | – |
| **TOTAL** | 82.6 | 874 | | 75.1 | 888 |

**Note:** ** Fewer than 10 cases   – not applicable

education agreed to having women in leadership positions compared to fewer proportions (86 percent) of their male counterparts. Similarly, occupations needing higher levels of education (such as professionals and clerical) tended to have higher proportions of the couples accepting women as leaders.

Furthermore, couples were slightly more likely to agree to women in leadership positions if they lived in the urban areas, were Christians, and were in monogamous relationships than if they resided in the rural areas, were Muslims or Traditionalists, and were in polygynous marriages. While between 76-86 percent of Christian couples agreed to women as administrative heads in the work place, between 66-68 percent of Muslim couples, and yet still fewer Traditionalists agreed. The lower proportions for Muslims and Traditionalist could be attributed to the relatively fewer public roles for women under these two religions.

The data also show that for wives in monogamous unions, 83 percent of them agreed that women could be administrative leaders compared to 77 percent of those in polygynous marriages. The proportions of monogamous husbands were 77 percent while only 65 percent of polygynous husbands agreed to women as leaders. While the choice of a partner did not make much difference for husbands on whether they agreed to have women as leaders, wives who chose their partners entirely by themselves were more likely to approve of women leaders than their counterparts whose marriages were arranged. Having a "free" hand in choosing a partner may give women and men a chance to develop a sense of maturity and feeling of being in control, thus they will be more sympathetic to women in leadership positions.

## Views on Women as Presidential Candidates

Although most couples in the GFAMS agreed to having women in administrative and leadership positions, as the national importance of the leadership position increases, lower proportions of the respondents accepted women as capable of occupying the position. Such was the case with regard to couples' views on women as presidential candidates. In fact, only about half of all couples agreed to the appropriateness of a woman president for Ghana. Reasons for and against a woman presidential candidate are presented in Figure 7.4.

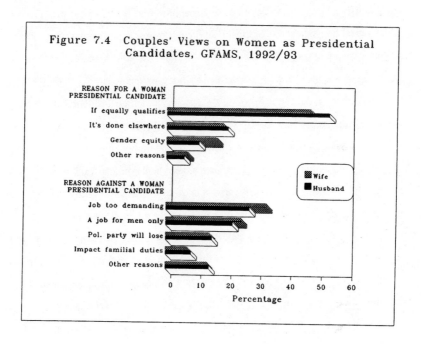

Figure 7.4   Couples' Views on Women as Presidential Candidates, GFAMS, 1992/93

An overwhelming majority of couples who agreed to the idea of a woman presidential candidate indicated that qualified women should be given the chance to run for the office. Slightly more men than women, though, believed that way. Almost a quarter of the respondents also felt that because women have had the chance to become presidents in other countries, Ghana should give it a try. However, other respondents felt that women presidential candidates were needed to bring about gender equity. It is interesting to note that while more husbands than wives mentioned "qualification," almost twice as many women as men indicated "gender equity" as a reason to support women presidential candidates.

For those couples who objected to a woman president, their main concerns were that the jobs will be too demanding for women, that the presidency was a job for men only, that any political party that presented a woman candidate was likely to lose elections, and that the job would negatively impact on the woman's family responsibilities. While about 50 percent of couples who disapproved of a woman president cited the "demands" of the job and male "prerogative," higher proportions of women than men expressed these views, indicating the cultural acceptance of men's place in the society as "natural" leaders even among women.

The cross-classification of couples' views on women as presidential candidates by selected background characteristics is presented in Table 7.6. Overall, more wives than husbands accepted the view of women becoming presidential aspirants. However, significantly more younger women agreed to a woman president compared to women 40 years or older. The reverse was true for men; more older men agreed than younger men. Whereas about 62 percent of wives under 30 years of age agreed that women could be presidential hopefuls, only 44 percent of their counterparts aged 40 years and above did agree to that. On the other hand, while about 44 percent of husbands aged 30 years or younger accepted that women could be presidential candidates, about 52 percent of older husbands agreed. Also, while higher proportions of urban wives than rural wives were for women presidential aspirants, higher proportions of rural husbands than their urban counterparts wanted to see women run for the office of the president.

An increase in female education in recent decades in the country may have given younger women some foot-hold in leadership positions in the formal sector of the economy and, therefore their vision of the possibility of a woman president in their lifetime than women of the older generation. This view may be supported by the data on the relationship between a wives' educational attainment and her support for a woman president. For example, while barely 50 percent of wives with no education did agree to a woman presidential candidate, 60 percent of those with elementary education did support the idea, yet still 70 percent of highly educated women expressed their support for a female presidential hopeful. The level of support did

**Table 7.6**  Percentage Distribution of Couples Who Agree to Having Women as Presidential Candidates, According to Selected Background Characteristics, GFAMS, 1992/93

| | WOMEN AS PRESIDENTIAL CANDIDATES | | | | |
| --- | --- | --- | --- | --- | --- |
| | Wife | | | Husband | |
| Background Characteristic | Percent | Number | | Percent | Number |
| AGE | | | | | |
| Under 30 | 61.7 | 329 | | 44.4 | 135 |
| 30-39 | 61.6 | 328 | | 50.5 | 382 |
| 40+ | 44.3 | 201 | | 52.1 | 365 |
| RESIDENCE | | | | | |
| Urban | 59.3 | 518 | | 46.8 | 538 |
| Rural | 54.8 | 343 | | 55.7 | 348 |
| LEVEL OF EDUCATION | | | | | |
| No education | 48.3 | 143 | | 45.9 | 37 |
| Elementary | 60.1 | 479 | | 49.5 | 380 |
| Sec/tec/trg.college | 52.7 | 186 | | 55.7 | 291 |
| Higher | 69.7 | 33 | | 43.9 | 157 |
| OCCUPATION | | | | | |
| Professional | 70.5 | 78 | | 52.8 | 212 |
| Clerical | 61.5 | 52 | | 48.4 | 93 |
| Sales | 54.1 | 172 | | 44.2 | 34 |
| Service/transport | 65.1 | 43 | | 54.2 | 120 |
| Farmer/fisherman | 58.3 | 12 | | 43.3 | 30 |
| Craftsman | 50.5 | 109 | | 50.5 | 188 |
| RELIGION | | | | | |
| Catholic | 55.0 | 151 | | 50.3 | 163 |
| Protestant | 58.7 | 586 | | 47.7 | 555 |
| Muslim | 56.8 | 37 | | 60.0 | 40 |
| Traditionalist | ** | ** | | 59.1 | 22 |
| Other religion | 50.9 | 55 | | 63.3 | 60 |
| No religion | 60.0 | 20 | | 47.5 | 40 |
| CHOICE OF PARTNER | | | | | |
| Entirely by me | 59.7 | 575 | | 49.2 | 669 |
| Help/consent of family | 54.8 | 230 | | 53.8 | 186 |
| Arranged by family | 42.3 | 26 | | 46.7 | 15 |
| TYPE OF MARRIAGE | | | | | |
| Customary | 58.0 | 590 | | 51.4 | 625 |
| Ordinance/Church | 48.9 | 131 | | 43.4 | 136 |
| Consensual | 66.4 | 113 | | 50.5 | 99 |
| Islamic | 56.5 | 23 | | 59.1 | 22 |
| FORM OF MARRIAGE | | | | | |
| Monogamous couple | 58.0 | 753 | | 50.3 | 783 |
| Polygynous husband | – | – | | 51.0 | 96 |
| Polygynous wife | | | | | |
| 1st ranked wife | 55.6 | 45 | | – | – |
| 2nd ranked wife | 51.8 | 56 | | – | – |
| TOTAL | 57.5 | 861 | | 50.3 | 886 |

**Note: ** Fewer than 10 cases      – not applicable

not only show a clear pattern, the proportions were generally higher than those of their male counterparts.

Couples were more likely to accept a woman president if they had chosen their partners entirely by themselves than if their partners had been arranged by the family. Couples were also more likely to agree to a woman president if they were in monogamous relationships or in polygynous marriages. Quite evident, especially in the case of wives, was that the more the family involvement in the choice of the partner, the lower the proportion agreeing to having female presidential candidates.

In general, data from the present study confirm that attitudes about gender/sex roles, responsibilities, as well as occupational and leadership preferences in Ghana are for the most part "traditional." The general patterns clearly fit common stereotypes of women and men doing typically feminine and masculine tasks respectively as defined by customary practices. Although higher education for girls and boys alike may be the aspiration of Ghanaian parents, with marriage and procreation still on their minds some parents may not encourage their daughters to pursue higher education. Such attitudes, of course, not only dampen the aspirations of females in the society, but also limit their potential to become completely independent and make autonomous decisions on matters affecting their interests both in the "private-domestic" and "public-political" arenas.

Propelled by the colonial experience and men's interpretations (or sometimes misinterpretations) of what constitute traditional and customary practices, African women for the most part have been marginalized in the affairs of the household as well as in the setting of political agendas and national priorities. Until recently, the existing socio-cultural and political order in most African societies that produce invisible and voiceless women had not been seriously challenged. Since the 1990's, some professional African women have been active in non-governmental organizations (NGO's) and other forums promoting consciousness raising, self-help development projects, and discussing discriminatory laws and practices (see, e.g., Nzomo, 1993, 1997; Dei, 1997; Manuh, 1997; Geisler, 1995).

In fact, Gwendolyn Mikell's words capture the challenges facing contemporary African women in the following statement:

> "....African women have become more aware of themselves as women and of their need to address their subordinate position in public life ...concerned about how to use African culture in assertive and positive ways as they seek solutions to the many problems facing them, their communities, and their states." (1997:28)

Among the many problems that women in Africa are confronted with are issues of their sexual rights and laws of inheritance of property. It is believed that strengthening the rights of women not only empowers them but promotes the welfare of children and the entire family. Thus, in the next chapter, we examine the views of Ghanaian couples in the GFAMS on sexual rights within marriage and property rights of surviving spouse and children.

**8**

# SEXUAL RIGHTS AND INHERITANCE

## SEXUAL RIGHTS

Although the ceremonies and processes that precede marriages and the rights inherent in them vary throughout Africa, several researchers have identified three essential elements that are common to most marriages on the continent: the marriage payment, the formal handing over of the bride by her parents to the groom and his parents, and finally the marriage ceremony. Of all these elements, the one that has attracted the most attention has been the marriage payment, commonly called bridewealth (Fortes, 1950; Nukunya, 1978; Assimeng, 1981; Lesthaeghe, 1989).

As a concept, bridewealth varies across ethnic groups in Ghana, nonetheless its payment is seen as a legal bond uniting the two families in both matrilineal and patrilineal systems. The act signifies the legal transfer of the rights of parents to their daughter to the groom and his family (Fiawoo, 1978b; Assimeng, 1981). While the completion of the payment of the bridewealth confers to the husband the productive, sexual and reproductive services of the wife, it also guarantees rights of protection for the wife. However, under Customary and Islamic law marriages in Ghana, the wife does not have any legal protection against the husband's acquisition of additional wives. Whereas a man married under these two marriage laws has the legal right to marry other women without being charged with bigamy, married women do not have similar legal rights, indicating a sexual double standard.

Thus, a Ghanaian wife's sexual rights in her husband are not absolute particularly in the potentially polygynous marriages. An extra-marital affair of a husband could be rationalized as part of a process towards marrying an additional wife (see, Preston-Whyte,1994). Thus, whereas African marriages confer uxorial rights unto the husband, there are no reciprocal rights for the wife and, therefore, she would not be expected to refuse to have sex with her husband under any circumstances (except prescribed periods such as during menstruation and when sick). In view of this, wives have limited control over the extra marital affairs of their husbands.

The sexual double standard in favor of men is part of the built-in traditional female subordination in all aspects of life, including sexuality (Awusabo-Asare et al., 1993). For instance, in the traditional courtship system, a man exchanges valued gifts in return for "matrimonial-like" services. In marriage the reciprocity includes the exchange of the woman's sexual and procreative services in return for maintenance (Dinan, 1983). This in part, is the exchange theory in marital relations. The two parties involved do exchange one commodity for the other within the relationship. The exchange may not be on equal terms and that is at the core of the domination of the partner who has the advantage over the other. And in most cases, it is the man who dominates in the relationship, and hence could enjoy sexual relations of social recognition with multiple partners.

Traditionally, the marriage of additional wives has been considered a status symbol for local dignities (Pool, 1972; Nukunya, 1978). In many of the rural areas, a predominant reason for plural marriages has been to acquire additional manual labor to expand the agricultural holdings and ensure the financial security of the household (Boserup, 1970, 1985; Pool, 1972). Furthermore, with the importance attached to procreation in many African societies, childlessness or low fecundity may often lead to the acquisition of additional wives by the husband (Pool, 1972; Nukunya, 1978). Even widows of reproductive age may be re-absorbed into the family of their deceased husbands (see, e.g., Welshman & Steward, 1995).

High fertility rates exist in polygynous relationships because, theoretically, wives may have a desire to prove their fertility to their husbands while men want to prove their sexual potency to their wives and family (Greenstreet, 1987). Consequently, plural marriages reduce the bargaining power of women as they compete for childbearing and affection of their husbands (Pool, 1972; ROG & UNICEF, 1990). Such competition often creates jealousy, insecurity and distrust within the household. Nonetheless, polygyny is also seen by others as a means of attaining female autonomy and independence through the sharing of domestic responsibilities and household chores (Pool, 1972; Nukunya, 1978; Brabin, 1984; Singh & Morey, 1987; Dorjahn, 1988).

In spite of the fact that the practice of polygyny in the open may be on the decline in many African societies, sexual relations with multiple partners have continued with a growing phenomenon called "outside wifeship" or "private polygyny" (Karanja, 1994:211). This is the common practice whereby married men who contracted their marriages under the Ordinance/Church laws resort to acquiring and economically maintaining girl-friends, concubines, or mistresses privately. Several scholars have argued that the practice of having outside wives, despite its lack of legal status, has been used by African elite men, in particular, to uphold the Western or Christian notion of monogamous marriage, while privately admiring the African traditional idea of polygynous relationships (Morgan [with Ohadike], 1975; Bleek, 1987; Karanja, 1987, 1994; Mann, 1994).

There are several reasons why African men acquire outside wives including egocentrism, procreation, pressure from family and friends, and the use of the practice as an alternate to divorce. For most outside wives, their motivations stem from economic support, status enhancement, procreation, pressure from peers and family, and the hope of becoming the next "legal" wife after a turbulent marriage fails (Karanja, 1994). All the above motivations notwithstanding, extra-marital affairs may have endured in Ghana as well as the rest of Africa because there appears to be little social or legal sanctions attached to the practice despite the risk of STDs and opposition from some elite women's groups. Thus, some women still perceive themselves as not having the right to refuse sex with a partner known to be promiscuous (Awusabo-Asare et al., 1993).

In the GFAMS, questions were asked on selected marital and sexual acts. These were: the rights of wives to refuse sexual demands from husbands, husbands' right to practice polygyny, husbands' right to have extra-marital affairs and wives' right to have extra-marital affairs. Questions were further asked to explore the circumstances under which a married couple had the right (or not) to those marital and sexual rights. The intention in asking questions on these issues was to find out how couples perceive their various rights within marriage. The issue of sexual rights is culture bound. But as female autonomy is generally a process, it is expected that women are going to demand more sexual rights within marriage as their individual and societal autonomy improve.

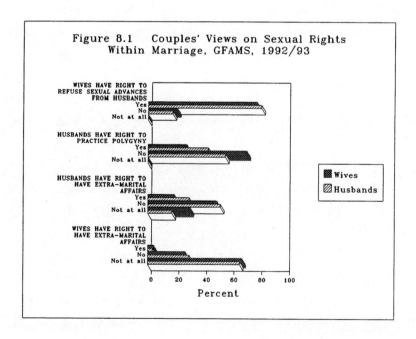

Figure 8.1    Couples' Views on Sexual Rights Within Marriage, GFAMS, 1992/93

Figure 8.1 illustrates the patterns of distribution of couples' views on the rights to refuse sexual demands, practice polygyny, and have extra-marital affairs. The sections below will discuss the findings on each of the four issues.

### Wives' Right to Refuse Sexual Demands From Husbands

It is very clear from Figure 8.1 that the majority of couples believe that women have the right to refuse their husbands' sexual advances. Barely one-fifth of both wives and husbands disagreed with the statement that wives have marital rights to refuse sex; neither wives nor husbands gave the extreme response of "not at all." Table 8.1 presents reasons for and against wives' right to refuse sexual advances from their husbands by place of residence.

**Table 8.1**   Reasons Why Wives Have the Right (or Not) to Refuse Sexual Demands From Their Husbands, According to Residence, GFAMS, 1992/93

| | Urban | | Rural | |
|---|---|---|---|---|
| REASON *FOR* WIFE'S RIGHT TO REFUSE SEX | Wife | Husband | Wife | Husband |
| Not in the mood | 34.7 | 31.0 | 36.5 | 40.1 |
| When sick | 32.8 | 44.8 | 30.6 | 35.2 |
| Menstrual period | 17.6 | 15.8 | 13.3 | 16.1 |
| Husband is promiscuous | 3.7 | 0.8 | 2.7 | 0.4 |
| Quarrel/unhappy | 3.5 | 1.3 | 5.1 | 2.2 |
| Other reasons | 7.8 | 6.3 | 11.8 | 6.0 |
| TOTAL | 100.0 | 100.0 | 100.0 | 100.0 |
| NUMBER | [461] | [480] | [255] | [267] |
| REASON *AGAINST* WIFE'S RIGHT TO REFUSE SEX | | | | |
| Marriage obligation | 48.9 | 45.7 | 50.5 | 53.1 |
| Gives men excuse to have extra-marital affairs | 26.1 | 34.6 | 10.9 | 4.2 |
| Against religion | 5.4 | 1.2 | 11.9 | 11.5 |
| Brings conflict/quarrel | 1.1 | 0.0 | 6.9 | 6.3 |
| Other reasons | 18.5 | 18.5 | 19.8 | 25.0 |
| TOTAL | 100.0 | 100.0 | 100.0 | 100.0 |
| NUMBER | [92] | [81] | [101] | [96] |

Looking at the urban couples' reasons in favor of wives' right to refuse sexual advances from husbands, a higher proportion of wives (35 percent) than husbands (31 percent) said that if the wife is not in the mood for sex, then she should have the right to refuse. While 45 percent of urban husbands agreed to sickness as basis for the wife rejecting the husband's sexual advances, only 33 percent of wives did agree. Thus, while the highest proportion of husbands saw mostly the physiological condition of the wife as a basis of refusing the husband's sexual advances, the wives saw it more in terms of the psychological condition of the woman.

Another important reason advanced was when the wife is in her menstrual period, a view held by between 13-18 percent of couples in the sample. Other reasons given include when the husband is promiscuous, or they have quarreled and/or wife is unhappy. However, it is noteworthy that in both situations, regardless of residence, more wives than husbands found promiscuity and unhappiness as good enough reasons to refuse sexual advances from the man. This again adds up to the importance of the wife's psychological preparedness as a basis for rejecting husband's sexual advances rather than the physiological conditions.

With regard to the 20 percent of couples who felt that wives do not have the right to refuse sexual advances from their husbands, marital obligation, plus the fact that refusal may give men the excuse to have extra-marital affairs, were the major reasons. These reasons hold true for urban and rural couples, except that among the latter an additional reason cited was that the act of sexual refusal was against their religious principles.

### *Wives' Right to Refuse Sexual Demands by Background Characteristics*:

A further insight into the rights of women to refuse sexual advances of husbands by respondents background characteristics is presented in Table 8.2. As should be expected, fewer wives and husbands dwelling in rural areas tended to agree that wives have the right to refuse sexual demands of husbands than their urban counterparts. While 84 percent of urban wives agreed, only 71 percent of their rural counterparts had such a realization. With respect to husbands, over 87 percent of

**Table 8.2**    Percentage Distribution of Couples' Views on Wives' Sexual Rights, According to Selected Background Characteristics, GFAMS, 1992/93

| Background Characteristic | WIVES HAVE THE RIGHT TO REFUSE SEXUAL DEMANDS | | | | | |
| | YES | | NO | | NOT AT ALL | |
| | Wife | Husband | Wife | Husband | Wife | Husband |
|---|---|---|---|---|---|---|
| AGE | | | | | | |
| Under 30 | 78.3 | 82.4 | 21.7 | 17.6 | 0.0 | 0.0 |
| 30-39 | 79.4 | 81.9 | 20.6 | 18.1 | 0.0 | 0.0 |
| 40+ | 79.8 | 82.5 | 20.2 | 17.5 | 0.0 | 0.0 |
| RESIDENCE | | | | | | |
| Urban | 84.1 | 87.3 | 15.9 | 12.7 | 0.0 | 0.0 |
| Rural | 71.0 | 74.2 | 29.0 | 25.8 | 0.0 | 0.0 |
| LEVEL OF EDUCATION | | | | | | |
| No education | 78.2 | 67.5 | 21.8 | 32.5 | 0.0 | 0.0 |
| Elementary | 77.9 | 77.6 | 22.1 | 22.4 | 0.0 | 0.0 |
| Sec/tec/trg. college | 82.2 | 86.4 | 17.8 | 13.6 | 0.0 | 0.0 |
| Higher | 85.3 | 88.2 | 14.7 | 11.8 | 0.0 | 0.0 |
| OCCUPATION | | | | | | |
| Professional | 90.1 | 86.9 | 9.9 | 13.1 | 0.0 | 0.0 |
| Clerical | 83.6 | 81.3 | 16.4 | 18.8 | 0.0 | 0.0 |
| Sales | 76.8 | 85.7 | 23.2 | 14.3 | 0.0 | 0.0 |
| Service/transport | 87.2 | 86.6 | 12.8 | 13.4 | 0.0 | 0.0 |
| Farmer/fisherman | 76.9 | 65.7 | 23.1 | 34.3 | 0.0 | 0.0 |
| Craftsman | 80.5 | 79.1 | 19.5 | 20.9 | 0.0 | 0.0 |
| RELIGION | | | | | | |
| Catholic | 74.7 | 85.2 | 25.3 | 14.8 | 0.0 | 0.0 |
| Protestant | 81.0 | 82.1 | 19.0 | 17.9 | 0.0 | 0.0 |
| Muslim | 74.4 | 78.6 | 25.6 | 21.4 | 0.0 | 0.0 |
| Traditionalist | 55.6 | 63.6 | 44.4 | 36.4 | 0.0 | 0.0 |
| Other religion | 78.3 | 85.0 | 21.7 | 15.0 | 0.0 | 0.0 |
| CHOICE OF PARTNER | | | | | | |
| Entirely by me | 80.9 | 82.4 | 19.1 | 17.6 | 0.0 | 0.0 |
| Help/consent of family | 72.2 | 81.9 | 27.8 | 18.1 | 0.0 | 0.0 |
| Arranged by family | 74.1 | 68.6 | 25.9 | 31.3 | 0.0 | 0.0 |
| TYPE OF MARRIAGE | | | | | | |
| Customary | 76.3 | 80.4 | 23.7 | 19.6 | 0.0 | 0.0 |
| Ordinance/Church | 81.8 | 82.7 | 18.2 | 17.3 | 0.0 | 0.0 |
| Consensual | 91.6 | 94.1 | 8.4 | 5.9 | 0.0 | 0.0 |
| Islamic | 64.0 | 68.2 | 36.0 | 31.8 | 0.0 | 0.0 |
| FORM OF MARRIAGE | | | | | | |
| Monogamous couple | 79.8 | 82.7 | 20.2 | 17.3 | 0.0 | 0.0 |
| Polygynous husband | – | 78.4 | – | 21.6 | – | 0.0 |
| 1st polygynous wife | 70.2 | – | 29.8 | – | 0.0 | – |
| 2nd+ polygynous wife | 73.3 | – | 26.7 | – | 0.0 | – |
| TOTAL | 78.9 | 82.1 | 21.1 | 17.9 | 0.0 | 0.0 |
| NUMBER | [711] | [739] | [190] | [161] | [0] | [0] |

urban residents agreed while only 74 percent agreed in the rural areas. It is possible that this trend may be due to more exposure of urban dwellers to divergent views on marriage, thus making them more "liberal" on women's rights than rural residents.

The wives' and husbands' responses by level of education shows that, generally, the higher the level of education, the higher the proportion of both wives and husbands that agreed that wives have the right to refuse sexual advances of their partners. This should be expected since with higher levels of education, the individual is expected to be more open-minded and objective in her/his analysis and judgement of issues. It is also worth noting that higher proportions of educated husbands accepted the wives' rights to refuse sexual advances than equally educated wives.

The pattern exhibited by occupational groups with respect to the issue of the right to refuse sexual advances by wives is quite interesting. While as much as between 87-90 percent of professional couples realized that wives have the right to refuse their husbands' sexual advances, only about 66 percent of husbands engaged in farming/fishing agreed to a wife's right to refuse sex. This could be explained by the relatively low level of education amongst this employment category, as such they are attached to traditional norms and values of the wife being virtually "owned" by the husband.

Christian couples had higher proportions of agreement on the rights of wives to reject their husbands' sexual advances. This may be due to their comparatively more relaxed views toward relationships generally compared to Traditionalists. Not surprisingly, only about half of wives with Traditional religions and 64 percent of husbands with similar religions agreed to the wife's right to refuse sex from the husband. Similarly, fewer couples married under Islamic law felt that wives do have the right to refuse to have sex with husbands than their counterparts who married under the Ordinance/Church or in consensual unions. Also, couples who chose their partners entirely by themselves, and monogamous couples, were more likely to accept wives' right to refuse sex with their husbands than couples whose family had been involved in their marriages, and those in polygynous relationships.

## Husbands' Right to Practice Polygyny

The data from Figure 8.1 indicate that the majority of couples, especially wives, in the GFAMS believe that the husband should not have the right to marry more than one wife. However, while 72 percent of wives disagreed with the right for men to have additional wives, only 56 percent of husbands objected. Table 8.3 presents the reasons in favor of or against the continued practice of polygyny.

**Table 8.3**  Reasons Why Husbands Have the Right (or Not) to Practice Polygyny, According to Residence, GFAMS, 1992-93

| REASON *FOR* HUSBAND'S RIGHT TO POLYGYNY | Urban | | Rural | |
|---|---|---|---|---|
| | Wife | Husband | Wife | Husband |
| If he can afford | 53.0 | 53.2 | 47.8 | 42.1 |
| It is customary | 19.0 | 12.3 | 27.7 | 8.2 |
| Unsatisfactory performance of duties | 11.0 | 18.2 | 6.9 | 18.0 |
| Unsatisfactory sexual performance | 3.0 | 3.4 | 2.5 | 5.5 |
| Wife's infertility | 3.0 | 3.4 | 3.1 | 7.7 |
| Other reasons | 11.0 | 9.4 | 11.9 | 18.6 |
| TOTAL | 100.0 | 100.0 | 100.0 | 100.0 |
| NUMBER | [100] | [203] | [159] | [183] |
| REASON *AGAINST* HUSBAND'S RIGHT TO POLYGYNY | | | | |
| Brings economic hardship | 30.2 | 40.8 | 34.7 | 31.7 |
| Brings conflict/quarrel | 43.7 | 29.3 | 31.6 | 29.9 |
| Spreads STDs | 10.4 | 8.2 | 1.1 | 3.0 |
| Against religion | 8.4 | 10.4 | 19.5 | 21.0 |
| It's cheating/adultery | 1.3 | 1.4 | 2.6 | 2.4 |
| Other reasons | 6.0 | 9.9 | 10.5 | 12.0 |
| TOTAL | 100.0 | 100.0 | 100.0 | 100.0 |
| NUMBER | [453] | [355] | [190] | [167] |

Reasons in favor of the practice include: if he can afford it, a customary practice, when the wife does not perform her normal duties satisfactorily, when she is infertile, and when her sexual performance is unsatisfactory. The single most important reason given by majority of wives and husbands in both rural and urban areas was if the husband can afford it, he should be allowed to practice it. That is to say if the man can materially, psychologically and sexually satisfy his wives, he should be allowed to marry them.

Traditionally, a wife's infertility had been a reason for the acquisition of additional wives by the husband. However, in the sampled population the proportions agreeing to polygyny because of infertility were quite low, creating the impression that most couples may not see marriage merely as a vehicle for producing children. Nonetheless, twice as many rural husbands cited infertility as grounds for polygyny than their urban counterparts or wives. In other words, procreation is considered an important reason for marriage from the perspective of rural husbands. This might be a reflection of the labor resource argument for high fertility predominance in the rural environment.

For both urban and rural couples, the strongest reasons against polygyny were that the practice brings economic hardships and creates conflict and quarrels; reasons given by about two-thirds of all couples who were not in favor of polygyny. Given the rapid rise in the cost of raising a family in contemporary Ghana, it comes as no surprise that men and women alike will be concerned about the economic drain of polygyny and its potential conflicts over scarce resources. Additionally, the data show that couples, particularly urban residents, were against polygyny for fear of the spread of sexually transmitted diseases (STDs).

*Husbands' Right to Practice Polygyny by Background Characteristics*:

Table 8.4 presents couples' views on whether or not husbands have the right to practice polygyny according to selected background characteristics. Although the age of the wife did not make much difference in attitudes toward polygyny, it appears that the proportions of husbands accepting polygyny increase with age. This declining acceptance of polygyny among young men, partly confirms the data reported earlier in Table 3.4 which indicated that there were fewer younger couples actually practicing polygyny than older couples, although they may agree to the practice of acquiring "outside wives."

On the whole, higher proportions of both wives and husbands in urban areas

**Table 8.4** Percentage Distribution of Couples' Views on Husbands' Right to Practice Polygyny, According to Selected Background Characteristics, GFAMS, 1992/93

| | HUSBANDS HAVE THE RIGHT TO PRACTICE POLYGYNY | | | | | |
| | YES | | NO | | NOT AT ALL | |
| Background Characteristic | Wife | Husband | Wife | Husband | Wife | Husband |
|---|---|---|---|---|---|---|
| **AGE** | | | | | | |
| Under 30 | 28.5 | 39.4 | 71.5 | 60.6 | 0.0 | 0.0 |
| 30-39 | 27.7 | 43.9 | 72.0 | 56.1 | 0.3 | 0.0 |
| 40+ | 27.5 | 45.0 | 72.1 | 55.0 | 0.3 | 0.0 |
| **RESIDENCE** | | | | | | |
| Urban | 16.9 | 36.8 | 83.0 | 63.2 | 0.2 | 0.0 |
| Rural | 45.7 | 54.8 | 54.0 | 45.2 | 0.3 | 0.0 |
| **LEVEL OF EDUCATION** | | | | | | |
| No education | 47.9 | 74.3 | 52.1 | 25.7 | 0.0 | 0.0 |
| Elementary | 29.6 | 56.8 | 70.0 | 43.2 | 0.4 | 0.0 |
| Sec/tec/trg. college | 10.4 | 33.9 | 89.6 | 66.1 | 0.0 | 0.0 |
| Higher | 15.2 | 25.6 | 84.8 | 74.4 | 0.0 | 0.0 |
| **OCCUPATION** | | | | | | |
| Professional | 16.7 | 33.8 | 82.1 | 66.2 | 1.3 | 0.0 |
| Clerical | 10.9 | 27.1 | 89.1 | 72.9 | 0.0 | 0.0 |
| Sales | 28.0 | 22.9 | 71.4 | 77.1 | 0.5 | 0.0 |
| Service/transport | 10.9 | 49.2 | 89.1 | 50.8 | 0.0 | 0.0 |
| Farmer/fisherman | 23.1 | 51.5 | 76.9 | 48.5 | 0.0 | 0.0 |
| Craftsman | 15.6 | 46.0 | 84.4 | 54.0 | 0.0 | 0.0 |
| **RELIGION** | | | | | | |
| Catholic | 34.2 | 38.2 | 65.8 | 61.8 | 0.0 | 0.0 |
| Protestant | 23.1 | 40.5 | 76.8 | 59.5 | 0.2 | 0.0 |
| Muslim | 63.9 | 66.7 | 36.1 | 33.3 | 0.0 | 0.0 |
| Traditionalist | 62.5 | 81.8 | 37.5 | 18.2 | 0.0 | 0.0 |
| Other religion | 27.6 | 45.8 | 70.7 | 54.2 | 1.7 | 0.0 |
| **CHOICE OF PARTNER** | | | | | | |
| Entirely by me | 24.5 | 41.8 | 75.2 | 58.2 | 0.3 | 0.0 |
| Help/consent of family | 33.0 | 52.2 | 67.0 | 47.8 | 0.0 | 0.0 |
| Arranged by family | 59.3 | 25.0 | 40.7 | 75.0 | 0.0 | 0.0 |
| **TYPE OF MARRIAGE** | | | | | | |
| Customary | 31.1 | 48.2 | 68.8 | 51.8 | 0.2 | 0.0 |
| Ordinance/Church | 10.4 | 14.4 | 89.6 | 85.6 | 0.0 | 0.0 |
| Consensual | 23.3 | 44.4 | 75.9 | 55.6 | 0.9 | 0.0 |
| Islamic | 69.6 | 95.5 | 30.4 | 4.5 | 0.0 | 0.0 |
| **FORM OF MARRIAGE** | | | | | | |
| Monogamous couple | 24.6 | 38.7 | 75.2 | 61.3 | 0.3 | 0.0 |
| Polygynous husband | – | 83.5 | – | 16.5 | – | 0.0 |
| 1st polygynous wife | 50.0 | – | 50.0 | – | 0.0 | – |
| 2nd+ polygynous wife | 57.1 | – | 42.9 | – | 0.0 | – |
| | | | | | | |
| TOTAL | 28.1 | 43.8 | 71.7 | 56.2 | 0.2 | 0.0 |
| NUMBER | [249] | [389] | [635] | [500] | [2] | [0] |

disagreed with the issue of the husband's right to practice polygyny, even though the proportions were higher for wives than husbands. While as many as 83 percent of wives in urban areas disagreed with polygyny, only 54 percent of wives in rural areas did. With respect to husbands, over 63 percent of urban residents were not in favor of the practice of polygyny compared to only 45 percent of their rural counterparts. As has been discussed before, the relatively lower proportions in rural areas may be more due to the effects of the dominant influence of "traditional" norms and values than the effects of "modernization" and the economic conditions in urban areas.

There seems to be an inverse relationship between level of education and proportion of both wives and husbands accepting men's right to practice polygyny. The higher the level of education of the wife or husband, the lower the proportion which agreed to the practice of polygyny. It is also noteworthy that comparatively lower proportions of wives than husbands agreed to polygyny at every level of education. Although higher education is generally associated with more modern and western values which include monogamy, it is probable that perhaps, due to the length of time it takes to acquire higher education, some highly educated women may prefer to be in polygynous unions than no marriage at all in a society that puts high premium on being married. This reasoning might explain why 15 percent of wives and 26 percent of husbands with higher education affirmed the right of men to practice polygyny.

As should be expected, the highest proportions of both wives and husbands agreeing to the existence of husbands' rights to practice polygyny were Muslims and Traditionalists. This is because both of these religious groups allow for the practice of polygyny in lieu of divorce and remarriage. While about two-thirds of couples affiliated with Traditional African religions and Islam agreed to the husband's right to have multiple wives, only between 23 to 40 percent of Christian couples agreed. The findings on the impact of religion on the acceptance of polygyny are confirmed by the respondent's type of marriage. As should be expected, almost 70 percent of

Muslim wives agreed that their husbands have the right to practice polygyny and virtually all Muslim husbands (96 percent) agreed. On the contrary, almost 90 percent of wives and husbands married under the Ordinance/Church disagreed to a man's right to have additional wives since the Ordinance as well as the Churches frown upon the practice.

It is obvious that those in polygynous union should be more sympathetic to the existence of rights for husbands to practice polygyny than monogamous couples. While only 39 percent of monogamous men agreed to the practice of polygyny, over twice as many polygynous men (84 percent) agreed. Similarly, while only a quarter of monogamous women agreed with the issue, over one-half of their polygynous counterparts did agree to the practice. What is also interesting is that slightly more second or lower ranked wives agreed to polygyny than first ranked wives. Since the marriages of first ranked wives might have started as monogamous, they may be less tolerant of the practice than higher order wives who may have enthusiastically just entered into their new relationships.

## Husbands' Right to Have Extra-Marital Affairs

As illustrated in Figure 8.1, couples in the GFAMS generally disagreed with the idea that husbands should have the right to have sexual relations outside of their marriage although more wives than husbands were vehemently opposed to the idea. Reasons for and against husbands' rights to extra-marital affairs are presented in Table 8.5. While the single most important reason given by urban wives and rural husbands for their acceptance of husbands' extra-marital affairs was affordability, more urban husbands mentioned wife's poor sexual performance. Among rural wives, while about 45 percent cited customary practices for accepting their husband's extra-marital affairs, only 14 percent of their urban counterparts saw it in that perspective. Similarly, higher proportions of rural husbands than urban husbands cited customary practice for accepting men's extra-marital affairs.

**Table 8.5**    Reasons Why Husbands Have the Right (or Not) to Have Extra-Marital Affairs, According to Residence, GFAMS, 1992-93

| REASON *FOR* HUSBAND'S RIGHT TO EXTRA-MARITAL AFFAIRS | Urban | | Rural | |
|---|---|---|---|---|
| | Wife | Husband | Wife | Husband |
| If he can afford | 29.8 | 15.1 | 21.8 | 23.5 |
| Unsatisfactory sexual performance | 26.3 | 22.4 | 11.8 | 18.3 |
| Unsatisfactory performance of duties | 21.1 | 17.1 | 5.9 | 18.3 |
| It is customary | 14.0 | 9.9 | 44.5 | 20.9 |
| Wife's infertility | 1.8 | 0.7 | 3.4 | 0.9 |
| Other reasons | 7.0 | 34.9 | 12.6 | 18.3 |
| | | | | |
| TOTAL | 100.0 | 100.0 | 100.0 | 100.0 |
| NUMBER | [57] | [152] | [119] | [115] |

| REASON *AGAINST* HUSBAND'S RIGHT TO EXTRA-MARITAL AFFAIRS | | | | |
|---|---|---|---|---|
| Brings economic hardship | 29.7 | 40.5 | 35.8 | 32.6 |
| Spreads STDs | 28.7 | 21.1 | 12.4 | 11.6 |
| Brings conflict/quarrel | 20.0 | 14.9 | 19.7 | 20.6 |
| Against religion | 7.2 | 7.0 | 16.5 | 17.6 |
| It's cheating/adultery | 4.5 | 5.0 | 2.8 | 4.7 |
| Other reasons | 9.9 | 11.4 | 12.8 | 12.9 |
| | | | | |
| TOTAL | 100.0 | 100.0 | 100.0 | 100.0 |
| NUMBER | [485] | [402] | [218] | [233] |

Also, urban wives were particularly concerned about their satisfactory performance of matrimonial duties, failure of which would give the husband a right to have sexual encounters outside marriage. This reason was given by 21 percent of wives in urban areas while only 6 percent of their rural counterparts found that as a good enough reason to accept a husband's affairs.

In both rural and urban areas, a significant number of couples (30-40 percent) indicated that they were opposed to the husband's right to engage in extra-marital affairs because such acts would divert economic resources away from the family. This is not surprising since most "outside" wives expect full economic support to be provided by their lovers as has been discussed above (see, e.g., Vellenga, 1983; Karanja, 1994). In addition to the economic hardships that a husband's affairs may bring, couples indicated that they disapproved affairs outside of marriage for fear of the spread of sexually transmitted diseases (STDs), escalating conflict, and religious immorality. As many as 21-29 percent of urban couples and 12-13 percent of their rural counterparts expressed concern about the health risks, while between 15-20 percent of all couples mentioned the potential for conflict that a husband's affairs would bring in their marital relationships.

### Husbands' Right to Have Extra-Marital Affairs by Background Characteristics

Respondents' opinions were further sought on the husband's right to have extra-marital affairs by selected background characteristics, the results of which are presented in Table 8.6. Generally, wives in rural areas compared to urban areas seemed to be more receptive to the idea that their husbands have the right to have affairs. While only 9 percent of urban wives agreed with the view, about four times as many rural wives (36 percent) did agree to the practice. Similarly, significantly more urban wives (38 percent) disagreed strongly to husbands' extra-marital affairs than their rural counterparts of whom only 19 percent vehemently opposed. This huge urban-rural difference might be explained by the fact that most rural wives' accept the husbands' engagement in affairs outside of marriage bonds as customary practice. For husbands, however, there were not much rural-urban differences in the proportions disagreeing; indeed, regardless of residence, around 50 percent of husbands disagreed to husbands' extra-marital affairs, and under 20 percent strongly opposed the practice.

The general picture shown by the data is that, the higher the level of education the lower the tendency to agree that husbands have the right to indulge in extra-marital affairs. However, the discrepancy between the levels of education is greater for wives than husbands. For instance, while only 3 percent of wives with higher education agreed to husbands' right to engage in extra-marital affairs, the proportion was 32 percent for wives without education. But for husbands, while about 22 percent of those with higher education felt men have the right to indulge in affairs outside of marriage, 32 percent of those without education also thought so.

**Table 8.6** Percentage Distribution of Couples' Views on Husbands' Right to Have Extra-Marital Affairs, According to Selected Background Characteristics, GFAMS, 1992/93

| | HUSBANDS HAVE THE RIGHT TO HAVE EXTRA-MARITAL AFFAIRS | | | | | |
| --- | --- | --- | --- | --- | --- | --- |
| | YES | | NO | | NOT AT ALL | |
| Background Characteristic | Wife | Husband | Wife | Husband | Wife | Husband |
| RESIDENCE | | | | | | |
| Urban | 9.0 | 28.7 | 53.3 | 54.4 | 37.7 | 16.9 |
| Rural | 35.6 | 31.6 | 45.0 | 50.0 | 19.3 | 18.4 |
| LEVEL OF EDUCATION | | | | | | |
| No education | 31.6 | 32.4 | 43.4 | 40.5 | 25.0 | 27.0 |
| Elementary | 21.4 | 36.6 | 48.2 | 48.5 | 30.3 | 14.9 |
| Sec/tec/trg. college | 6.4 | 26.6 | 58.4 | 55.4 | 35.3 | 19.0 |
| Higher | 3.0 | 21.5 | 57.6 | 60.8 | 39.4 | 17.7 |
| OCCUPATION | | | | | | |
| Professional | 7.8 | 22.0 | 54.5 | 57.5 | 37.7 | 20.6 |
| Clerical | 7.3 | 26.0 | 58.2 | 61.5 | 34.5 | 12.5 |
| Sales | 18.8 | 30.3 | 54.5 | 63.6 | 26.7 | 6.1 |
| Service/transport | 6.5 | 34.7 | 45.7 | 44.9 | 47.8 | 20.3 |
| Farmer/fisherman | 30.8 | 18.2 | 61.5 | 54.5 | 7.7 | 27.3 |
| Craftsman | 7.5 | 33.9 | 62.3 | 47.6 | 30.2 | 18.5 |
| RELIGION | | | | | | |
| Catholic | 30.0 | 25.0 | 46.7 | 58.5 | 23.3 | 16.5 |
| Protestant | 16.1 | 32.4 | 50.1 | 50.7 | 33.8 | 16.8 |
| Muslim | 13.9 | 17.9 | 58.3 | 61.5 | 27.8 | 20.5 |
| Traditionalist | 37.5 | 50.0 | 50.0 | 36.4 | 12.5 | 13.6 |
| Other religion | 19.6 | 22.0 | 57.1 | 52.5 | 23.2 | 25.4 |
| CHOICE OF PARTNER | | | | | | |
| Entirely by me | 14.4 | 29.6 | 50.3 | 51.7 | 35.4 | 18.6 |
| Help/consent of family | 28.5 | 32.8 | 51.8 | 55.9 | 19.7 | 11.3 |
| Arranged by family | 29.6 | 6.7 | 40.7 | 66.7 | 29.6 | 26.7 |
| TYPE OF MARRIAGE | | | | | | |
| Customary | 23.0 | 32.8 | 50.0 | 51.8 | 27.0 | 15.4 |
| Ordinance/Church | 10.4 | 11.6 | 54.5 | 66.7 | 35.1 | 21.7 |
| Consensual | 11.4 | 39.8 | 42.1 | 37.8 | 46.5 | 22.4 |
| Islamic | 8.3 | 15.0 | 66.7 | 55.0 | 25.0 | 30.0 |
| FORM OF MARRIAGE | | | | | | |
| Monogamous couple | 16.8 | 28.5 | 51.6 | 53.8 | 31.6 | 17.6 |
| Polygynous husband | – | 39.4 | – | 43.6 | – | 17.0 |
| 1st polygynous wife | 37.8 | – | 31.1 | – | 31.1 | – |
| 2nd+ polygynous wife | 34.5 | – | 46.6 | – | 19.0 | – |
| CO-RESIDENCE | | | | | | |
| Yes | 17.6 | 29.8 | 50.3 | 52.8 | 31.5 | 17.4 |
| No | 34.1 | 29.3 | 44.3 | 52.5 | 21.6 | 18.2 |
| | | | | | | |
| TOTAL | 19.3 | 29.8 | 50.1 | 52.7 | 30.6 | 17.5 |
| NUMBER | [166] | [263] | [432] | [465] | [264] | [154] |

In terms of occupational differences, while less than 10 percent of professional women and those who work in the service and transportation sector agreed to husbands' affairs, as many as one-third of women in the farming/fishing business agreed. With regard to the religious differences, the data show that although in general less than half of all couples agreed to a husband's right to have extra-marital affairs, more couples who adhere to Traditional religion agreed than those in any other religion. But an intriguing finding was that although Muslims and Traditionalists both permit plural marriages, it appears that opposition to husband's extra-marital affairs was stronger among adherents of the former compared to the latter. For instance, while between 38-50 percent of Traditionalists said that husbands could indulge in extra-marital affairs, only between 14-18 percent of Muslim couples agreed. Similarly, Muslim couples were among those who saw no justification for sexual relationship outside marriage. This may be explained by the fact that the acceptance of plural marriages in the Muslim faith does not necessarily give the husband a license for promiscuous behavior.

Nevertheless, the difference in the attitudes of monogamous and polygynous couples toward husbands' right to extra-marital affairs also confirms our expectations. Overall, couples in polygynous relationships tend to be more sympathetic to the practice than their counterparts in monogamous marriages. While only about 17 percent of wives in monogamous marriages said that their husbands have the right, over twice as many polygynous wives (regardless of rank) said so. Similarly, fewer monogamous husbands than their counterparts with multiple wives agreed to husbands' rights to have sexual encounters outside marriage bonds. Perhaps, polygynous wives were less critical of men's sexual affairs outside marriage because polygynous relations often begin as extra-marital affairs and that these people now legally married, at one time or the other, were parties to such relationships.

The data also indicate that while the magnitude of wives' opposition to extra-marital affairs depended on co-residential status, husbands' views did not appear to be influenced by the living arrangement. Thus, whereas only about 18 percent of wives living in the same house as their spouse agreed to husbands' involvement in extra-marital affairs, 34 percent of their counterparts living apart from their spouses said so. Most likely, not living together made some of these women quite "liberal" in their ideas about husbands' sexual rights.

### Wives' Right to Have Extra-Marital Affairs

When discussing the rights of wives to have extra-marital affairs, the percentage distributions are quite revealing. The strong opposition of both women and men to wives' indulgence in sexual affairs outside of marriage is illustrated in Figure 8.1 above. Overall, an overwhelming majority of couples (about 96 percent) were opposed to the idea with over two-thirds adamantly opposing it. In other words, wives' right to extra-marital affairs is seriously frowned upon in the society by women and men alike. It is less agreeable to Ghanaians for wives to indulge in extra-marital affairs than husbands.

Table 8.7 outlines the reasons for and against wives' right to engage in extra-marital relationships. For the few couples who felt that the wife had that right the acceptable grounds included dissatisfaction with her husband's performance of his marital duties, his unsatisfactory sexual performance, and adultery on his part. Irrespective of residence, the majority of respondents gave a husband's unsatisfactory performance of his duties as the basis for a wife's right to extra-marital affairs. About two-thirds of urban wives as well as one-third of urban husbands and rural couples gave this reason as their basis for wives indulgence in affairs outside marriage. Also, between 14-18 percent of urban couples and slightly over 20 percent of rural couples felt that the wife had a right to engage in extra-marital affairs if the husband's sexual performance was unsatisfactory.

For the great majority of couples, however, a wife having an affair outside marriage was considered an act against custom and religion, disgraceful, disrespectful, and adulterous. Regardless of residence, around 40 percent of all couples felt that it was against custom and societal expectations to permit married women to engage in extra-marital affairs.

**Table 8.7**    Reasons Why Wives Have the Right (or Not) to Have Extra-Marital Affairs, According to Residence, GFAMS, 1992/93

| REASON FOR WIFE'S RIGHT TO EXTRA-MARITAL AFFAIRS | Urban | | Rural | |
|---|---|---|---|---|
| | Wife | Husband | Wife | Husband |
| Poor performance of duties | 62.9 | 38.2 | 34.8 | 31.6 |
| Poor sexual performance | 14.3 | 17.6 | 21.7 | 21.1 |
| Husband cheating/adultery | 5.7 | 29.4 | 21.7 | 10.5 |
| Other reasons | 17.1 | 14.7 | 21.7 | 36.8 |
| | | | | |
| TOTAL | 100.0 | 100.0 | 100.0 | 100.0 |
| NUMBER | [35] | [34] | [23] | [19] |

| REASON AGAINST WIFE'S RIGHT TO EXTRA-MARITAL AFFAIRS | | | | |
|---|---|---|---|---|
| Against custom/society | 35.7 | 40.2 | 37.8 | 44.0 |
| Against religion | 18.4 | 12.8 | 28.5 | 20.5 |
| It's cheating/adultery | 14.6 | 15.5 | 7.5 | 8.7 |
| Disgraceful/disrespectful | 13.2 | 9.8 | 14.4 | 15.7 |
| Spreads STDs | 6.0 | 5.4 | 1.5 | 1.5 |
| Other reasons | 12.1 | 16.4 | 10.2 | 9.6 |
| | | | | |
| TOTAL | 100.0 | 100.0 | 100.0 | 100.0 |
| NUMBER | [521] | [523] | [333] | [332] |

Furthermore, 18 percent of urban wives, 29 percent of rural ones, as well as 13 percent of urban husbands and 21 percent of the rural ones cited religion as a basis to oppose extra-marital affairs of wives. Also, the data show that more urban couples than rural couples were against wives having relationships outside marriage because they saw such acts as cheating and also that they are capable of spreading STDs. On the other hand, more rural couples than their urban counterparts found extra-marital affairs disgraceful and disrespectful on the part of wives who indulge in it.

*Wives' Right to Have Extra-Marital Affairs by Background Characteristics*

The strong opposition of the respondents in the GFAMS to the right of wives to engage in affairs outside of marriage is further confirmed in Table 8.8. Generally, the act was vehemently opposed by over two-thirds of both wives and husbands across almost all of the categories of the selected background variables such as residence, occupation, religion, choice of partner, marriage type, form of marriage, and co-residential status. However, in terms of the relationship between educational level and views on wives' extra-marital affairs, it appears that for both wives and husbands, the higher the level of education, the lower the proportion that approves of the act, indicating that the highly educated couples may be more moderate in their disapproval than their counterparts with no schooling.

Also, it is striking to note that although tiny proportions of respondents across the religious categories agreed to wives' indulgence in extra-marital affairs, no Muslim or Traditionalist wife agreed that they could engage in affairs outside of marriage. This observation is further confirmed by the fact that Muslim and Traditionalist couples registered some of the strongest opposition to wives' extra-marital affairs. For example, as high as 79 percent of Muslim wives did not see any circumstance under which wives' sexual affairs outside of marriage could be justified, compared to 63 percent of Catholic wives and 70 percent of Protestant wives. Similarly, higher proportions of Muslim husbands than husbands of any other religious group reported strong opposition to wives' right to have extra-marital affairs. As has been discussed earlier on in this chapter, although Muslims and Traditionalists are permitted to practice polygyny, their adherence to tradition and strong religious faith may motivate them to condemn sexual relationships outside of marriage for couples, particularly for wives who are supposed to occupy "submissive" positions under both of these religions.

On the whole, the findings from the GFAMS about attitudes of both women and men toward extra-marital affairs are quite revealing. While a significant majority

**Table 8.8** Percentage Distribution of Couples' Views on Wives' Right to Have Extra-Marital Affairs, According to Selected Background Characteristics, GFAMS, 1992/93

| Background Characteristic | WIVES HAVE THE RIGHT TO HAVE EXTRA-MARITAL AFFAIRS | | | | | |
| | YES | | NO | | NOT AT ALL | |
| | Wife | Husband | Wife | Husband | Wife | Husband |
|---|---|---|---|---|---|---|
| RESIDENCE | | | | | | |
| Urban | 4.4 | 3.2 | 25.0 | 29.0 | 70.5 | 67.9 |
| Rural | 4.3 | 4.0 | 30.5 | 31.0 | 65.2 | 64.9 |
| LEVEL OF EDUCATION | | | | | | |
| No education | 6.3 | 5.0 | 25.7 | 25.0 | 68.1 | 70.0 |
| Elementary | 4.4 | 2.7 | 25.8 | 30.1 | 69.8 | 67.3 |
| Sec/tec/trg. college | 2.0 | 3.8 | 28.6 | 28.6 | 69.4 | 67.6 |
| Higher | 2.9 | 3.8 | 44.1 | 32.7 | 52.9 | 63.5 |
| OCCUPATION | | | | | | |
| Professional | 2.5 | 3.8 | 27.5 | 34.3 | 70.0 | 62.0 |
| Clerical | 3.6 | 5.3 | 34.5 | 21.3 | 61.8 | 73.4 |
| Sales | 4.4 | 2.9 | 25.6 | 31.4 | 70.0 | 65.7 |
| Service/transport | 6.4 | 2.6 | 25.5 | 31.9 | 68.1 | 65.5 |
| Farmer/fisherman | 0.0 | 0.0 | 30.8 | 39.4 | 69.2 | 60.6 |
| Craftsman | 3.6 | 3.7 | 30.0 | 33.2 | 66.4 | 63.1 |
| RELIGION | | | | | | |
| Catholic | 4.4 | 4.8 | 32.3 | 31.5 | 63.3 | 63.6 |
| Protestant | 5.0 | 2.7 | 25.0 | 28.4 | 70.0 | 68.9 |
| Muslim | 0.0 | 4.8 | 21.1 | 19.0 | 78.9 | 76.2 |
| Traditionalist | 0.0 | 4.5 | 37.5 | 22.7 | 62.5 | 72.7 |
| Other religion | 1.7 | 5.2 | 34.5 | 34.5 | 63.8 | 60.3 |
| CHOICE OF PARTNER | | | | | | |
| Entirely by me | 4.8 | 3.5 | 26.4 | 29.7 | 68.7 | 66.8 |
| Help/consent of family | 3.0 | 4.3 | 29.5 | 31.4 | 67.5 | 64.3 |
| Arranged by family | 3.8 | 0.0 | 19.2 | 25.0 | 76.9 | 75.0 |
| TYPE OF MARRIAGE | | | | | | |
| Customary | 5.4 | 3.7 | 27.5 | 30.9 | 67.2 | 65.4 |
| Ordinance/Church | 2.3 | 2.9 | 33.1 | 30.1 | 64.7 | 66.9 |
| Consensual | 2.6 | 4.0 | 17.9 | 23.0 | 79.5 | 73.0 |
| Islamic | 0.0 | 0.0 | 28.0 | 22.7 | 72.0 | 77.3 |
| FORM OF MARRIAGE | | | | | | |
| Monogamous couple | 4.4 | 3.4 | 27.3 | 30.3 | 68.3 | 66.3 |
| Polygynous husband | – | 4.2 | – | 25.3 | – | 70.5 |
| 1st polygynous wife | 0.0 | – | 27.7 | – | 72.3 | – |
| 2nd+ polygynous wife | 6.9 | – | 24.1 | – | 69.0 | – |
| CO-RESIDENCE | | | | | | |
| Yes | 4.3 | 3.6 | 26.8 | 29.2 | 69.0 | 67.2 |
| No | 5.5 | 3.1 | 31.9 | 33.7 | 62.6 | 63.3 |
| | | | | | | |
| TOTAL | 4.4 | 3.5 | 27.2 | 29.8 | 68.5 | 66.7 |
| NUMBER | [39] | [31] | [242] | [263] | [610] | [589] |

of couples believe that husbands and wives do not have the right to have sexual affairs outside of marriage, their opposition was much stronger to the wife having an affair than the husband. This belief among others clearly signifies the presence of sexual double standards in a patriarchal society such as exists in Ghana, whereby men and women in the society are measured on the same issue by different and usually unequal yardsticks.

Since most Ghanaian wives relative to their husbands have fewer economic resources for their own survival and the well-being of their children, they are vulnerable to obeying the wishes of their men by exchanging sexual favors for economic benefits and status enhancement. Under such circumstances, women may be less likely to refuse sexual advances from their husbands or question their husbands' extra-marital affair for fear of being abandoned or ending up with co-wives. Indeed, as Lockwood (1995) points out, in many African societies, ideas about sexual behavior and about keeping a spouse happy all fall within the large context of marital and gender relations. Thus, both women and men alike are often socialized to accept such standards as values and traditional practices, and therefore are reluctant to re-examine and critique them.

## INTESTATE SECESSION

Among the common reasons why societies have historically defined the circles within which its members can marry are the wish to avoid incest, establish links to ensure security, widen sphere of influence and establish acceptable mode for the transfer of property (Goody, 1969). The transfer of property rights to surviving spouse(s) and children has also been a right within marriage that has not traditionally benefitted women, particularly those whose husbands die without leaving a legal document (e.g., a will) specifying disposal of self-acquired property.

Lineage relations through kinship and marriage (and in some cases, slavery) have been established to be compatible with the mode of production, and also to facilitate the transfer of property (Clark, 1994:124). In Ghana, customary and state laws govern both testate and intestate successions. For each ethnic group, Customary law clearly defines the lines of succession, which can be altered only through a written or oral will. In theory, any person of sound mind can dispose of his/her self-acquired property in any manner deemed fit. However, the argument has been that it "was once an individual's self-acquired property of a remote ancestor which became vested in the wide family" (Ollennu & Woodman, 1985:35). Therefore, it is expected that any member of the family will add to the family property that he/she came to inherit.

While alive, an Akan father is expected to set up his children to succeed in life, either through gifts or by assisting them to acquire skills or their own property so that they will not inherit directly from him after his death. However, in principle, children and wives do not belong to the husband's family but to the wives' matrikin. Such arrangement gives women and their children the right to own land and inherit property only in the matrikinship group to which they belong (Ollennu, 1966; Manuh, 1997).

In the case of a male succession, an uterine brother of the deceased is the first in line to inherit the self-acquired property and any family property in the care of the deceased. In the absence of an uterine brother, the next person is a son of an uterine sister. The third preference is either an uterine sister or one of the sons of the deceased's mother's sisters. For a female succession, the first preference is the mother of the deceased, if still alive, followed by an uterine sister, and lastly the eldest daughter of the deceased. However, the mother or sister of the deceased may defer the succession to the daughter of the deceased if she is deemed old enough to take care of the mother's property (Awusabo-Asare, 1990).

To facilitate the transfer of property, one of the preferred forms of marriage among the Akan was cross-cousin marriage. That is, marriage to the son or daughter of one's mother's brother or one's father's sister. Through that marriage, it is expected that part of the self-acquired property of the deceased, inherited by either the brother or the sister's son, would also be at the disposal of the children of the deceased (Bittles, 1994; Awusabo-Asare, 1990).

Inheritance practices of the patrilineal societies (e.g., the Ewe) are in sharp contrast to the practices among the Akan. Since the family of inheritance is made up of the offspring of brothers from the same patriarch among the Ewes, the first preference of succession in the case of a male is the paternal brother of the deceased followed by the eldest son. For a female, the first preference is the sister followed by the daughter.

In both the matrilineal and patrilineal form of inheritance, Customary law differentiates between succession to self-acquired property and an office held by the deceased, if (s)he held one. If there are arrangements for the succession to the office of the deceased among the group, the person inheriting the self-acquired property of may not necessarily inherit the office of the deceased.[5]

**Evolution of Ghana's Intestate Succession Law**

In general, governments make or promulgate laws in order to streamline aspects of life which may not be compatible with the aspirations of a modern state. Over the last century, the inheritance systems in Ghana have undergone significant transformations, just like many other socio-cultural practices. This is partly due to colonialism and associated religion and way of life, the expansion of the global economy absorbing Ghana into the world capitalist system, and the internal dynamics of socio-cultural changes in the country (Dickson, 1969; Clark, 1994).

Official laws on marriage and inheritance in Ghana date back to 1884 with the passing of the Ordinance and Islamic Marriages Acts by the colonial administration which provided alternatives to Customary transfer of property. The Marriage Ordinance of 1884 vested one-third of self-acquired intestate property in the surviving spouse and the rest in the children, if any. The law also made monogamy the only form of legal marriage. When the changes in the devolution of self-acquired property

---

[5]One of the arrangements for inheritance of an office is rotation among qualified members of the extended family.

and marriage system became known, Ghanaians protested (Ollennu, 1966). In 1909, the sections of the law on the devolution of intestate self-acquired property and monogamy were amended. The revised versions allocated a third of self-acquired property to the lineage and permitted polygyny to be practiced under the Customary and Islamic Marriage Laws (Ollennu, 1966; Luckham, 1976; Vellenga, 1983).

With the status of all wives and children to inherit property still not clearly defined under the existing laws, the post-independence government of Ghana established the Ollenu Commission on Inheritance in 1959 to study the issues and make recommendations to the government (Luckham, 1976; Manuh, 1997). Although the Ollenu Commission's recommendations were never implemented due to political instability and opposition from the traditional society, review of the country's inheritance laws continued with the Law Reform Commission whose reports of 1969, 1975, and 1977 formed the basis for the new Intestate Succession Law (Manuh, 1997).

The laws on marriage and inheritance were passed in 1985 by the government of the Provisional National Defence Council (PNDC) as:

- the administration of intestate self-acquired property (PNDCL 111);
- registration of all Customary marriages contracted in the country (PNDCL 112);
- the registration of communal (Stool/Skin,[6] family and kin) property in the custody of individuals (PNDCL 113 and 114).

It had become necessary to make changes in the system of inheritance for several reasons. First, modernization generally has eroded some of the props for the customary system of inheritance. For instance, cross-cousin marriage is not as common as it used to be. Second, inter-marriage between the matrilineal Akan and the other patrilineal groups has created some difficult situations: where a matrilineal Akan female marries a man from any of the patrilineal groups, the children have

---

[6]Stools and Skins are symbols of authority in Southern Ghana (Forest zone) and Northern Ghana (Savannah zone), respectively.

inheritance from both the father's patriclan and the mother's matriclan. On the other hand, children from a marriage between an Akan male and a female from one of the patriclans have no automatic inheritance. Third, there have been situations whereby widows have been left destitute as a result of the strict application of the Customary law of succession (Kuenyehia, 1993; Vellenga, 1983).

Thus, in recognition of the fact that the existing laws were unjust to surviving dependents, the new laws represent attempts to influence the direction of the transfer of self-acquired property in favor of a surviving spouse to encourage conjugal joint investment (Kludze, 1983). Thus, citing the growing importance of the nuclear family over the extended family in the country, and the tension between the two systems over transfer of property upon the intestate death of a spouse, PNDCL 111 gives a larger portion of the estate of the deceased to the surviving spouse and children (Republic of Ghana [ROG] Gazette, 1985; Awusabo-Asare, 1990). This law not only compensates the surviving spouse's services to the deceased, but also acknowledges that the surviving spouse is the best person to look after the children.

### Diffusion of the Intestate Succession Law

A decade after the promulgation of the Intestate Succession Law, it should be possible to assess people's knowledge and attitudes about the law. In the GFAMS, respondents were asked to state their knowledge of PNDCL 111, if they were aware of attempts to implement the law, and reactions to the content of the law. Our aim was to examine the diffusion of information about the law and some of the barriers (constraints and resistance) to the implementation of the tenets of the law.

The results of the GFAMS indicate that regardless of background characteristics, a majority of wives and husbands overwhelmingly felt that PNDCL 111 is good and acceptable as indicated in Table 8.9. But some disparities with regard to education, type and form of marriage, and in-laws' influence are worth noting. For example, the proportions of couples who believed that the law provides security to

**Table 8.9** Percentage Distribution of Couples' Views About Intestate Succession Law (PNDCL 111), According to Selected Background Characteristics, GFAMS, 1992/93

| Background Characteristic | VIEWS ABOUT PNDCL 111 | | | | | | | | | | | |
|---|---|---|---|---|---|---|---|---|---|---|---|---|
| | Good & Acceptable | | Security for Women & Children | | Peace for Family & Spouse | | Other Views | | Total | | Number | |
| | Wife | Hus. | Wife | Hus. | Wife | Hus. | Wife | Hus. | Wife | Hus. | Wife | Hus. |
| **AGE** | | | | | | | | | | | | |
| Under 30 | 82.1 | 90.7 | 8.9 | 5.3 | 1.6 | 1.3 | 7.4 | 2.7 | 100.0 | 100.0 | 190 | 75 |
| 30-39 | 82.5 | 81.3 | 9.9 | 9.2 | 3.3 | 3.1 | 4.2 | 6.5 | 100.0 | 100.0 | 212 | 294 |
| 40+ | 77.6 | 81.5 | 11.2 | 9.8 | 3.4 | 1.8 | 7.8 | 6.9 | 100.0 | 100.0 | 116 | 275 |
| **RESIDENCE** | | | | | | | | | | | | |
| Urban | 70.6 | 74.4 | 17.7 | 14.2 | 4.5 | 3.6 | 7.2 | 7.8 | 100.0 | 100.0 | 265 | 359 |
| Rural | 92.5 | 92.7 | 1.6 | 2.4 | 0.8 | 0.7 | 5.1 | 4.2 | 100.0 | 100.0 | 254 | 287 |
| **LEVEL OF EDUCATION** | | | | | | | | | | | | |
| No education | 88.2 | 92.3 | 2.6 | 7.7 | 1.3 | 0.0 | 7.9 | 0.0 | 100.0 | 100.0 | 76 | 26 |
| Elementary | 83.5 | 85.8 | 8.1 | 7.5 | 2.1 | 0.4 | 6.3 | 6.3 | 100.0 | 100.0 | 284 | 240 |
| Sec/tec/trg.college | 72.8 | 82.9 | 16.7 | 6.1 | 5.3 | 2.6 | 5.3 | 8.3 | 100.0 | 100.0 | 114 | 228 |
| Higher | 76.7 | 73.3 | 16.7 | 16.3 | 3.3 | 5.9 | 3.3 | 4.4 | 100.0 | 100.0 | 30 | 135 |
| **OCCUPATION** | | | | | | | | | | | | |
| Professional | 74.1 | 83.9 | 17.2 | 8.9 | 3.4 | 2.8 | 5.2 | 4.4 | 100.0 | 100.0 | 58 | 180 |
| Clerical | 70.7 | 74.0 | 17.1 | 17.8 | 4.9 | 2.7 | 7.3 | 5.5 | 100.0 | 100.0 | 41 | 73 |
| Sales | 64.9 | 73.9 | 24.7 | 8.7 | 5.2 | 8.7 | 5.2 | 8.7 | 100.0 | 100.0 | 77 | 23 |
| Service/transport | 79.2 | 81.7 | 12.5 | 8.5 | 8.3 | 1.2 | 0.0 | 8.5 | 100.0 | 100.0 | 24 | 82 |
| Farmer/fisherman | ** | 76.9 | ** | 19.2 | ** | 0.0 | ** | 3.8 | 100.0 | 100.0 | ** | 26 |
| Craftsman | 72.7 | 78.4 | 3.6 | 10.8 | 3.6 | 3.6 | 20.0 | 7.2 | 100.0 | 100.0 | 55 | 111 |
| **RELIGION** | | | | | | | | | | | | |
| Catholic | 82.1 | 85.1 | 10.5 | 8.3 | 2.1 | 0.8 | 5.3 | 5.8 | 100.0 | 100.0 | 95 | 121 |
| Protestant | 83.3 | 83.6 | 10.1 | 9.3 | 2.3 | 2.9 | 4.3 | 4.2 | 100.0 | 100.0 | 348 | 409 |
| Muslim | 90.0 | 82.8 | 5.0 | 6.9 | 0.0 | 0.0 | 5.0 | 10.3 | 100.0 | 100.0 | 20 | 29 |
| Traditionalist | ** | 85.7 | ** | 7.1 | ** | 0.0 | ** | 7.1 | 100.0 | 100.0 | ** | 14 |
| Other religion | 48.6 | 60.5 | 13.5 | 11.6 | 8.1 | 2.3 | 29.7 | 25.6 | 100.0 | 100.0 | 37 | 43 |

**Table 8.9 cont'd**    Percentage Distribution of Couples' Views About Intestate Succession Law (PNDCL 111), According to Selected Background Characteristics, GFAMS, 1992/93

| Background Characteristic | VIEWS ABOUT PNDCL 111 | | | | | | | | | | | |
| --- | --- | --- | --- | --- | --- | --- | --- | --- | --- | --- | --- | --- |
| | Good & Acceptable | | Security for Women & Children | | Peace for Family & Spouse | | Other Views | | Total | | Number | |
| | Wife | Hus. | Wife | Hus. | Wife | Hus. | Wife | Hus. | Wife | Hus. | Wife | Hus. |
| CHOICE OF PARTNER | | | | | | | | | | | | |
| Entirely by me | 81.7 | 82.8 | 10.8 | 9.0 | 2.3 | 2.2 | 5.2 | 6.0 | 100.0 | 100.0 | 344 | 465 |
| Help/consent of family | 79.5 | 81.8 | 7.5 | 9.1 | 3.4 | 1.9 | 9.6 | 7.1 | 100.0 | 100.0 | 146 | 154 |
| Arranged by family | 86.7 | 90.9 | 13.3 | 0.0 | 0.0 | 0.0 | 0.0 | 9.1 | 100.0 | 100.0 | 15 | 11 |
| TYPE OF MARRIAGE | | | | | | | | | | | | |
| Customary | 83.5 | 83.5 | 8.5 | 8.3 | 2.2 | 2.5 | 5.8 | 5.8 | 100.0 | 100.0 | 364 | 448 |
| Ordinance/Church | 73.8 | 78.2 | 15.0 | 11.8 | 5.0 | 0.9 | 6.3 | 9.1 | 100.0 | 100.0 | 80 | 110 |
| Consensual | 75.4 | 84.9 | 11.5 | 8.2 | 3.3 | 4.1 | 9.8 | 2.7 | 100.0 | 100.0 | 61 | 73 |
| Islamic | 90.9 | 66.7 | 9.1 | 16.7 | 0.0 | 0.0 | 0.0 | 16.7 | 100.0 | 100.0 | 11 | 12 |
| FORM OF MARRIAGE | | | | | | | | | | | | |
| Monogamous couple | 82.4 | 83.1 | 9.5 | 9.1 | 2.6 | 1.7 | 5.5 | 6.1 | 100.0 | 100.0 | 454 | 573 |
| Polygynous husband | – | 75.8 | – | 9.1 | – | 7.6 | – | 7.6 | 100.0 | 100.0 | – | 66 |
| 1st polygynous wife | 72.0 | – | 8.0 | – | 4.0 | – | 16.0 | – | 100.0 | 100.0 | 25 | – |
| 2nd + polygynous wife | 72.7 | – | 18.2 | – | 3.0 | – | 6.1 | – | 100.0 | 100.0 | 33 | – |
| IN-LAW INFLUENCE ON PROPERTY ACQUISITION | | | | | | | | | | | | |
| Yes | 66.7 | 68.1 | 11.1 | 16.7 | 4.8 | 0.0 | 17.5 | 15.3 | 100.0 | 100.0 | 63 | 72 |
| No | 83.7 | 84.4 | 9.1 | 7.9 | 2.4 | 2.6 | 4.7 | 5.1 | 100.0 | 100.0 | 449 | 572 |
| TOTAL | 81.3 | 82.5 | 9.8 | 9.0 | 2.7 | 2.3 | 6.2 | 6.2 | 100.0 | 100.0 | 519 | 646 |

Note: ** fewer than 10 cases     – not applicable

women and children increased with increasing education. This pattern is clearer for wives in the sample than husbands.

Furthermore, couples (but wives in particular) were more likely to believe that the law provided women and children with security if they resided in the urban area, were formally-employed, and were second or lower order ranked in polygynous unions than if they lived in the rural area, were employed in the non-formal sectors of the economy, and were first ranked in polygynous relationships. Compared to couples who married under the Customary law, those who married under Ordinance, Church, or Islamic laws were more likely to view PNDCL 111 as good for women and children. Consistent with our expectations, both wives and husbands were more likely to believe that the law provides women and children with security if they perceive their in-laws to have influence on their acquisition of property than not.

As for the knowledge of PNDCL 111, the results presented in Figures 8.2a & 8.2b indicate that regardless of rural-urban residence, couples have varying interpretations of the law. In fact, of all couples who have heard about PNDCL 111, only about 20 percent had accurate knowledge about the law--which is that surviving spouse, children and family inherit from the deceased spouse. The most common misinterpretation of PNDCL 111 was the idea that the wife and children inherit the property when the husband dies, a view shared by a significant number of rural couples (72 percent) and about one-third of urban couples. Furthermore, about one-fifth of urban residents shared a misconception that PNDCL 111 was supposed to distribute inheritance between surviving spouse and children only, without any compensation for the extended family. Also, another one-fifth of urban residents confused PNDCL 111 with PNDCL 112 which called for the registration of all marriages legally contracted in the country under the existing marriage laws.

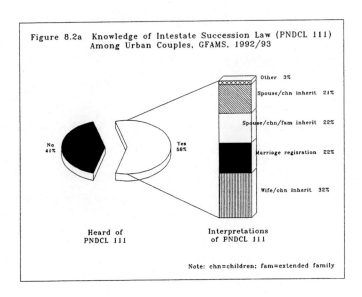

Figure 8.2a   Knowledge of Intestate Succession Law (PNDCL 111)
Among Urban Couples, GFAMS, 1992/93

Other  3%

Spouse/chn inherit  21%

Spouse/chn/fam inherit  22%

Marriage regisration  22%

Wife/chn inherit  32%

No
41%

Yes
59%

Heard of
PNDCL 111

Interpretations
of PNDCL 111

Note: chn=children; fam=extended family

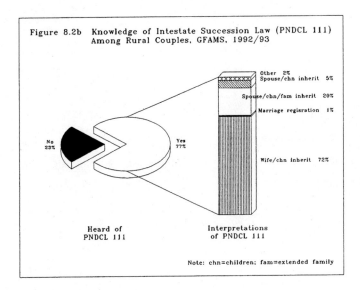

Figure 8.2b   Knowledge of Intestate Succession Law (PNDCL 111)
Among Rural Couples, GFAMS, 1992/93

Other  2%
Spouse/chn inherit  5%

Spouse/chn/fam inherit  20%

Marriage regisration  1%

Wife/chn inherit  72%

No
23%

Yes
77%

Heard of
PNDCL 111

Interpretations
of PNDCL 111

Note: chn=children; fam=extended family

The diverse ways that men and women in the GFAMS interpreted PNDCL 111 is confirmed by the almost even spread of the percentage distribution across all the categories of the selected background factors presented in Table 8.10. While a number of the background variables did not make much difference in terms of knowledge of PNDCL 111, the educational level of the respondent seems to have an effect on the correct interpretation of the law. Generally, the proportions of couples who knew about the law increased as educational attainment increased. For example, whereas 40 percent of women with higher education knew about the law, only 17 percent of women with elementary school education gave the correct interpretation. Similarly, 33 percent of men with higher education knew about the law compared to only 19 percent of their counterparts with elementary school education.

Couples who were married under the Ordinance/Church and Customary laws appeared to be well informed about the new inheritance law than those married under the Islamic law. While about a quarter of monogamous husbands were knowledgeable about the law, only 14 percent of husbands in polygynous relations were, even though a quarter of senior wives in polygynous relations were familiar with the terms of the inheritance law. And if couples perceived that their in-laws influenced them on acquisition of physical property, they were more likely to report familiarity with the inheritance law.

It is clear from the analysis above that while the Intestate Succession Law (PNDCL 111) enacted in Ghana in 1985 may be a relief for the surviving spouse and children as they are awarded the lion's share of the self-acquired property of the deceased, couples from the GFAMS sampled population seemed to be confused as to what the correct interpretation of the law was. As with the introduction of any new phenomenon, there is an implicit assumption that the new idea will diffuse through the society. However, about 10 years after the promulgation, this has not happened, as the results of our study indicate.

**Table 8.10** Percentage Distribution of Couples by Their Knowledge of Intestate Succession Law (PNDCL 111), According to Selected Background Characteristics, GFAMS, 1992/93

| Background | KNOWLEDGE OF PNDCL 111 | | | | | | | | | | | |
|---|---|---|---|---|---|---|---|---|---|---|---|---|
| | Wife/Chn & Family Inherit | | Only Wife & Chn Inherit | | Only Spouse & Chn Inherit | | Marriage Registration | | Total | | Number | |
| Characteristic | Wife | Hus. | Wife | Hus. | Wife | Hus. | Wife | Hus. | Wife | Hus. | Wife | Hus. |
| **AGE** | | | | | | | | | | | | |
| Under 30 | 21.2 | 16.7 | 53.4 | 59.0 | 11.6 | 9.0 | 13.8 | 15.4 | 100.0 | 100.0 | 189 | 78 |
| 30-39 | 16.5 | 24.7 | 59.2 | 50.7 | 12.6 | 10.4 | 11.7 | 14.2 | 100.0 | 100.0 | 206 | 288 |
| 40+ | 20.2 | 24.5 | 50.5 | 44.4 | 20.2 | 19.7 | 9.2 | 11.3 | 100.0 | 100.0 | 109 | 274 |
| **RESIDENCE** | | | | | | | | | | | | |
| Urban | 18.5 | 25.6 | 37.7 | 30.0 | 21.5 | 21.4 | 22.3 | 23.1 | 100.0 | 100.0 | 260 | 360 |
| Rural | 19.6 | 20.8 | 73.9 | 72.8 | 5.7 | 5.3 | 0.8 | 1.1 | 100.0 | 100.0 | 245 | 283 |
| **LEVEL OF EDUCATION** | | | | | | | | | | | | |
| No education | 18.7 | 21.7 | 70.7 | 78.3 | 4.0 | 0.0 | 6.7 | 0.0 | 100.0 | 100.0 | 75 | 23 |
| Elementary | 17.1 | 19.0 | 57.5 | 62.8 | 11.3 | 7.4 | 14.2 | 10.7 | 100.0 | 100.0 | 275 | 242 |
| Sec/tec/trg.college | 19.1 | 22.7 | 45.5 | 41.5 | 25.5 | 18.3 | 10.0 | 17.5 | 100.0 | 100.0 | 110 | 229 |
| Higher | 40.0 | 33.3 | 33.3 | 28.8 | 23.3 | 22.7 | 3.3 | 15.2 | 100.0 | 100.0 | 30 | 132 |
| **OCCUPATION** | | | | | | | | | | | | |
| Professional | 26.3 | 29.1 | 50.9 | 36.9 | 14.0 | 19.6 | 8.8 | 14.5 | 100.0 | 100.0 | 57 | 179 |
| Clerical | 23.1 | 22.9 | 28.2 | 37.1 | 30.8 | 15.7 | 17.9 | 24.3 | 100.0 | 100.0 | 39 | 70 |
| Sales | 20.3 | 29.2 | 53.2 | 45.8 | 10.1 | 20.8 | 16.5 | 4.2 | 100.0 | 100.0 | 79 | 24 |
| Service/transport | 21.7 | 15.7 | 30.4 | 45.8 | 26.1 | 16.9 | 21.7 | 21.7 | 100.0 | 100.0 | 23 | 83 |
| Farmer/fisherman | ** | 18.5 | ** | 66.7 | ** | 7.4 | ** | 7.4 | 100.0 | 100.0 | ** | 27 |
| Craftsman | 15.4 | 25.2 | 36.5 | 44.1 | 26.9 | 13.5 | 21.2 | 17.1 | 100.0 | 100.0 | 52 | 111 |
| **RELIGION** | | | | | | | | | | | | |
| Catholic | 11.1 | 22.3 | 68.9 | 52.9 | 11.1 | 18.2 | 8.9 | 6.6 | 100.0 | 100.0 | 90 | 121 |
| Protestant | 20.9 | 25.7 | 49.7 | 43.6 | 15.6 | 14.5 | 13.8 | 16.2 | 100.0 | 100.0 | 340 | 408 |
| Muslim | 31.6 | 20.7 | 47.4 | 65.5 | 10.5 | 6.9 | 10.5 | 6.9 | 100.0 | 100.0 | 19 | 29 |
| Traditionalist | ** | 23.1 | ** | 46.2 | ** | 7.7 | ** | 23.1 | 100.0 | 100.0 | ** | 13 |
| Other religion | 18.4 | 19.0 | 68.4 | 64.3 | 10.5 | 11.9 | 2.6 | 4.8 | 100.0 | 100.0 | 38 | 42 |

**Table 8.10 cont'd**   Percentage Distribution of Couples by Their Knowledge of Intestate Succession Law (PNDCL 111), According to Selected Background Characteristics, GFAMS, 1992/93

| | KNOWLEDGE OF PNDCL 111 | | | | | | | | | | | |
| Background Characteristic | Wife/Chn & Family Inherit | | Only Wife & Chn Inherit | | Only Spouse & Chn Inherit | | Marriage Registration | | Total | | Number | |
| | Wife | Hus. | Wife | Hus. | Wife | Hus. | Wife | Hus. | Wife | Hus. | Wife | Hus. |
| --- | --- | --- | --- | --- | --- | --- | --- | --- | --- | --- | --- | --- |
| **CHOICE OF PARTNER** | | | | | | | | | | | | |
| Entirely by me | 19.9 | 22.2 | 48.2 | 45.4 | 16.8 | 16.1 | 15.6 | 16.3 | 100.0 | 100.0 | 334 | 465 |
| Help/consent of family | 19.4 | 28.5 | 68.1 | 58.3 | 8.3 | 7.9 | 4.2 | 5.3 | 100.0 | 100.0 | 144 | 151 |
| Arranged by family | 0.0 | 27.3 | 86.7 | 45.5 | 0.0 | 18.2 | 13.3 | 9.1 | 100.0 | 100.0 | 15 | 11 |
| **TYPE OF MARRIAGE** | | | | | | | | | | | | |
| Customary | 20.4 | 21.1 | 56.4 | 51.2 | 11.5 | 12.4 | 11.7 | 15.3 | 100.0 | 100.0 | 358 | 445 |
| Ordinance/Church | 18.4 | 33.6 | 51.3 | 40.9 | 23.7 | 22.7 | 6.6 | 2.7 | 100.0 | 100.0 | 76 | 110 |
| Consensual | 13.8 | 24.7 | 50.0 | 41.1 | 15.5 | 15.1 | 20.7 | 19.2 | 100.0 | 100.0 | 58 | 73 |
| Islamic | 10.0 | 16.7 | 60.0 | 66.7 | 20.0 | 8.3 | 10.0 | 8.3 | 100.0 | 100.0 | 10 | 12 |
| **FORM OF MARRIAGE** | | | | | | | | | | | | |
| Monogamous couple | 19.7 | 24.9 | 53.6 | 46.6 | 14.9 | 15.4 | 11.8 | 13.1 | 100.0 | 100.0 | 442 | 571 |
| Polygynous husband | – | 13.8 | – | 64.6 | – | 6.2 | – | 15.4 | 100.0 | 100.0 | – | 65 |
| 1st polygynous wife | 25.0 | – | 58.3 | – | 4.2 | – | 12.5 | – | 100.0 | 100.0 | 24 | – |
| 2nd + polygynous wife | 6.3 | – | 75.0 | – | 6.3 | – | 12.5 | – | 100.0 | 100.0 | 32 | – |
| **IN-LAW INFLUENCE ON PROPERTY ACQUISITION** | | | | | | | | | | | | |
| Yes | 20.6 | 35.2 | 61.9 | 52.1 | 14.3 | 11.3 | 3.2 | 1.4 | 100.0 | 100.0 | 63 | 71 |
| No | 18.9 | 22.1 | 54.5 | 48.2 | 13.3 | 14.7 | 13.3 | 14.9 | 100.0 | 100.0 | 435 | 570 |
| **TOTAL** | 19.0 | 23.5 | 55.2 | 48.8 | 13.9 | 14.3 | 11.9 | 13.4 | 100.0 | 100.0 | 505 | 643 |

**Note:** ** fewer than 10 cases     – not applicable

Theoretically, the spread of information of this nature goes through a *diffusion* process (Knowles & Wareing, 1985). First described by Haggerstrand, a Swedish geographer, the diffusion of any new information or ideas is influenced by six elements. These are the *item* to be diffused, the *environment*, the *path, origin*, the *destination* and *time*. Generally, the diffusion of a new idea starts with a small group of people (*the innovators*) and gradually spreads through the population. After the innovators, the item spreads to a small group of people (*the early adopters*), followed by the *early majority*, and later the *late majority*. It is expected that there will be a small group of people (*the laggards*) who will resist the change (Knowles & Wareing, 1985:150). The speed with which any information spreads will depend upon the environment, the path, the origin and the destination as well as the barriers associated with the item.

In the case of the Intestate Succession Law, the item to be diffused runs counter to some deep-seated traditions, especially among the matrilineal Akan who considers wives and husbands as separate economic entities in marriage. The law transfers self-acquired property from the matriclan to wife and children (the conjugal family), who in the matrilineal system belong to a different matriclan. Succession is part of a wide range of socio-cultural norms and practices that govern the identification of a person with a group, as well as the ownership and the transfer of property.

To minimize the opposition to the law while increasing the rate of diffusion, there is the need for the government and other grassroots organizations working to improve the well-being of the Ghanaian family to publicize and explain the importance of the law to people over a long period. Widespread dissemination of information would not only legitimize the proper transfer of intestate property, but would also protect women and children from greedy members of the extended family.

# 9

## CONCLUSIONS

At the core of the processes of sustainable human development is the institution of the family. The family is generally acknowledged as the basic unit of society, and therefore what happens to it under conditions of rapid social and economic change should be of crucial concern to researchers and policy-makers. In spite of this universal recognition of the importance of the family, research on family structures and relation seems to have been neglected in demographic study of Africa compared to the emphasis given to research on fertility, mortality and migration in the last 2-3 decades. The situation now is contrary to that of the period prior to the 1970s when a number of studies were conducted on the demography of the African family. For instance, there was the African Family Studies Project directed from the Australian National University in the 1960s and the 1970s.

In the 1970s, the locus of demographic research shifted towards quantification, family planning and reducing population growth (see for instance, Agyei-Mensah, 1997; Bourgeois-Pichat, 1970). The publications of books such as the *The Time Bomb* by Ehrlich (1968) and *Limits to Growth* by Meadows et al., (1972) influenced demographic research of the 1970s including the conduct of the World Fertility Survey (WFS). Between 1973 and 1984, the WFS used standard questionnaire to conduct surveys to investigate human fertility in 42 developing countries and 20 developed countries (Cleland & Scott, 1987). The view then was that it was important to understand the factors responsible for the high fertility, particularly in Third World Countries.

In 1987, the Population Crisis Committee (PCC) reported that there were 30 countries with conditions of extreme human suffering in the developing world, including Ghana and 23 other African countries. Among the most significant findings from the study was the fact that there was a high correlation (r=.83) between population growth and the human suffering index. Without exception, every country associated with the high suffering ratings had high population growth rates (PCC, 1987). Consistent with Malthusian population theory and other major demographic studies (see e.g., Coale & Hoover, 1958; Simon, 1981; Higgens et al., 1982), the PCC's finding suggests that rapid population growth hinders social and economic progress for individuals, families, and societies in general. Without comparable growth in the economies of African countries, rapid population increase, of the magnitude observed in much of the continent, could lead to more conflicts over resource allocation and economic hardships.

Lessons learned from research on family planning, health transition and the status of women within the family and their level of autonomy in decision making have re-kindled interest in the study of family dynamics in many parts of the developing world including Africa. The general thesis is that it is when women are able to make independent decisions on a wide range of issues including those on reproductive health that fertility begins to decline. Nonetheless, there is a lack of consensus among researchers as to how to define "female autonomy."

Using a Euro-American world view, female autonomy has come to be equated with formal education, occupation in the modern sector of the economy, independent income, and control of sexuality. But others believe that such individual characteristics as education or employment do not address the social context within which people operate (Caldwell, 1986; Schuler & Hashemi 1994; Kaufmann & Cleland, 1994; Mason, 1995; Oheneba-Sakyi & Takyi, 1997). Goldsheider (1995), for instance, argues that in order to comprehend the content of long-term intergenerational and gender relations that make up the core of the lives of many people, researchers need to move beyond the individual and focus on the larger community/societal context.

Conscious of the multi-faceted nature of the female autonomy concept, we used multiple indicators to capture elements of autonomy at both the individual and institutional levels in the present study (named the Ghana Female Autonomy Micro Study [GFAMS]). Women's autonomy at the individual level was conceptualized as a composite of formal education, employment status, control of independently-earned income, and communication and decision making on a wide range of family issues. At the institutional level, gender role obligations and responsibilities, "gender-appropriate" education and leadership roles, and sexual and marital rights including rights to inherit property were used as measures of women's autonomy in the society.

The GFAMS, therefore, was an attempt to obtain data for detailed analysis on family types and relations in contemporary Ghana, as a case study of the African situation. The focus was female autonomy in a rapidly changing society, and the main objective was to find out how changes in power relations between wives and husbands affect certain major aspects of family life such as fertility, contraception, gender roles, and other family-related behavior. In this final chapter, we present our conclusions and discuss the limitations and some policy implications of the study.

Historically, it has been assumed by Goode (1963) and Pool (1972), among others, that family systems move from a so-called "traditional" type to a "modern" one. The suggestions have been that the differences between these two ideal types can easily be determined in terms of family decision making, distribution of power, communication, and division of labor in household--whether activities are shared or whether one spouse exercises a dominant position at the expense of the other partner. In this transformation from the traditional to the modern family, the role of "modernization," commonly interpreted through formal education, urbanization, and industrialization, has often been emphasized. In relation to these assumptions, some of the critical questions which the present study tried to answer were the following:

- Where does the Ghanaian family fall along this continuum from a traditional to a modern family type?
- Is there indeed a "Ghanaian" family type or several types in a transitional process?
- What are the structural implications of these family types for social behavior such as contraception and fertility outcomes?

Earlier attempts to answer some of these questions in the Ghanaian context had been made by Oppong (1970; 1974), and Caldwell (1976). The GFAMS had attempted to build upon these earlier studies to test some of the assumptions and hypotheses. The general hypothesis for this study was that women's autonomy (which is itself influenced by individual and societal factors) would influence family-related activities including contraception and fertility behavior.

**SUMMARY OF FINDINGS FROM THE GFAMS**

Our study demonstrates that researching the family in an African setting, although difficult, is possible. Researching about the family involves probing into aspects of customary beliefs and practices, asking questions about private life, and challenging people to re-assess some of their deeply held beliefs. Questions on such topics as discrimination against women, marital infidelity, family size, contraception, and sexual coercion are often regarded by couples as highly personal and they do not like to discuss them in public. Even fairly innocuous questions about how much money a husband gives to the wife for housekeeping may seem justifiably threatening to a husband who either gives too little or not at all in a society which regards this as a husband's duty. In spite of these difficulties, people were prepared to discuss these issues partly due to the changing perception of inter-spousal communication and emerging acceptance of the culture of answering some questions about private life.

A more serious difficulty relates to the problem of interpretation of the real meaning of the responses. For example, the fact that a man does not give his spouse housekeeping money ("chop" money--as it is commonly called in Ghana) or buy her clothes may not necessarily imply failure in the performance of his matrimonial duties. There are husbands who believe that the best way of handling household budgetary arrangements is to provide some capital or other facilities for the wife to earn enough income on a regular basis to take care of the housekeeping. Thus, a fisherman may, for example, allow his wife to sell the catch and use whatever profit she makes to care for the household. Similarly, other husbands arrange to procure capital for their wives to set up small businesses, with the understanding, of course, that profit accruing from the trade or business would be used by the wives for housekeeping needs.

Further observations from our study point to the fact that it may no longer be appropriate to see marriage arrangements as fitting idealistically mutual exclusive cells such as "arranged by family," or "entirely chosen by partner himself/herself," nor can we also independently classify such marriages as customary, ordinance, church, or consensual, since these are dynamic processes that usually overlap. Marriage arrangements in African societies are complex, and attempting to put them into certain pre-determined modes may leave the respondent with no choice other than to say what the researcher wants to hear. Even living arrangements of couples often change in response to the varying demands of the larger extended family or the couple itself. For example, a wife who moves to the family house or hometown to deliver a child may find herself for one reason or the other staying there for years. Some wives may also move in or out of the marital home on a regular basis for other reasons including observing post-partum abstinence, going to take care of aged parents, responding to family crises or just taking a vacation.

These complications notwithstanding, studying the dynamic processes of family relations is too important to be ignored. What this micro-study has shown is that there is a need for social science researchers to refine concepts and devise appropriate methodologies in order to depict more accurately the social and economic reality of the African family. Using indigenous knowledge to interpret the family situation, the GFAMS has aided us to assess the effects of continued social change on human reproduction, family dynamics, and spousal relations in an African context.

The research findings presented in this book have provided empirical support to our understanding of the nature of marital relations among a select sample of Ghanaian couples. The results of the study confirm that a number of factors help to explain marriage systems and fertility behavior in Ghana. Although the majority of couples indicated that they chose their partners entirely by themselves, some form of family involvement of partner choice as well as marriage of multiple wives continue to exist side by side with new forms such as church, ordinance, and consensual marriages. Marriages contracted solely under Customary law are still the most preferred form of marriages in spite of over a century of Ordinance Marriage law in the country. The influence of the family on choice of marriage partner, though, was evidently higher for females than males, and decreased for both women and men as their level of education increased.

Although across every social category, husbands in our study had more children and desired more than wives, the structural changes that seem to be occurring in the Ghanaian marriage systems and fertility behavior appear to be associated with age, urban residence, and formal education, among other things. Supposedly, for women who have more children than they desire, it is positive changes in education which will enhance their capacity toward fertility reduction.

Also, our research findings showed the existence of a gap between knowledge and the use of modern contraceptive methods in Ghana as had been reported in other studies. However, compared to previous studies there appeared to be a trend toward increasing use of condoms, possibly for the prevention of HIV/AIDS and other sexually transmitted diseases. As expected, educated couples, urban residents, those not in arranged marriages, and those desiring less children were more likely to use modern contraception. For the vast majority of women who did not use a method, their partners' disapproval played a major role in their decision.

Conjugal relations for both wives and husbands increased with increased education, and couples had strong conjugal bonding if they had chosen their partners by themselves. Most couples reported discussing issues including children's education, social issues, and acquisition of property. However, urban couples generally discussed pregnancy prevention more than rural couples, and women with more than high school education indicated that they primarily initiated discussions with their spouses on how to avoid unwanted pregnancy.

Similarly, joint decision making in children's educational matters, purchase of household items, family size, and contraception was higher for women who possessed some autonomy by way of higher education, urban living, and freedom in their choice of marriage partner. Thus, the observed patterns in family communication and decision making reflect a changing society where the influence of education "emancipates" women (and to some extent men) from traditional practices that recognize the man's authority in certain familial domains.

The GFAMS data showed that women and men alike had independent sources of income, exhibited some control over how the money they earned should be disposed of, and contributed to various household expenditures based on reflections of their "gendered" roles, responsibilities, and obligations. Likewise, our findings confirmed that attitudes about occupational, administrative, and political leadership preferences in Ghana are for the most part "traditional." There is still the stereotyping of jobs into feminine and masculine ones as defined by customary practices, in spite of the high educational aspirations that most parents had for their daughters and sons.

While most couples felt that wives and husbands should not have the right to sexual relations outside of marriage, there was stronger opposition to the wife having an affair than the husband. This finding and the fact that some respondents (mostly men), defended polygyny as a legal form of marriage indicate the acceptance of sexual double standards in the society. However, despite some of the misinterpretations about the provisions of the current law of inheritance embodied in the Intestate Succession Law passed by the government of the Provisional National Defence Council (PNDC) in 1985, it appeared that most couples welcomed the law as a way to guarantee the economic security of women and children.

It is clear that dynamic changes are occurring, and will continue to occur in all facets of the Ghanaian family. Continuous changes will emanate from several sources, prominent of which are formal education, economic trends, migration, the HIV/AIDS situation, and legal demands such as the Intestate Succession Law.

## Formal Education

Since political independence from Britain in 1957, Ghana has made significant advances in education although rural residents receive less education than urban residents, and female education still lags behind that of men. However, in recent years, the Ghanaian government has embarked upon educational reforms to improve adult literacy through the Non-Formal Education Program (NFEP), and to increase access for all children, particularly girls through the Free and Compulsory Universal Education [F-CUBE] (GSS & MI, 1994). Continued improvements in the education of Ghanaians would not only foster egalitarian relationships between the sexes, but would also increase parental responsibilities toward children's education. The cost of formal education reverses the inter-generational flow of wealth from parents to children, and this according to Caldwell (1982), contributes to fertility decline.

## Economic Trends

In the 1970s and 1980s, Ghana's economy experienced a rapid decline. Between 1975 and 1983, gross national product declined at a rate of 1 percent per annum and the inflation rate was around 122 percent in 1983 (Alderman, 1994). During that period, there were shortages of basic items including detergents. To redress the decline in the economy, the government adopted a Structural Adjustment Program (SAP) which included withdrawal of subsidies of social services such as education and health and items such as fuel and agricultural inputs. These changes which shifted most of the cost of education and health to the family have contributed to the economic cost of raising children in the country, motivating couples to re-evaluate their fertility intentions (Anyinam, 1989).

## Migration

*Emigration:*   The economic stagnation and political uncertainties in Ghana during the 1970s and 80s also triggered a wave of emigration from the country. Significant numbers of Ghanaians left for Nigeria and other neighboring countries. Those who could afford left for Europe, North America and other parts of the world. At the peak of the outflow, emigrants accounted for nearly a tenth of the 1980 population of 12 million (Zacharia & Conde, 1981). In the U.S., for instance, Ghanaians are well represented among recent African immigrants (Takyi, 1993b). Ghana is considered to be one of the ten countries that has experienced diasporization in the last two decades (Van Hear, 1998).

*Rural-Urban Migration:* As Ghana's economy continues to modernize, its towns and cities have grown rapidly, surpassing even the country's population growth rate. In a span of about 50 years, the percent of Ghanaians who live in cities or towns increased nearly three-fold from 13 percent in 1948 to about 36 percent in 1995 (Nabila, 1988; GSS & MI, 1994; GSS, 1995). Results of the Ghana Living Standard Survey (GLSS 2) indicate that the majority of all migrants to urban areas go to join family members, for marriage-related reasons, to escape family problems, to look for jobs, and to receive education or training (GSS, 1995).

In both international outflows and rural-urban migration, the domination of male migrants has led to separation of couples, children, and extended family members. Such separations have contributed to recent increases in the rates of divorce and female-headed households in the country (Lloyd & Gage-Brandon, 1993; GSS, 1996). Also, the living arrangements of married couples have been altered in the urban areas. In the cities, housing constraints have promoted separate residences for some couples, while economic realities have forced others who can find accommodation to live together.

With an increasing number of people becoming cosmopolitan, their belief systems and attachment to the traditional family norms are becoming weak. Moreover, the economic costs of raising children in urban areas and overseas, and the exposure to different norms of family life, in themselves, may prompt migrants to delay marriage, and/or desire fewer children than they would otherwise like to have. And, although, most migrants try to maintain some emotional and economic ties to their ancestral homes, the distance away from home limits their active participation in the day-to-day activities of the traditional extended family.

While traditional polygyny may be on the decline in the cities and among the elite, adapting to the global and urban environment may also mean "freedom" from traditional control of sexuality. This new found freedom has been credited with exposure to a wide range of sexual behaviors such as commercial sex, non-marital multiple partnerships, and other casual sex that expose individuals and families to the risks of STDs and HIV/AIDS infection (Anarfi, 1993; Carael, 1994; Schoepf, 1997). In effect, migration will continue to bring about changes in the traditional forms of nuptiality patterns in Ghana.

## HIV/AIDS Situation

Although the issue of HIV/AIDS was not specifically explored in the GFAMS, a number of couples in the survey had made general references to the fear of the spread of STDs as a reason against the continued practice of polygyny and sexual freedom for both wives and husbands. Since the 1980's, HIV/AIDS has become one of the major demographic issues that has affected the African family. The HIV/AIDS situation in sub-Saharan Africa has gained a lot of attention in recent times for a number of reasons. First, as a morbid condition which feeds into mortality, it is a field of study in its own right. Second, it has implications for fertility since in the African context, about 80 percent of all HIV infection is through heterosexual sex, the same process used for procreation (see, e.g., Gregson et al., 1997).

When the GFAMS was conducted in 1992/93, officially diagnosed HIV/AIDS cases in Ghana was about 11,000 (National AIDS/STD Control Program [NACP], 1998). At that time, the general view in the country was that HIV/AIDS was a problem for commercial sex workers and their permanent male partners mostly from

Cote d'Ivoire, Nigeria, other West African Countries, and Europe (Adomako, 1991; Anarfi, 1993). However, by the end of 1998, the number of officially reported cases was over 27,692, putting Ghana in the category of a moderately infected country with a prevalence rate of 135 per 100,000 population (NACP, 1998).

In general, the current prevalence of HIV/AIDS in the country is relatively low compared to other countries in African sub-region. But even with the available data, the seriousness of the situation cannot be underestimated since it has profound implications for fertility levels, mortality, productivity, long-term medical care, and the general health of the nation.

While educational campaigns about all the known ways of transmission and proper protection against this deadly disease have to be innovative and aggressive, focusing on the cultural context of gender relations is equally essential. Women are more at risk than men because their powerless positions in relationships leave them with fewer options to use condoms or practice safer sex. As Schoepf argues in her article on AIDS and gender relations in Africa "...those who have reduced their risk are women with decision-making autonomy based on their capacity to support themselves without resorting to sex within or outside of marriage" (1997:329).

### Intestate Succession Law (PNDCL 111)

To increase the economic capacity for surviving spouses to support themselves and their children, the Government of Ghana passed the Intestate Succession Law in 1985. The aim of this law was to shift the transfer of property of the deceased away from the extended family to the surviving nuclear unit. This law not only compensates the surviving spouse's services to the deceased, but also acknowledges that the spouse is the best person to look after the children of the deceased. Hence, under this law the surviving spouse and children get a significant proportion of the physical property of the deceased spouse.

Over a decade after its passage, it appears that people know about the existence of the law but not necessarily all its provisions. Although, as expected, this overturning of customary practices has invoked tensions in family relations, we believe that when this law becomes publicized and institutionalized in Ghana, women and children may become more economically secure than they have been in the past. According to Manuh, "...to the extent that the law exists and people have to regulate their affairs in interpersonal matters with reference to it, it can be said to be a positive development that may oblige parents to accept full economic responsibility for the children they procreate" (Manuh, 1997:91-92). In the process of accepting the provisions of the new law, large family sizes may not be necessary to build strong kin networking, thus compelling couples to examine their fertility outcomes.

Female autonomy impacts on decision making with regards to fertility, contraception use, economic well-being, sexuality, and other family-related behavior in diverse ways, with both positive and negative feedback loops. As a concept, it provides a framework for examining the existing as well as future trends in demographic behavior. Although conducted before the United Nation's International Conference on Population and Development (ICPD) in Cairo in 1994, the GFAMS seems to have addressed some of the underlying factors supporting the implementation of effective reproductive health programs (e.g., sexual rights within marriage) set forth in the *Program for Action*, the document that emerged from the Cairo conference.

## LIMITATIONS OF STUDY

However, in spite of the usefulness of the GFAMS as a case study, we need to acknowledge some limitations with regard to geographical scope, limited coverage of adolescence family behavior, and the use of age data.

First, the present study was conducted in the southern coastal zone which in many ways is different from the rest of the country. In terms of ecological, economic, and cultural characteristics, Ghana can be divided roughly into two areas. These are: (1) the southern zone (comprising the coastal and middle belt regions) with most of the nation's industries, modern infrastructure, tree crop cultivation, and minerals, and

(2) the northern zone, which lags behind the south in modern infrastructure and productive land.

It is, however, the different cultural characteristics in terms of ethnic background, lineage and kinship systems, type of religion, and extent of contacts with the outside world that make the divisions important for the study of social, economic and cultural changes upon which female autonomy, modern contraceptive use, and fertility behavior rest (Fortes, 1949; Goody [J.R.], 1969; Goody, [E.N.], 1973; Oppong,1973; Clark, 1994; Binka et al., 1995; Adongo et al., 1998). Thus, to obtain a comprehensive picture of female autonomy in Ghana similar studies would have to be conducted in the northern zone.

Second, there were few adolescent couples in the GFAMS sample, thus we were unable to analyze their behavior patterns. These are young adults whose life course will have implications for the levels of fertility in the future because they are yet to go through their full fertility experience. It will be useful in subsequent studies to target adolescent couples and compare their perceptions of female autonomy, sexuality, family forms, decision making, and fertility behavior with older adults.

Finally, in a society where many respondents are neither literate nor numerate, a researcher often has to treat responses on the age data with some caution. As is the case in Ghana and several other African countries, exact dates of occurrence of events may not be reported, contributing to age heaping--preference for certain digits (usually 0 or 5). Moreover, with events such as marriages which have the tendency to consist of long processes of customary ceremonies and rites, it is often difficult to establish dates of occurrences with precision. To get around the date(s) issue, we resulted to the use of estimation in the data collection process and used the conventional 5-year or 10-year intervals in the data analysis whenever appropriate. These techniques conform to the standard practice of data collection and analysis in world-wide demographic surveys (see, e.g., GSS & IRD, 1989; GSS & MI, 1994).

**POLICY IMPLICATIONS OF THE STUDY**

Ghana formulated a comprehensive policy on population in 1969. One of the basic aims of the policy was to persuade couples to limit the number of children they would wish to have. At that time, total fertility was between 6 and 7 children per woman. With a declining mortality, population growth rate was estimated at about 2.7 percent per year. The target was to reduce population growth rate to 1.7 percent by the beginning of the 1990s. However, by 1988, total fertility was around 6.5 children and population growth rate was 3.0 percent per annum. As a result of these observations, the Population Policy was revised in 1994 with the view to developing new strategies to achieve fertility decline in the country.

A major reason for the little apparent change in the level of fertility lies in the obvious fact that the traditional value system which underpinned and sustained high fertility had itself not changed significantly over the past few decades. Secondly, the decision on whether or not to have a child, how many, and even whether or not to use contraception, still seems to be largely influenced by factors such as extended kin perceptions or husband-dominance in inter-spousal relations. Thirdly, in spite of over half a century of formal education, female participation rates are still very low.

Selection of the necessary intervention strategies by policy-makers to influence fertility behavior needs to be based on empirical knowledge about changes in inter-spousal relations, female autonomy and kin-family relations. As has been demonstrated in this book, the greater the degree of sharing in critical decision making, and the greater the degree of communication between spouses, the greater the desire to postpone an unwanted pregnancy and therefore lower fertility.

The new Population Policy of 1994 recognized the importance of empirical research on family dynamics as a basis for policy formation. The *Action Plans* developed to ensure full implementation of the 1994 policy objectives specifically recommend a series of studies on inter-spousal communication and multi-media campaigns on ways in which such knowledge can be used to induce changes in fertility behavior (Government of Ghana, 1994:18).

For generations, the institution of the family perpetuated through marriages and social networking might have served most Africans well. Sharing and reciprocity reflected in group solidarity and communal spirit have provided a sense of belonging and security for individuals and their families. However, for the last century, the family in several African societies has undergone tremendous transformations in attempts to adjust to colonialism, postcolonial male dominance, economic ups and downs, and indigenous notions of gender segregation and gender complementarity of roles. As pointed out by Mikell (1997), the new realities and challenges posed by the modern state and global forces compel African women of the 1990's "... to be moving toward a consensus that this feminist position must include types of political involvement, and an assertive female autonomy that represents some movement away from traditional gender limitations for women while still being culturally sustainable." (Mikell, 1997:342).

The importance of information on female autonomy specifically, and intra-family relations generally goes far beyond the needs of family planning or population policy interventions. The two recent United Nations' conferences: (1) the International Conference on Population and Development in Cairo, Egypt, 1994 and (2) the International Women's Conference in Beijing, China, 1995, brought the world's attention to the urgent need to address a number of critical issues relating to the denial of fundamental human rights to women, and the need therefore to empower them. These issues include violence, deprivation, and discrimination against women in various spheres of life. It is, however, within the family or domestic setting that much of that violence and deprivation takes place. In order to formulate the right policies to meet the challenges of Cairo and Beijing with regard to improving the situation of African women and children, there is the need to increase the training of personnel with indigenous knowledge to conduct prospective studies to examine changes in attitudes and behavior that affect the African family over time.

# REFERENCES

Adler, P. A. et al. 1992. "Socialization to Gender Role: Popularity Among Elementary School Boys and Girls." *Sociology of Education*, 65:169-187.

Adomako, A. 1991. "To be or Not to be a Prostitute: The Example of Ghanaian Prostitutes in the Netherlands." Paper *Presented at DAWS Seminar on Women and Development*, Institute of African Studies, University of Ghana, Legon, Accra.

Adongo, P. B. et al. 1998. "The Influence of Traditional Religion on Fertility Regulation Among the Kassena-Nankana of Northern Ghana. *Studies in Family Planning*, 29(1):23-40.

Agyei-Mensah, S. 1997. *Fertility Change in a Time and Space Perspective: Lessons From Ghana*. Ph.D. Thesis submitted to the Department of Geography of the Norwegian University of Science and Technology, Trondheim, Norway.

Agyeman, D. K. et al. 1990. *African Population Initiative for the 1990s*. Report prepared for the World Bank. Cape Coast: University of Cape Coast.

Aidoo, A. A. 1994. "Asante Queen Mothers in Government and Politics in the Nineteenth Century." In *The Black Woman Cross-Culturally*, pp. 65-77. Steady, F. C. (ed.). Rochester, VT: Schenkman Books, Inc.

Akuffo, A. D. 1990. "Dimensions of Sex Discrimination: The Ghanaian Working Women's Experience." *Greenhill Journal of Administration*, 7(3&4):76-107.

Akuffo, F. O. 1987. "Teenage Pregnancies and School Drop-Outs: The Relevance of Family Live Education and Vocational Training to Girls' Employment Opportunities." In *Sex Role, Population and Development in West Africa*, pp. 54-164. Oppong, C. (ed.). Portsmouth, NH: Heinemann.

Alderman, H. 1994. "Ghana: Adjustment's Star Pupil?" In *Adjusting to Policy Failure in African Economies*, pp. 23-52. Sahn, D. E. (ed.). Ithaca: Cornell University.

Allot, A. 1960. *Essays in African Law*. London: Butterworth.

Anarfi, J. K. 1993. "Sexuality, Migration and AIDS in Ghana." In *Sexual Networking and HIV/AIDS in West Africa*, pp. 45-68. Supplement to Vol. 3, *Health Transition Review*. Caldwell J. C. et. al. (eds.). Canberra: Australian National University.

Anyinam, C. 1989. "The Social Cost of the International Monetary Fund Adjustment Program for Poverty: The Case of Health Care Development in Ghana." *International Journal of Health Services*, 19(3):531-547.

Appiah, R. 1985. "Knowledge and Use of Contraception." In *Demographic Patterns in Ghana: Evidence From the Ghana Fertility Survey 1979-80*, pp. 97-142.

Singh, S. et al., (eds.). Voorburg, The Netherlands: International Statistical Institute.

Aryee, F. 1978. "Urbanization and the Incidence of Plural Marriages." In *Marriage, Fertility and Parenthood in West Africa*, Vol 4, pp. 367-379. Oppong, C. et al., (eds.). Canberra: Australian National University.

Aryee, F. 1985. "Nuptiality Patterns in Ghana." In *Demographic Patterns in Ghana: Evidence From the Ghana Fertility Survey 1979-80*, pp. 17-48. Singh, S. et al., (eds.). Voorburg, The Netherlands: International Statistical Institute.

Assimeng, M. 1981. *Social Structure of Ghana: A Study in Persistence and Change*. Tema, Ghana: Ghana Publishing Corp.

Awusabo-Asare, K. 1988. *Education and Fertility in Ghana*. Unpublished Ph.D. Dissertation submitted to the Department of Geography, University of Liverpool.

Awusabo-Asare, K. 1990. "Matriliny and the New Intestate Succession Law of Ghana." *Canadian Journal of African Studies*, 24:1-16.

Awusabo-Asare, K. & Agyeman, D. K. 1993. "Social Science and the Challenge of the AIDS Epidemics: Ghana Data." In *Proceedings of the 22nd Conference of the International Union for the Scientific Studies of Population (IUSSP)*, Vol. 4:357-368. Liege, Belgium: IUSSP.

Awusabo-Asare et al. 1993. "Women's Control Over Their Sexuality and the Spread of STDs and HIV/AIDS in Ghana." In *Sexual Networking and HIV/AIDS in West Africa*, pp. 29-43. Caldwell, J. C. et al., (ed.), Supplement to *Health Transition Review*, 3. Canberra: Australian National University.

Benneh, G. et al. 1989. *Twenty Years of Population Policy in Ghana*. Accra, University of Ghana: Population Impact Project.

Binka, F. N. et al. 1995. "The Navrongo Community Health and Family Planning Project." *Studies in Family Planning*, 26(3):121-39.

Birdsall, N. 1977. "Analytical Approaches to the Relation of Population Growth and Development." *Population and Development Review*, 3:63-102.

Bittles, A. H. 1994. "The Role and Significance of Consanguinity as a Demographic Variable." *Population and Development Review*, 20 (3):561-584,693,695.

Blanc, A. K., & Lloyd, C. B. 1990. "Fertility, Women's Employment and Childrearing Over the Life Cycle in Ghana." *Paper Presented at the Annual Meeting of the Population Association of America, Toronto, Canada, May 3-5*.

Blau, P. 1964. *Exchange and Power in Social Life*. New York: John Wiley and Sons.

Bledsoe, C. 1990. "Transformations in Sub-Saharan African Marriage." *Annals, AAPSS*, 510 (July):115-125.

Bledsoe, C. et al. 1994. "Constructing Natural Fertility: The Use of Western Contraceptive Technologies in Rural Gambia." *Population and Development Review*, 20:81-113.

Bleek, W. 1981. "The Unexpected Repression: How Family Planning Discriminates Against Women in Ghana." *Review of Ethnography*, 7(25):193-198.

Bleek, W. 1987. "Family and Family Planning in Southern Ghana." In *Sex Role, Population and Development in West Africa*, pp. 138-153. Oppong, C. (ed.). Portsmouth, NH: Heinemann.

Bongaarts, J., 1990. "The Measurement of Wanted Fertility." *Population and Development Review*, 16 (4):487-506.

Boserup, E. 1970. *Women's Role in Economic Development*. London: George Allen & Unwin.

Boserup, E. 1985. "Economic and Demographic Interrelationships in Sub-Saharan Africa." *Population and Development Review*, 11(3):383-397.

Bourgeois-Pichat, J. 1970. *Main Trends in Demography*. London: Allen and Unwin.

Brabin, L. 1984. "Polygyny: An Indicator of Nutritional Stress in African Agricultural Societies." *Africa*, 54(1):31-45.

Brody, E. B. et al. 1976. "Fertility-Related Behavior in Jamaica." In *Cultural Factors and Population in Developing Countries*, pp. 15-30. Occasional Monograph Series No.6, ICP Work Agreement Reports. Washington, DC: Interdisciplinary Communications Program, Smithsonian Institution.

Bukh, J. 1979. *The Village Woman in Ghana*. Uppsala: Scandinavia, Institute of African Studies.

Bulatao, R. A. 1984. *Reducing Fertility in Developing Countries: A Review of Determinants and Policy Levers*. Washington, DC: The World Bank.

Cain, M. T. 1984. *Women's Status and Fertility in Developing Countries: Son Preference and Economic Security*. Working Paper No. 110. Population Council, New York.

Cain, M. T. et al. 1979. "Class, Patriarchy, and Women's Work in Bangladesh." *Population and Development Review*, 5:405-438.

Caldwell, J. C. 1976. "Marriage and the Family in Sub-Saharan Africa with Special Reference to Research Programs in Ghana and Nigeria." In *Family and Marriage in Some African and Asiatic Countries*, pp. 359-371. Huzayyin, S. A. & Acsadi, G. T. (eds.). Cairo Demographic Center (CDC) Research Monograph Series, #6. Cairo, Egypt: CDC.

Caldwell, J. C. 1980. "Mass Education as a Determinant of the Timing of the Fertility Decline." *Population and Development Review*, 6:225-255.

Caldwell, J.C. 1982. *Theory of Fertility Decline*. New York: Academic Press, Inc.

Caldwell, J. C. 1986. "Routes to Low Mortality in Poor Countries." *Population and Development Review*, 12(2):171-220.

Caldwell J. C. & Caldwell, P. 1987. "The Cultural Context of High Fertility in Sub-Saharan Africa." *Population and Development Review*, 13(3):409-438.

Caldwell, J. C. & Caldwell, P. 1988. "Is the Asian Family Planning Program Model Suited to Africa?" *Studies in Family Planning*, 19:19-28.

Caldwell, J. C. & Caldwell, P. 1993. "The South African Fertility Decline." *Population and Development Review*, 19(2):225-262.

## 198 References

**198** References

Caldwell, J. C. et al. 1982. "The Causes of Demographic Change in Rural South India: A Micro Approach." *Population and Development Review*, 8:689-727.

Caldwell, J. C. et al. 1992. "Fertility Decline in Africa: A New Type of Transition?" *Population and Development Review*, 18(2):211-242.

Caldwell, J. C. et al. 1994. "Methodological Advances in Studying the Social Context of AIDS in West Africa." In *Sexual Networking and AIDS in Sub-Saharan Africa: Behavioral Research and the Social Context*, pp. 1-12. Orubuloye et al., (eds.). Canberra: Australian National University.

Carael, M. 1994. "The Impact of Marriage Change on the Risks of Exposure to Sexually Transmitted Diseases in Africa." In *Nuptiality in Sub-Saharan Africa: Contemporary Anthropological and Demographic Perspectives*, pp. 255-273. Bledsoe, C. & Pison, G. (eds.). Oxford: Clarendon Press.

Casterline, J. B. et al. 1986. "The Age Difference Between Spouses: Variations Among Developing Countries." *Population Studies*, 40:353-374.

Central Bureau of Statistics (CBS). 1983. *Ghana Fertility Survey 1979-80: First Report*. Accra, Ghana.

Central Statistical Authority. 1988. *Rural Household Income, Consumption, and Expenditure Survey of 1988*. Addis Ababa, Ethiopia.

Chaudhury, R. H. 1982. *Social Aspects of Fertility, With Reference to Developing Countries*. New Delhi:Vikas.

Chronicle of Higher Education. 1991. "Average Salaries for Men and Women by Rank." *Chronicle of Higher Education*, April 3:A14.

Clark, G. 1994. *Onions are my Husband: Survival and Accumulation by West African Market Women*. Chicago: University of Chicago Press.

Cleland, J. & Scott, C. 1987. "Introduction." In *The World Fertility Survey: An Assessment*, pp. 1-4. Cleland, J. & Scott, C. (eds.). New York, NY: Oxford University Press.

Clignet, R. & Sween, J. 1969. "Social Change and Type of Marriage." *American Journal of Sociology*, 75:123-145.

Coale, A. J. & Hoover, E. M. 1958. *Population Growth and Economic Development in Low-income Countries: A Case Study of India's Prospects*. Princeton: Princeton University Press.

Cochrane, S. 1979. *Fertility and Education: What do we Really Know?* World Bank Staff Occasional Papers, No. 26. Baltimore, MD: Johns Hopkins Press.

Cochrane, S. & Sai, F. T. 1993. "Excess Fertility." In *Disease Control Priorities in Developing Countries*, pp. 333-361. Jamison, D. T. et al., (eds.). Oxford: Oxford University Press; Washington, DC: World Bank.

Cornia, G. A. et al. 1987. *Adjustment With a Human Face*. Oxford: The Clarendon Press for UNICEF.

Costello, M. & Palabrica-Costello, M. 1988. "Religious Differences in Fertility in Southern Philippines: How Fares the Status of Women and Fertility Model?" *Paper Presented at Rockefeller Foundation Workshop on the Status of Women and Fertility, Bellagio, Italy.*

Dare, L. O. & Cleland, J. 1994. "Reliability and Validity of Survey Data on Sexual Behavior: Preliminary Results of Field Tests." In *AIDS Impact and Prevention in the Developing World: The Contribution of Demography and Social Science, Supplement to Vol 3, Health Transition Review*. Canberra: Australian National University.

Dasgupta, P. 1994. "The Population Problem." In *Population: The Complex Reality*, pp. 151-180. Graham-Smith, F., Sir (ed.). Golden, CO: North American Press.

Date-Bah, E. 1982. *Sex Inequalities in an African Urban Labor Market: The Case Study of Accra-Tema*. Geneva: International Labor Organization.

Dei, C. H. 1997. "Women and Grassroots Politics in Abidjan, Cote d'Ivoire." In *African Feminism: The Politics of Survival in Sub-Saharan Africa*, pp. 206-231. Mikell, G. (ed.). Philadelphia: University of Pennsylvania Press.

Desai, S. & Jain, D. 1994. "Maternal Employment and Changes in Family Dynamics: The Social Context of Women's Work in Rural South India." *Population and Development Review*, 20(1):115-36, 249-52.

Dickson, K. B. 1969. *A Historical Geography of Ghana*. Cambridge: Cambridge University Press.

Dinan, C. 1983. "Sugar Daddies and Gold-Diggers: The White-Collar Single Women in Accra." In *Female and Male in West Africa*, pp. 344-366. Oppong, C. (ed.). London: George Allen & Unwin.

Disch. E. 1997. Reconstructing Gender: A Multicultural Anthology. Mountain View, CA: Mayfield Publishing Company.

Dorjahn, V. R. 1988. "Changes in Temne Polygyny." *Ethnology*, 27:367-390.

Dormor, D. J. 1994. "The Status of Women and Mortality." *Genus*, L(3-4):13-45.

Dow, T. E., et al. 1994. "Wealth Flow and Fertility Decline in Rural Kenya, 1981-92." *Population and Development Review*, 20(2):343-364.

Dyson, T. & Moore, M. 1983. "On Kinship Structure, Female Autonomy, and Demographic Behavior in India." *Population and Development Review*, 9: 35-60.

Ebin, V. 1982. "Interpretation of Infertility: The Aowin of South West Ghana." In *Ethnography of Fertility and Birth*, pp. 141-159. MacCormarck, C. P. (ed.). New York: Academic Press.

Edwards, J. N. 1969. "Family Behavior as Social Exchange." *Journal of Marriage and the Family*, 31:518-526.

Ehrlich, P. R. 1968. *The Time Bomb*. New York, NY: Ballantine Books, Inc.

Ekechi, F. K. 1996. "Perceiving Women as Catalysts." *Africa Today*, 43(3):235-250.

Estes, R. J. 1988. "Toward a Quality-of-Life Index: Empirical Approaches to Assessing Human Welfare Internationally." In *The Third World: States of Mind and Being*, pp. 23-36. Norwine, J. & Gonzalez, A. (eds). Boston, MA: Unwin Hyman.

Eyetsemitan, F. 1997. "Age, Respect and Modernization in Africa: Toward a Psychosocial Understanding." *The Western Journal of Black Studies,* 21(2):142-145.

Ezeh, A. C. 1993. "The Influence of Spouses Over Each Other's Contraceptive Attitudes in Ghana." *Studies in Family Planning,* 24(3):163-174.

Farooq, G. M. & Simmons, G. B. (eds.). 1985. *Fertility in Developing Countries: An Economic Perspective on Research and Policy Issues.* New York: St. Martin's Press.

Ferrante, J. 1998. *Sociology: A Global Perspective.* Belmont, CA: Wadsworth Publishing Company.

Ferree, M. & Hall, E. J. 1996. "Rethinking Stratification from a Feminist Perspective: Gender, Race and Class in Mainstream Textbooks." *American Sociological Review,* 61(6):929-50.

Fiawoo, D. K. 1978a. "Some Patterns of Foster Care in Ghana." In *Marriage, Fertility and Parenthood in West Africa,* pp. 278-288. Oppong, C., et al., (eds.). Canberra: Australian National University.

Fiawoo, D. K. 1978b. "Women and Customs in Ghana." In *Background Papers to the Seminar on Ghanaian Women in Development,* pp. 54-70. National Council on Women and Development (NCWD), Accra, Ghana.

Fisher, I. 1999. "Sometimes a Girl's Best Friend is Not Her Father." *The New York Times,* A4, March 2.

Fortes, M. 1949. *The Web of Kinship Among the Tallensi.* London: Oxford University Press.

Fortes, M. 1950. "Kinship and Marriage Among the Ashanti." In *African Systems of Kinship and Marriage,* pp. 252-284. Radcliffe-Brown, A. R. & Forde, D. (eds.). London: Oxford University Press.

Fosu, G. B. 1986. "Fertility and Family Planning in Accra." *Journal of Biosocial Science,* 18(1):11-22.

Gage, A. J. 1995. "Women's Socioeconomic Position and Contraceptive Behavior in Togo." *Studies in Family Planning,* 26(5):264-277.

Gaisie, S. K. 1968. "Social Structure and Fertility." *Ghana Journal of Sociology,* 4(2):88-99.

Gaisie, S. K. 1969. *Dynamics of Population Growth in Ghana.* Accra-Tema: Ghana Publishing Corporation.

Gaisie, S. K. 1981. "Child-Spacing Patterns and Fertility Differentials in Ghana." In *Child-Spacing in Tropical Africa,* pp. 237-253. Page, H. J. & Lesthaeghe, R. (eds.). New York: Academic Press, Inc.

Gaisie, S. K. & DeGraft Johnson, K. T. 1976. *The Population of Ghana.* Committee for International Coordination of National research in Demography (CIRCRED) series.

Geisler, G. 1995. "Troubled Sisterhood: Women and Politics in Southern Africa, Case Studies from Zambia, Zimbabwe and Botswana." *African Affairs,* 94(377):545-578.

Ghana Government. 1984. *1984 Population Census: Preliminary Report*. Accra: Central Bureau of Statistics.

Ghana Statistical Service (GSS). 1991. *Quarterly Digest of Statistics*, Vol. IX (4). Accra, Ghana.

Ghana Statistical Service (GSS). 1995. *Ghana Living Standards Survey, 1991/92*. Accra, Ghana.

Ghana Statistical Service (GSS). 1996. *Ghana Living Standards Survey Report on the Second Round (GLSS 2)*. Accra, Ghana.

Ghana Statistical Service & Institute for Resource Development/Macro Systems, Inc., (GSS & IRD). 1989. *Ghana Demographic and Health Survey 1988*. Columbia, Maryland: GSS & IRD.

Ghana Statistical Service & Macro International, Inc., (GSS & MI). 1994. *Ghana Demographic and Health Survey 1993*. Accra, Ghana & Calverton, MD.

Goldscheider, F. K. 1995. "Interpolating Demography with Families and Households." *Demography*, 32(3):459-470.

Goode, W. J. 1963. *World Revolution and Family Patterns*. London: The Free Press of Glencoe.

Goody, E. N. 1973. *Contexts of Kinship: An Essay of the Family Sociology of the Gonja of Northern Ghana*. Cambridge: Cambridge University Press.

Goody, J. R. 1969. *Comparative Studies in Kinship*. Stanford, CA: Stanford University Press.

Government of Ghana, 1994. *Government of Ghana Action Plans, Vol IV*. Accra, Ghana.

Greenstreet, M. 1987. *The Ghanaian Woman: Development Through Education and Family Planning*. Legon, Accra, University of Ghana: Population Impact Project.

Gregson, S. et al. 1997. "HIV and Fertility Change in Rural Zimbabwe." In *Evidence of Socio-Demographic Impact of AIDS in Africa*, pp. 89-112. Awusabo-Asare, K. et al., (eds.) Supplement 2 to Vol. 7, *Health Transition Review*. Canberra: Australian National University.

Hagan, G. P. 1983. "Marriage, Divorce and Polygyny." In *Female and Male in West Africa*, pp. 192-203. Oppong, C. (ed.). London: George Allen & Unwin.

Harrison, K. A. 1997. "The Importance of the Educated Healthy Woman in Africa." *The Lancet*, 349 (9052):644-647.

Hart, K. 1973. "Informal Income Opportunities and Urban Employment in Ghana." *Journal of Modern African Studies*, 11:61-89.

Helitzer-Allen, D. et al. 1994. "Obtaining Sensitive Information: The Need for More Than Focus Groups." *Reproductive Health Matters*, 3:75-82.

Henn, J. K. 1989. "Women in the Rural Economy: Past, Present, and Future." In *African Women South of the Sahara*, pp. 1-18. Hay, M. J. & Stichter, S. (eds.) New York: Longman, Inc.

Higgens, G. M. et al.1982. *Potential Population Supporting Capabilities of Lands in the Developing World. Technical Report of Land Resources for*

*Populations of the Future Project*, by United Nations FAO, with the International Institute for Applied Systems and Analysis and UNFDP. Rome: FAO.

Ho-Won, J. 1995. "Liberal Economic Reform in Ghana: A Contested Political Agenda." *Africa Today*, 42(4):82-104.

Isiugo-Abanihe, U. C. 1983. *Child Fostering in West Africa: Levels, Determinants and Consequences*. Philadelphia, PA: Unpublished Ph.D. Dissertation submitted to the University of Pennsylvania.

Isiugo-Abanihe, U. C. 1985. "Child Fosterage in West Africa." *Population and Development Review*, 11(1):53-73.

Isiugo-Abanihe, U. C. 1994. "Parenthood in Sub-Saharan Africa: Child Fostering and its Relationship with Fertility." In *The Onset of Fertility Transition in Sub-Saharan Africa*, pp. 163-174. Locoh, T. & Hertrich, V. (eds.). Liege, Belgium: International Union for the Scientific Studies of Population (IUSSP).

Jonah, K. 1989. "The Social Impact of Ghana's Adjustment Program, 1983-86." In *The IMF, the World Bank and the African Debt, Vol 2, The Social and Political Impact*, pp. 140-152. Onimode, B. (ed.). London: The Institute for African Alternatives, Zed Book Ltd.

Kar, S. B. & Talbot, J. M. 1980. "Attitudinal and Nonattitudinal Determinants of Contraception: A Cross-Cultural Study." *Studies in Family Planning*, 11:51-64.

Karanja, W. W. 1987. "'Outside Wives' and 'Inside Wives' in Nigeria: A Study of Changing Perceptions of Marriage." In *Transformations of African Marriage*, pp. 247-61. Parkin, D. & Nyamwaya, D. (eds.). Manchester: Manchester University Press.

Karanja, W. W. 1994. "The Phenomenon of 'Outside Wives': Some Reflections on its Possible Influence on Fertility." In *Nuptiality in Sub-Saharan Africa: Contemporary Anthropological and Demographic Perspectives*, pp. 194-214. Bledsoe, C. & Pison, G. (eds.). Oxford: Clarendon Press.

Kasarda, J. D. et al. 1986. *Status Enhancement and Fertility: Reproductive Responses to Social Mobility and Educational Opportunity*. Orlando, Florida: Academic Press, Inc.

Kaufmann, G. & Cleland, J. 1994. "Maternal Education and Child Survival: Anthropological Responses to Demographic Evidence." *Health Transition Review*, 4(2):196-9.

Kaufmann, G. L. & Meekers, D. 1998. "The Impact of Women's Socioeconomic Position on Marriage Patterns in Sub-Saharan Africa." *Journal of Comparative Family Studies*, 29(1):101-14.

Kludze, A. K. P. 1983. "Property Law and Rural Development in Ghana." *Rural Africana*, 17:57-67.

Knodel, J. et al. 1987. *Thailand's Reproductive Revolution: Rapid Fertility Decline in a Third-World Setting*. Madison: University of Wisconsin Press.

Knoke, D. & Bohrnstedt, G. W. 1994. *Statistics for Social Data Analysis*. Itasca, IL: F.E. Peacock Publishers, Inc.

Knowles, R. & Wareing, J. 1985. *Economic and Social Geography*. London, Heinemann.

Kritz, M. M., & Gurak, D. T. 1989. *Women's Position, Education and Family Formation in Sub-Saharan Africa*. Cornell University, Population and Development Program, Working Paper Series 1.06. Ithaca, New York.

Kuenyehia, A. 1978. "Women and Family Law in Ghana." In *Background Papers to the Seminar on Ghanaian Women in Development*, pp. 316-337. National Council on Women and Development (NCWD), Accra, Ghana.

Kuenyehia, A. 1993. "Distribution of Matrimonial Property on Dissolution of Marriage: A Re-appraisal." *University of Ghana Law Journal*, 18:94-108.

Kuznets, S. 1966. *Modern Economic Growth: Rate, Structure, and Spread*. New Haven, CT: Yale University Press.

Lebeuf, A. M. D. 1963. "The Role of Women in Political Organization of African Societies." In *Women of Tropical Africa*, pp. 93-120. Paule, D. (ed.). London: Routledge & Kegan Paul.

Lesthaeghe, R. J. 1989. "Production and Reproduction in Sub-Saharan Africa: An Overview of Organizing Principles." In *Reproduction and Social Organization in Sub-Saharan Africa*, pp. 13-59. Lesthaeghe, R. J. (ed.). Berkeley, CA: University of California Press.

Lesthaeghe, R. J. et al. 1981. "Child-Spacing and Fertility in Lagos." In *Child-Spacing in Tropical Africa: Tradition and Change*, pp. 147-179. Page, H. J. & Lesthaeghe, R. J. (eds.). Academic Press, London.

Lesthaeghe, R. J., & Wilson, C. 1986. "Modes of Production, Secularization and the Pace of Fertility Decline in Western Europe." In *The Decline of Fertility in Europe*, pp. 261-292. Coale, A. J. & Watkins, S. C. (eds.). Princeton, N.J: Princeton University Press.

Lim, L. L. 1988. "The Impact of Islam on Female Status and Fertility in Malaysia." *Paper Presented at Rockefeller Foundation Workshop on the Status of Women and Fertility, Bellagio, Italy*.

Lloyd, C. B. 1986. "Women's Work and Fertility, Research Findings and Policy Implications From Recent United Nations Research." *Paper Presented at Rockefeller Foundation Workshop on the Status of Women and Fertility, July 8-11, Bellagio, Italy*.

Lloyd, C. B. & Gage-Brandon, A. J. 1993. "Women's Role in Maintaining Households: Family Welfare and Sexual Inequality in Ghana." *Population Studies*, 47(1):115-131.

Lockwood, M. 1995. "Structure and Behavior in the Social Demography of Africa." *Population and Development Review*, 21(1):1-32,216-7,219.

Lucas, D. & Ware, H. 1981. "Fertility and Family Planning in the South Pacific." *Studies in Family Planning*, 12(8-9):303-315.

Luckham, Y. 1976. "Law and the Status of Women in Ghana." *Columbia Human Rights Law Review*, 8(1):69-94.

Mann, K. 1994. "The Historical Roots and Cultural Logic of Outside Marriage in Colonial Lagos." In *Nuptiality in Sub-Saharan Africa: Contemporary Anthropological and Demographic Perspectives*, pp. 167-193. Bledsoe, C. & Pison, G. (eds.). Oxford: Clarendon Press.

Manuh, T. 1997. "Wives, Children, and Intestate Succession in Ghana." In *African Feminism: The Politics of Survival in Sub-Saharan Africa*, pp. 77-95. Mikell, G. (ed.). Philadelphia: University of Pennsylvania Press.

Mason, K. O. 1984. *The Status of Women: A Review of Its Relationships to Fertility and Mortality*. New York: Population Science Division, Rockefeller Foundation.

Mason, K. O. 1987. "The Impact of Women's Social Position on Fertility in Developing Countries." *Sociological Forum*, 2(4):718-745.

Mason, K. O. 1993. "Family Change and Support of the Elderly in Asia: What Do We Know?" *Asia-Pacific Population Journal*, 7(3):13-22.

Mason, K. O. 1995. *Gender and Demographic Change; What do we Know?* Liege, Belgium: International Union for the Scientific Studies of Population (IUSSP).

Mason, K. O & Palan, V. T. 1981. "Female Employment and Fertility in Peninsular Malaysia: The Maternal Role Incompatibility Hypothesis Reconsidered." *Demography*, 18(4):549-575.

Mason, K. O. & Taj, A. M. 1987. "Differences Between Women's and Men's Reproductive Goals in Developing Countries." *Population and Development Review*, 13 (4):611-638.

McGinn, T. et al. 1989. "Male Knowledge, Use and Attitudes Regarding Family Planning in Burkina Faso." *International Family Planning Perspectives*, 15(3):84-87.

Meadows, D. H. et al. 1972. *The Limits to Growth*. London: Pan Books.

Mikell, G. 1997. "Conclusions: Theorizing and Strategizing About African Women and State Crisis." In *African Feminism: The Politics of Survival in Sub-Saharan Africa*, pp. 333-346. Mikell, G. (ed.). Philadelphia: University of Pennsylvania Press.

Mikell, G. 1997. "Introduction." In *African Feminism: The Politics of Survival in Sub-Saharan Africa*, pp. 1-50. Mikell, G. (ed.). Philadelphia: University of Pennsylvania Press.

Miller, D. L. 1995. "Toys for Boys." In *Sociology*, 5th ed., Annotated Instructors' Edition, pp. IM26-IM28. Schaefer, R.T. & Lamm, R. P. New York: McGraw-Hill.

Miller, D. L. 1998. "Toys are Getting Better! Context Analysis of a Major Toy Catalog." In *Sociology*, 6th ed., Annotated Instructors' Edition, pp. IM30-IM33. Schaefer, R. T. & Lamm, R. P. New York: McGraw-Hill.

Miller, J. & Garrison, H. H. 1982. "Sex Roles: The Division of Labor at Home and in the Workplace." In *Annual Review of Sociology*, pp. 237-262. Turner, R. (ed.). Palo Alto, CA: Annual Reviews.

Morgan, R. W., with Ohadike, P. O. 1975. "Fertility Levels and Fertility Change." In *Population Growth and Socio-Economic Change in West Africa*, pp. 187-235. Caldwell, J. C. (ed.). New York, NY: Columbia University Press.

Muhuri, P. K. et al. 1994. *Socioeconomic Defferentials in Fertility. DHS Comparative Studies*, No. 13. Macro International, Demographic and Health Surveys (DHS). Calverton, MD: DHS.

Nabila, J. S. 1988. *Urbanization in Ghana*. Legon, Accra: Population Impact Project.

NACP. 1998. *Ghana, National AIDS/STD Control Program*. Accra: Ghana.

Namboodiri, K. & Suchindran, C. M. 1987. *Life Table Technique and Their Applications*. Orlando, Florida: Academic Press, Inc.

National Commission on Working Women. 1984. *Women's Work: Undervalued, Underpaid*. Washington, DC: National Commission on Working Women.

New Patriotic Party. 1993. *The Stolen Verdict: Ghana November 1992 Presidential Elections*. Accra, Ghana: New Patriotic Party.

Nukunya, G. K. 1969. *Kinship and Marriage Among the Anlo Ewe*. London: Athlone Press, University of London.

Nukunya, G. K. 1978. "Women and Marriage." In *Background Papers to the Seminar on Ghanaian Women in Development*, pp. 1-22. National Council on Women and Development (NCWD), Accra, Ghana.

Nzioka, C. 1998. *Male Participation in the Decision-Making on Family Planning and Modern Contraceptive Use in Kenya: Problems and Prospects*. Report submitted to the Special Programme on Research and Training in Human Reproduction, World Health Organisation, Geneva.

Nzomo, M. 1993. "Engendering Democratization in Kenya: A Political Perspective." In *Democratic Change in Africa: Women's Perspectives*, pp. 5-15. Kabira, W. M. et al., (eds.). Nairobi: Association of African Women for Research and Development (AAWORD).

Nzomo, M. 1997. "Kenyan Women in Politics and Public Decision Making." In *African Feminism: The Politics of Survival in Sub-Saharan Africa*, pp. 232-254. Mikell, G. (ed.). Philadelphia: University of Pennsylvania Press.

O'Laughlin, B. 1974. "Mediation of Contradiction: Why Mbum Women Do Not Eat Chicken." In *Women, Culture, and Society*, pp. 301-318. Rosaldo, M. & Lamphere, L. (eds.). Stanford, CA: Stanford University Press.

Oheneba-Sakyi, Y. 1992. "Determinants of Current Contraceptive Use Among Ghanaian Women at the Highest Risk of Pregnancy." *Journal of Biosocial Science*, 24(4):463-475.

Oheneba-Sakyi, Y. & Takyi, B. K. 1997. "Effects of Couples' Characteristics on Contraceptive Use in Sub-Saharan Africa: The Ghanaian Example." *Journal of Biosocial Science*, 29(1):33-49.

Ollennu, N. A. 1966. *The Law of Testate and Intestate Succession in Ghana.* London: Sweet and Maxwell.

Ollennu N. A. & Woodman, G. 1985. *Principles of Customary Land Law in Ghana.* Birmingham, CAL Press (2nd edition).

Olusanya, P. O. 1971. "Status Differentials in the Fertility Attitudes of Married Women in Two Communities in Western Nigeria." *Economic Development and Cultural Change*, 19:641-651.

Oppong, C. 1970. "Conjugal Power and Resources: An Urban African Example." *Journal of Marriage and the Family*, 32:676-680.

Oppong, C. 1973. *Growing up in Dagbon.* Accra-Tema: Ghana Publishing Corporation.

Oppong, C. 1974. *Marriage Among a Matrilineal Elite: A Study of Ghanaian Senior Civil Servants.* London: Cambridge University Press.

Oppong, C. 1982. *Middle Class African Marriage.* London: George Allen & Unwin.

Oppong, C. 1983a. "Women's Roles, Opportunity Costs and Fertility." In *Determinants of Fertility in Developing Countries*, pp. 439-473. Bulatao, R. A. & Lee, R. D. (eds.). New York: Academic Press.

Oppong, C. 1983b. *Paternal Costs, Role Strains and Fertility Regulation: Some Ghanaian Evidence.* Geneva: ILO Working Paper, #134.

Oppong, C. 1987. "Responsible Fatherhood and Birth Planning." In *Sex Role, Population and Development in West Africa*, pp. 165-178. Oppong, C. (ed.). Portsmouth, NH: Heinemann.

Oppong, C. 1993. "Some Roles of Women: What Do We Know? -- Conceptual and Methodological Issues in Sub-Saharan Africa." *Paper Presented at the IUSSP Seminar on Women and Demographic Change in Sub-Saharan Africa, Dakar, Senegal.*

Oppong, C. & Abu, K. 1984. *The Changing Maternal Role of Ghanaian Women: Impacts of Education, Migration and Employment.* Geneva: ILO Population and Labor Policies Program Working Paper, #143.

Owen, M. 1996. *A World of Widows.* Atlantic Highlands, NJ: Zed Books.

Page, H. 1989. "Childrearing Versus Childbearing: Coresidence of Mother and Children in Sub-Saharan Africa." In *Reproduction and Social Organization in Sub-Saharan Africa*, pp. 401-441. Lesthaeghe, R. J. (ed.). Berkeley, CA: University of California Press.

Parsons, T. & Bales, R. 1955. *Family, Socialization and Interaction Processes.* Glencoe, IL: Free Press.

Pescosolido, B. A. 1992. "Beyond Rationale Choice: The Social Dynamics of How People Seek Help." *American Journal of Sociology*, 94(4):1096-1138.

Pool, J. E. 1972. "A Cross-Comparative Study of Aspects of Conjugal Behavior Among Women of Three West African Countries." *Canadian Journal of African Studies*, VI(ii):233-259.

Population Crisis Committee (PCC). 1987. *Human Suffering Index.* Camp, S. L & Speidel, J. J. (eds.). Washington, D.C.

Preston-Whyte, E. 1994. "Gender and the Lost Generation: The Dynamics of HIV Transmission Among Black South African Teenagers in KwaZulu/Natal." In *AIDS Impact and Prevention in the Developing World: Demographic and Social Science Perspectives*, pp. 241-256. Cleland, J. & Way, P. (eds.). Supplement to Vol. 4, *Health Transition Review*. Canberra: Australian National University.

Pritchett, L. H. 1994. "Desired Fertility and the Impact of Population Policies." *Population and Development Review*, 20(1):1-55.

Radcliffe-Brown, A. R. 1950. "Introduction." In *African Systems of Kinship and Marriage*, pp. 1-85. Radcliffe-Brown, A. R. & Forde, D. (eds.). London: Oxford University Press.

Rattray, R. S. 1923. *Ashanti*. London: Oxford University Press.

Rattray, R. S. 1929. *Ashanti Law and Constitution*. London: Oxford University Press.

Republic of Ghana [ROG] Gazette. 1985. "Intestate Succession Law." *Provisional National Defence Council Laws on Intestate Succession, 1985; Customary Marriage and Divorce (Registration), 1985; Administration of Estates (Amendments), 1985; Head of Family (Accountability), 1985*. Accra, Ghana: Information Services Department.

Republic of Ghana (ROG) Statistical Service. 1989. *Ghana Living Standards Survey: First Year Report, September 1987-August 1988*. Accra, Ghana.

Republic of Ghana & United Nations Children's Fund (ROG & UNICEF). 1990. *Children and Women in Ghana: A Situation Analysis*. Accra, Ghana: ROG & UNICEF.

Robertson, C. 1983. "The Death of Makola and Other Tragedies: Male Strategies Against a Female-Dominated System." *Canadian Journal of African Studies*, 17(3):469-95.

Robertson, C. 1989. "Women in the Urban Economy." In *African Women South of the Sahara*, pp. 33-50. Hay, M.J. & Stichter, S. (eds.). New York: Longman Inc.

Schaefer, R. T. 1998. *Racial and Ethnic Groups*. New York, NY: Addison-Wesley Educational Publishers, Inc.

Schaefer, R. T. & Lamm, R. P. 1998. *Sociology*. New York, NY: McGraw-Hill.

Schatz, S. 1994. "Structural Adjustment in Africa: A Failing Grade So Far." *The Journal of Modern African Studies*, 32(4):679-692.

Schoepf, B. G. 1997. "AIDS, Gender, and Sexuality During Africa's Economic Crisis." In *African Feminism: The Politics of Survival in Sub-Saharan Africa*, pp. 310-332. Mikell, G. (ed.). Philadelphia: University of Pennsylvania Press.

Schuler, S. R. & Hashemi, S. M. 1994. "Credit Programs, Women's Empowerment, and Contraceptive Use in Rural Bangladesh." *Studies in Family Planning*, 25(2):65-76.

Shah, N. A. 1974. "The Role of Inter-Spousal Communication in Adoption of Family Planning Methods: A Couple Approach." *Pakistan Development Review*, 13: 454-469.

Simmons, O. G. & Culagovski, M. 1975. "If They Know, Why They Don't Use? Selected Factors Influencing Contraceptive Adoption in Rural Latin America." *Paper Presented at the Annual Meeting of the Population Association of America, Seattle, April 17-19.*

Simon, J. L. 1981. *The Ultimate Resource.* Princeton, N.J: Princeton University Press.

Singh, R. D. & Morey, M. J. 1987. "The Value of Work-at-Home and Contributions of Wives' Household Service in Polygynous Families: Evidence From an African LDC." *Economic Development and Cultural Change,* 35:743-765.

Slakey, F. 1997. "Cattle, Education, and the Masai Identity." *The Chronicle of Higher Education,* 44(15):A72, Dec 5.

Takyi, B. K. 1993a. *The Status of Women and Fertility Behavior in Sub-Saharan Africa: The Effects of Female Labor Force Participation and Gender Preferences on Fertility in Ghana.* Ann Arbor, MI: UMI.

Takyi, B. K. 1993b. "The Socio-Demographic Characteristics of the Foreign-Born Population in New York State: A Look at African Immigrants." *Paper Presented at the Annual Meeting of the New York State Sociological Association,* October 15-16, Potsdam, N.Y.

Teachman, J. D. 1985. "Historical and Subgroup Variations in the Association Between Marriage and First Childbirth: A Life-Course Perspective." *Journal of Family History,* 10:379-401.

Thomas, D. & Muvandi, I. 1995. *How Fast is Fertility Declining in Botswana and Zimbabwe?* World Bank Discussion Paper, No. 258. Washington, DC: World Bank.

Toungara, J. M. 1997. "Changing the Meaning of Marriage: Women and Family Law in Cote d'Ivoire. In *African Feminism: The Politics of Survival in Sub-Saharan Africa,* pp. 53-76. Mikell, G. (ed.). Philadelphia: University of Pennsylvania Press.

U.S. Bureau of the Census. 1991. *Money Income and Poverty Status of Families and Persons in the U.S., 1990.* Current Population Reports, Series P-60, No. 174. Washington, DC: Government Printing Office, August, pp. 104-107.

U.S. Department of Labor. Bureau of Labor Statistics. 1991. *Employment and Earnings.* Washington, DC: Government Printing Office, January, pp. 185-90, 223-27.

United Nations Children's Fund (UNICEF). 1994. *The Progress of Nations.* New York, NY: UNICEF House.

United Nations Children's Fund (UNICEF). 1998. *The Status of the World's Children, 1999.* New York, NY: UNICEF House.

United Nations Economic Commission For Africa (UNECA). 1984. *Law and the Status of Women in Ghana*. E/ECA/ATRCW/84/2256. African Training and Research Center on Women, Research Series. Addis Ababa: Ethiopia.

Van Hear, N. 1998. *New Diasporas*. London: University College of London Press.

Vellenga, D. D. 1971. "Attempts to Change the Marriage Laws in Ghana and the Ivory Coast." In *Ghana and the Ivory Coast: Perspectives on Modernization*, pp. 125-150. Foster, P. & Zolberg. A. R. (eds.). Chicago: University of Chicago Press.

Vellenga, D. D. 1983. "Who is a Wife? Legal Expression of Heterosexual Conflicts in Ghana." In *Female and Male in West Africa*, pp. 144-155. Oppong, C. (ed.). London: George Allen & Unwin.

Ware, H. 1977. "Women's Work and Fertility in Africa." In *The Fertility of Working Women*, pp. 1-34. Kupinsky, (ed.). New York: Praeger.

Welshman, N. & Stewart, J. (eds.) 1995. *Widowhood, Inheritance Laws, Customs and Practices in Southern Africa*. Harare, Zimbabwe: Women and Law in Southern Africa Research Project.

West Africa. 1992. "The National Population Council, Ghana." *West Africa*, 3926, December, 14-20:2155.

Westoff C. F. & Ochoa, L. H. 1991. *Unmet Need and the Demand for Family Planning*. Demographic and Health Survey Comparative Studies, No. 5. Columbia, MD.

Woodman, G. 1988. "How State Courts Create Customary Law in Ghana and Nigeria." In *Indigenous Law and the State*, pp. 181-220. Morse, B. & Woodman, G. (ed.). Holland: Foris Publications.

World Wide Government Directory. 1996. *Women's League Table*. UN Division for the Advancement of Women. New York, NY: United Nations.

Zacharia, K. & Conde, J. 1981. *Migration in West Africa: Demographic Aspects. A Joint World Bank and OEC Study*. London: Oxford University Press.

## APPENDIX A

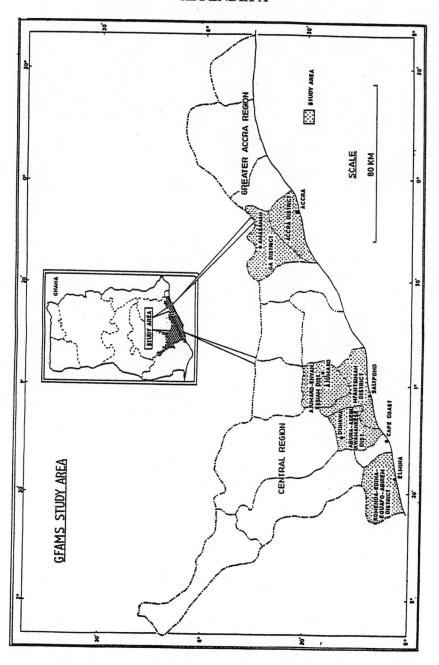

# AUTHOR INDEX

# SUBJECT INDEX

ideal for women, 126, 127
*Odikro*, 132
Old age, 48, 121, 132
Ollenu Commission, 169
*Omanhene*, 132
Ordinance, 16, 38, 44-47, 56, 69, 79, 80, 83, 89, 96, 97, 106, 107, 113, 115, 116, 137, 141, 147, 151, 152, 155, 157, 160, 161, 165, 175, 183, 184
Ordinance/Church, 45, 47, 56, 69, 80, 83, 89, 97, 106, 107, 113, 115, 116, 137, 141, 147, 151, 152, 155, 157, 160, 165, 175
Outside wives, 147

Paid work (*see* Non-familial work)
Parliamentary election, 21
Patriarchal (patriarchy), 4, 9, 74, 94, 166
Patriclan, 170
Patrilineal, 35, 94, 145, 168, 169
Physical property, 3, 81, 89, 96
Pill, 62, 63, 65, 68, 71, 73
Planned Parenthood Association of Ghana (PPAG), 62
Plural marriages (*see also* Polygyny), 146, 147, 161
PNDCL [111] (*see* Intestate Succession Law)
PNDCL (112), 169, 173
PNDCL (113), 169
PNDCL (114), 169
Policy implications, 25, 181, 192
Polygyny, 9, 14, 16, 24, 37, 46, 47, 60, 147-149, 153-157, 164, 169, 185, 188
Population Crisis Committee, 180
Population Impact Project (PIP), 26
Population Planning for National Progress and Prosperity, 62
Post-independence, 169
Postpartum sexual abstinence, 84-87, 89
Power relations, 10, 74, 86, 88, 181
Pregnancy prevention, 3, 78, 81, 83, 84, 185
Preliminary results, 25
Private-domestic arena, 142
Private polygyny (*see* Outside wives)
Program for Action, 190
Promiscuous behavior, 161
Provisional National Defence Council (PNDC) government, 169, 185
Public leadership roles for women, 131-134
Public-political arena, 142

Queenmother(s), queens, 132 (*see also* Yaa Asantewaah)
Questionnaire, 23-25, 179

Region, 22, 23, 26, 133, 189
Reproductive behavior (*see* Children ever born [CEB], Family size, Fertility Behavior)
Research design, 25
Resources (*see also* Capital)
  access to, 88
  economic, 20, 98, 158, 166
  financial, 120
  political, 4
  utilization of, 114
Riddles, 120
Right(s)
  of husbands to have extra-marital affairs, 148, 157, 159
  of husbands to practice polygyny, 148, 153-155
  of wives to have extra-marital affairs, 148, 162, 164, 165
  of wives to refuse husbands' sexual advances/demands, 149, 150, 152, 166
  to dispose of property, 6
  to own/acquire property, 6, 98, 143, 185
Risk(s)
  of pregnancy, 12, 54
  of STDs, 147
  of HIV/AIDS (*see* HIV/AIDS)
Royal birth, 13, 133
Rural-urban migration, 34, 187 (*see also* Urbanization)

Sampling
  frame, 22
  method, 22
School
  drop-out, 12
  fees, 111, 116, 117, 124, 125
Schooling, 12, 36, 39, 44, 46, 87, 164 (*see also* Education)
Segregation of roles, 10 (*see* Gender roles)
Self-acquired/individual property, 14, 36, 166-170, 175, 178
Self-esteem, 98
Sexual
  demands/advances, 148-151
  double standards, 14, 15, 166, 185

## STUDIES IN AFRICAN ECONOMIC
## AND SOCIAL DEVELOPMENT